DARK
TOWERS

ALSO BY DAVID ENRICH

The Spider Network: The Wild Story of a Math Genius, a Gang of Backstabbing Bankers, and One of the Greatest Scams in Financial History

DARK TOWERS

DEUTSCHE BANK, DONALD TRUMP, AND AN EPIC TRAIL OF DESTRUCTION

DAVID ENRICH

CUSTOM
HOUSE

To everyone who has struggled with mental health issues—
and to those who have helped them.

In memory of Letty and Henry, whose lives inspire me,
and Madelyn, whose daughter inspires me.

CONTENTS

PART I

PART II

This book is based primarily on interviews I conducted with and materials I received from nearly two hundred people: past and present Deutsche Bank employees, from the highest-ranking executives and board members to low-level staff; their family members, friends, lawyers, and rivals; consultants and contractors who worked at the bank; current and former regulators, prosecutors, and other government officials; and others with direct knowledge of the events described in the book. Some of these people shared emails, letters, photos, bank documents, audio and video recordings, and other primary-source materials. Most agreed to help me on the condition that I not identify them as sources. When faced with conflicting accounts of specific incidents, I have used the descriptions that strike me as the most plausible, based on factors including the credibility of different sources. In some cases, I have included dissenting accounts in footnotes.

I also drew on decades of journalism and academic research—as well as court filings, government documents, bank archives, and recordings and transcripts of conversations—about Deutsche Bank, the banking industry, and the book's characters. Those sources are detailed at the end of the book.

DARK
TOWERS

PROLOGUE

It was a little before one P.M. when a wiry American emerged from the Tube station into a drizzle, the type of dreary January weather that earns London its reputation as a depressing place during the long winter months. The man looked around Sloane Square. Normally, even in this dark season, the block was pretty and bustling with shoppers. This Sunday in early 2014, it was desolate.

Val Broeksmit didn't feel well. He had woken up groggy from the previous night's drug-fueled jam session with his band. Then, on the crowded Underground train on his way to Chelsea, he had been jolted by a surge of negative energy, like a dark spirit had brushed past him. He lit a cigarette and trudged toward the entrance to the Saatchi Gallery, his head down in a futile attempt to stay dry. He was scheduled to have brunch at the gallery's café with his parents. The last time he'd seen them was a month earlier, in December 2013, before they'd set off for the Caribbean and then a vacation in Oman. Val had just turned thirty-eight. While he was a talented musician with thirty-four albums to his name (none, alas, were chart-toppers), he lived off the largesse of his father, Bill, who had spent many years as a senior executive at Deutsche Bank, one of the world's largest financial institutions.

Tall, skinny, and scraggly—his friends sometimes told him he resembled a tramp—Val was determined on this Sunday not to get an earful from his mother about looking like a slob. He wore slacks, a blue blazer, and a black woolen cap.

At exactly one o'clock, Val arrived at the arched brick wall that snaked around the Saatchi Gallery. He was notorious in his family for never being on time, but here he was, and his obsessively punctual parents were nowhere to be seen. "Where are you guys?" he texted his mother, Alla. She didn't respond.

Val wandered across the pedestrianized street, perusing a row of boutiques and overpriced shops. He came across the Taschen bookstore, which specialized in coffee-table books about art and culture. For the past couple of years, Val had been collecting rare first editions—the older and more famous the author, the better. He was so into his hobby that he had done volunteer work for an organization that gathered unwanted books from estate sales and distributed them to needy children. Val would sift through the stacks, searching for hidden gems, and pilfer them for his own little library.

The bookstore was mostly empty. Val browsed its shelves until something caught his eye: an enormous volume with a shimmering silver cover, priced at £650 (about $1,000). It was a limited edition collection of Harry Benson's iconic photos of the Beatles, including the one of a pillow fight in a Paris hotel room. The book was signed by the photographer, and its pages were so luxuriously metallic that Val could see his reflection in them. He started to daydream about convincing his parents to buy it for him as a belated birthday gift.

Val's iPhone buzzed, interrupting his reverie. The call was from a blocked number. Val answered it. A woman with a thick accent—Val was pretty sure it was his parents' housekeeper, Belle—was on the line.

"Emergency! Emergency!" she shouted. "Your father! Your father!"

Val asked what she was talking about, but he couldn't get a coherent answer from her. The only thing he could think was that he needed to get to his parents' flat, which was about a mile away in the posh Kensington neighborhood. He put the Beatles book down, raced outside, and hailed a black cab. "Twenty-one Evelyn Gardens," he instructed the driver.

The ten-minute drive felt endless. The cab seemed to crawl through London's traffic-choked streets, past stately townhouses and brick apartment blocks and high-end restaurants and organic grocery stores. Bundled locals hurried along the rain-slicked sidewalks, nearly keeping pace with the taxi. Val went through the possible scenes he might encounter when he arrived. Maybe his father was hurt? Maybe there was a big family argument? Or maybe it was just that Bill was locked out of his computer and needed his tech-savvy son's help?

The taxi pulled onto Evelyn Gardens, a wide, quiet street that, instead of having a median, allowed cars to park in the middle as well as on the sides. Now, in addition to the BMWs and Audis and mopeds, an ambulance was stationed at the curb. Val paid the cabby and sprinted across the street.

His parents lived in a flat on the third floor of a white-trimmed redbrick building. Its heavy black door, normally opened only via a buzzer, was ajar. Val galloped up two flights of stairs. The door to his parents' apartment was wide open.

In the middle of the hallway, Bill Broeksmit was lying on his back, his eyes closed. A neck brace tilted his head back at an unnatural angle. A paramedic's plastic tube jutted from his mouth. Val's mother was curled in the fetal position on the dark wooden floor, her head resting on a pillow next to her husband's face. She was wailing. Belle kneeled beside her, stroking her hair.

"What the fuck is this?" Val screamed.

"He killed himself," his mother gasped. "He hung himself with Daisy's leash."

Two years later, in January 2016, Jacques Brand arrived at Deutsche Bank's American headquarters on Wall Street in Lower Manhattan. A former consultant and a longtime investment banker at Lehman Brothers, Brand was the CEO of Deutsche's U.S. businesses, and his mission was to instill some modicum of discipline, ethics, and control on an outfit where recklessness, chaos, and greed had long been the organizing principles. If there was one thing that Brand had learned in his years at Lehman, it was that there was no point in generating lots of revenue if you didn't understand and control the risks you were taking. That wasn't happening at Deutsche. Thus, shortly before taking over back in 2012, he had recruited Bill Broeksmit to the board that oversaw the American operations. Brand (everyone called him Jack) figured that the best way to ensure the business got cleaned up was to inject himself and folks who shared his priorities, like Bill, into more of the day-to-day activities that previously had been left to the whims of lower-level executives who had powerful financial incentives—otherwise known as annual bonuses—to prioritize short-term profits over long-term stability.

The process of combing out the bank's knots and tangles was a grueling, sometimes hundred-hour-a-week, not-always-successful slog, and by early 2016, Brand, a native of Ghana, a triathlon competitor, and a father of three with graying hair and a toothy smile, was in the early stages of negotiating his exit from Deutsche. He believed that during his nearly four years in the job, he'd developed a pretty solid grasp of what was going on, good and bad, inside his little kingdom. He'd grown accustomed to being appalled by what he found, until gradually each incremental problem was downgraded from shocking to surprising to just another day at Deutsche. It had seemed like a perpetual avalanche, but by now he thought he'd seen and dealt with every-thing at this crazy bank.

And then one day he walked through 60 Wall Street's cavern-ous marble lobby, rode the elevator up to the executive suites, and realized that no, in fact, he had not seen everything.

At a meeting with a few colleagues that morning, someone mentioned that a division of the bank in New York planned to make a large loan to Donald Trump. The proposed loan came from Deutsche's "private banking" group, which was devoted to serving the richest of the rich. The loan was ostensibly to pay for upgrade work at a golf resort, Turnberry, that Trump owned in Scotland. At the time, though, Trump was running for president, and it was hard to avoid the suspicion that the loan he was re-questing might have something to do with the fact that he was burning through gobs of his own cash on the campaign trail.[1]

Brand was stunned. Somehow, he hadn't realized that Trump—the real estate mogul, the reality-TV impresario, the race-baiting demagogue, and at that moment the front-runner for the Republican presidential nomination—was one of his company's most important clients. In fact, for nearly two decades, Deutsche had been the only mainstream bank consistently will-ing to do business with Trump. It had bankrolled his develop-ment of luxury high-rises, golf courses, and hotels. The bank had doled out well over $2 billion in loans to Trump and his compa-nies; at this moment in 2016, he owed the bank about $350 mil-lion, making Deutsche his biggest creditor. And that was despite two divisions of the bank, on separate occasions, having sworn to never again do business with The Donald because of his annoy-ing habit of stiffing his lenders, not just Deutsche but also banks like Citigroup and JPMorgan Chase. Deutsche had become the

key force allowing Trump to bounce back from multiple bankruptcies, to purchase and develop marquee properties, to recast
himself as a successful businessman, to become a viable candidate for president.

Brand couldn't believe that the folks in his wealth-management
division thought it would be a good idea to dispense tens of millions *more* to Trump, especially right now, in the middle of this
violent brawl of a presidential campaign. For the first time in a
while, he was genuinely aghast. "Why are we doing business
with him?" Brand fumed. He paused and thought about the matter at hand—whether Deutsche would go further down this path.
"The answer is no," he snapped to colleagues.

For the past several years, Deutsche's relationship with Trump
had been managed by a banker named Rosemary Vrablic. Serving Trump and his extended family—including the Kushner
clan—had become central to her job, and she wasn't about to let
the opportunity to make another loan to her prized client just slip
away. Vrablic, a slim, stylish woman with short gray hair, was
accustomed to getting her way. She was a rainmaker, generating
tens of millions of dollars in income for the bank each year. Until
recently she had reported directly to one of the bank's highest-
ranking U.S. executives, leapfrogging an entire level of managers. She also had enjoyed a strong relationship with the bank's
co-CEO, Anshu Jain, who accompanied her on visits to rich and
famous customers, including Trump. On the previous occasions
when rival executives had tried to scuttle her loans to Trump,
warning that he was a deadbeat and that other divisions of the
bank had imposed bans on working with him, Vrablic had
counted on her superiors to dismiss the objections, no matter how
valid, as based on professional envy. And they had.

By 2016, though, as Vrablic tried to push through yet one more
loan to Trump, she was more isolated. Her longtime boss, the

man who'd hired her at Deutsche, had recently left. So had Jain, forced to resign months earlier. Vrablic appealed Jack Brand's decision to an internal committee that evaluated proposed transactions that posed potential risks to the bank's reputation. The panel, consisting of Deutsche executives, risk managers, and lawyers in the United States, met every couple of weeks. Given Trump's high profile, this was a special situation, and so an emergency meeting was convened on the twentieth floor of Deutsche's Wall Street skyscraper, around the corner from the New York Stock Exchange. After hearing a quick summary of the proposed loan, the committee unanimously voted to reject it. "It was an affront to all of our senses," recalls an executive involved in the deliberations.

That should have been the end of the matter, but Vrablic and her colleagues appealed the committee's decision to Frankfurt, where the bank was headquartered. Christian Sewing, a Deutsche lifer who had recently taken over responsibility for its international wealth-management and private-banking business, heard the proposal and he, too, balked. Sewing already knew that Trump was an important bank client, but the combination of Trump's awful business record and the fact that he was now a serious contender for the American presidency meant it was time to cut ties, or at least to stop adding to them. Sewing said no, a larger committee in charge of monitoring the entire bank's risks also vetoed it, and in March 2016 the loan died before it was born.

After decades of making expedient, easy choices with the single-minded purpose of maximizing immediate profits, Deutsche had internalized a painful lesson: Its long-standing inability to say no—to clients, to shareholders, to testosterone-fueled traders and managers—was potentially lethal. It was a big part of the reason Deutsche was teetering on the brink of financial ruin, with a sizable contingent of the financial world bracing (and in some cases hoping) for it to fall over that cliff's edge. Finally, the bank's top executives had opted to turn down a short-term business opportunity for the sake of their institution's long-term health.

It was too late.

For its first twelve decades, Deutsche Bank had been little more than a lender to German and other European companies and, more widely, a funder of infrastructure and development projects. But these activities weren't very lucrative, and starting in the late 1980s, this proud national icon was seduced by the siren song of Wall Street riches. A crew of Americans—led by a charismatic salesman named Edson Mitchell and his sidekick and best friend, Bill Broeksmit—would arrive to give Deutsche a dramatic makeover. Before long, it was competing alongside hard-charging U.S. investment banks, trading stocks and bonds and peddling complex financial products of all shapes and sizes. English replaced German as Deutsche's official language. The locus of power shifted from Frankfurt and Berlin to London and New York. To the chagrin of the German industrialists, bankers, union leaders, and politicos who had long called the shots, American investment bankers and traders increasingly dominated the bank's upper ranks. High-risk trading became an end unto itself, rather than a means to serve clients.

This new strategy worked well—until it didn't. Deutsche's investment bankers and traders cranked out one record-breaking year after another, and soon the Wall Street division was responsible for most of Deutsche's revenue and profits. Executives and rank-and-file bankers got rich. So did shareholders.

But it was an ascent fueled by greed, sloppiness, hubris, and criminality, and when the reckoning came, it was brutal. Deutsche's risk-taking—the product of years of make-money-at-all-costs mismanagement—was out of control. Painful financial decisions had been punted far down the road. Its computer systems didn't talk to each other. Neither did its German and American executives. Managers were incentivized to shirk responsibilities. Different subsidiaries competed against each other for business. Even by the amoral standards of Wall Street, Deutsche exhibited a jarring lack of interest in its clients' reputations. It would soon become enveloped in scandals related to money laundering, tax evasion, manipulating interest rates, manipulating the prices of precious metals, manipulating the currencies markets, bribing foreign officials, accounting fraud, violating international sanctions, ripping off customers, and ripping off the German, British, and United States governments. (The list went on.) A straight line connected the corporate culture that permitted those crimes to the corporate culture that permitted the bank to become Donald Trump's chief financial enabler. By the time of his inauguration as president, Deutsche's very survival was in doubt.

This is the story of Deutsche Bank's rise and fall. It is about the men who transformed a sleepy German lender into what was, for a time, the largest bank in the world, but who also set the stage for the ensuing catastrophe. It is about one well-intentioned and honest man who tried to save the bank but couldn't save himself, and about his son, who embarked on a quest to understand his father's demise. And it is about the consequences—dead people, doomed companies, broken economies, and the forty-fifth president of the United States—that Deutsche Bank wrought on the world.

PART I

CHAPTER 1

A CRIMINAL ENTERPRISE

On September 8, 1883, a private four-coach train chugged into Gold Creek, Montana. It was packed with hundreds of American and European dignitaries—members of Congress, diplomats, high-ranking judges, Ulysses S. Grant. On its way from Chicago, the Northern Pacific Special had made a number of stops so that its passengers could admire waterfalls, scenic vistas, and President Chester A. Arthur, who had greeted the travelers in Minneapolis. In dusty Gold Creek—an old mining outpost on its way to becoming a ghost town—a contingent of Crow Indians performed war dances for men in bowler hats and women in ruffled dresses. A newly constructed pavilion, bedecked with gold-mining pickaxes and sprigs of greenery, afforded seating for a thousand spectators.

Henry Villard—slim, balding, and sporting a well-manicured brown mustache—stood before the crowd in a black coat, hat, and necktie, ready for his moment in the limelight. Thirty years earlier, Villard—then going by his given name, Heinrich Hilgard—had emigrated to America, a penniless, sickly German eighteen-year-old who spoke zero English. He had worked in wheat fields and at a lumber yard and on a wood-burning train and as a bartender before eventually landing a job for a German-language newspaper. That was the springboard for a reporting career in which he would cover Abraham Lincoln and the Civil War and, in the process, become a respected syndicated journalist. After the war, his pedigree established, Villard married the daughter of the great abolitionist and progressive William Lloyd Garrison. But all of that was not enough for Villard: He wanted fame and fortune. And the greatest fame and fortune to be had at the end of the nineteenth century were in the railroads.

Charismatic and charming, Villard exuded a fearless, infectious confidence. Like many master showmen, he also had a tendency for exaggeration and a taste for his own celebrity—not to mention blind spots when it came to weighing risks, keeping track of money, and focusing on details. Banking on his national heritage and promising riches, he convinced German institutions to entrust him with millions of dollars to invest in American railroads. Using other people's money, he refashioned himself as an up-and-coming industrial baron. He soon achieved fame and fortune—his initial investments in railroads paid off handsomely—and bought a brick mansion that stretched a full block along New York's Madison Avenue, its interior decorated in grand Renaissance style and its mahogany floors inlaid with mother-of-pearl.* It was about a quarter of a mile away from the future Trump Tower, where another rich man, needing to prove himself to the world, would live in comparable gaudiness.[1]

In September 1883, the forty-five-year-old Villard had journeyed to southwestern Montana to mark the completion of his company's Northern Pacific Railway, a key segment of the transcontinental railroad. Always the self-publicist, he arranged for

---

* Today, Villard's mansion is preserved as the historic wing of the New York Palace Hotel.

photographers to capture him swinging a large hammer to drive in the ceremonial last spike, then mounting a shiny black locomotive, festooned in American flags, like a big-game hunter standing atop his conquered prey. The audience—including a German banker named Georg von Siemens—cheered.

Yet as Villard celebrated for the crowd and cameras in Gold Creek, his overextended company was unraveling financially, crushed by a massive and unsustainable load of debt. Within weeks of the last-stake ceremony, Northern Pacific defaulted on its loans. Creditors seized Villard's Madison Avenue mansion. A group of banks bailed out his prized railroad on the condition that he resign from the company. Villard stepped down but refused to accept blame for the debacle, insisting that he was the victim of bad luck and economic forces outside his control. It was scant comfort to creditors who lost their money.

Georg von Siemens was among those losers. His fledgling bank had helped sell $20 million of bonds that had financed Northern Pacific's breakneck expansion. The bonds were now worth pennies on the dollar. At a normal bank, a customer's default typically spelled the end of the relationship, or at least the onset of a much more conservative posture. But Siemens's bank wasn't normal, and it would soon pave the way for Villard's comeback.[2]

Thirteen years earlier, in April 1870, Siemens's tiny bank had opened for business in Berlin, chartered by "highest decree" of His Majesty the King of Prussia. Its offices were a short walk down Französische Straße from the Berlin stock exchange, inside a dilapidated shingled building, reached by a treacherous staircase. He chose an almost generic name for his new company: Deutsche Bank.

A group of German businessmen had established the bank

along with Siemens to facilitate international commerce, especially between German and other European companies—and most important, to free German firms from relying on the dominant British banks to finance their international growth. Deutsche Bank didn't provide banking services to individuals; its sole focus was on rapidly growing industries. Deutsche Bank's mission was decidedly imperial. It saw its role as helping Germany's business community—and Germany itself—establish far-flung beachheads. Within two years, the bank had outposts in China and Japan. By the 1880s, it was lending money to German companies in South America and the United States and financing the czar's Russian railroads. Projects in the Balkans and the Middle East followed, including a railway stretching from Istanbul to Baghdad.[3]

Siemens was the bank's first leader. A portly, cigar-chomping man (and a cousin of the founder of the giant eponymous electrical company), he didn't know much about banking. "I nevertheless try to look very erudite, give the occasional shrug, grin from ear to ear—this is my sneering smile—and secretly refer, when I get home, to my encyclopedia or dictionary," he confided to a family member.[4] Siemens was boisterous and brimming with creative energy; details were not his strong suit. These shortcomings were not lost on Siemens's colleagues. "The transactions on which my brilliant colleague embarked stood on what were to some extent artificial foundations," Hermann Wallich, whose job at the bank was to serve as the check on Siemens's impulsivity, wrote in his memoirs. The public had no idea, though, "and my colleague was hailed as a genius."[5]

The year after Northern Pacific's implosion, Villard retreated to Germany to lick his wounds. There he got to know Siemens. The two men bonded over their shared visions of progressive politics, of an electrified future, of a coming American Century. Siemens had become infatuated with the young, scrappy, and hungry country on his trip to Gold Creek, and he was dying to have his bank do more business in the United States. A few years after Villard burned the bank, Siemens again placed his faith— and Deutsche's money—in the aspiring tycoon.

In 1886, Villard returned to New York with a mandate to scout out investments for Deutsche Bank. He quickly ginned up opportunities; Deutsche sold a total of more than $60 million of railroad securities to German investors, playing an important role financing the development of America's rail network. Soon he convinced Deutsche Bank to lend him millions to invest in his old railroad so that he could be installed, once again, as its leader. As his great-granddaughter would write in a biography more than a century later: "Armed to the teeth with German capital, Henry Villard could return to the railroad wars."[6] Soon, American newspapers were hailing him as "The Railroad King" and a "genius of financial operations."

Villard might have been a visionary, but he was not a financial genius. He was reckless, and this became clearer each time he returned to Berlin to plead for millions of dollars in additional loans. Despite signs that Northern Pacific was once again facing financial distress, Deutsche kept backing Villard. At times Siemens even encouraged Villard to move faster to spend the bank's money. Rarely, it seems, did Siemens ask for collateral to protect the bank and its investors. "It is a little hard to understand why Deutsche Bank gave Villard such a wide berth," a biographer of the bank wrote with considerable understatement in 2008.[7]

Partly thanks to Deutsche Bank's generosity, the Northern Pacific by the 1890s was massive: thousands of miles of track, tens of millions of acres of land. But that expansion had been bankrolled by hundreds of millions of dollars of debt. For the second time in a decade, Villard's railroad had grown dangerously over-leveraged. In 1893, the interest on that debt was nearly $11 million a year, which was in addition to the company's roughly $25 million in annual operating expenses. By contrast, the railroad's annual revenue averaged $10 million. Then, on top of that irreconcilably lopsided ledger, a great financial crisis descended on the United States and Europe, and Northern Pacific went from treading water to sinking fast. Twice in 1893, Villard traveled to Germany to beg for more money, and twice the bank—by now grudgingly—threw millions of dollars of good money after bad.[8] It wasn't enough. A defeated but unapologetic Villard, now gout-stricken and with a silver comb-over, sent a self-pitying cable to Deutsche that August to inform his sponsors that Northern Pacific was bankrupt. Once again he blamed circumstances outside his control.[9] Deutsche was stuck with millions of dollars in losses—a painful blow at the time—and many of its furious clients, to whom Deutsche had sold Northern Pacific bonds, suffered ruinous hits.

A century later, in 1995, a German historian would write: "This was the first (but not the last) time that the bank had the wool pulled over its eyes by a man who employed great personal charm and shrewd publicity to win over investors and repeatedly mobilize fresh sources of credit, but whose business rested on thoroughly rickety foundations."[10]

While the Villard experience was bad, it was not catastrophic. Deutsche kept growing, propelled by the rapid industrialization of Germany, Europe, and the world. By 1903, its Berlin headquarters occupied an entire city block. A decade later, benefiting in part from acquisitions of domestic competitors, it was the world's sixth-largest bank, with nearly 10,000 employees.[11] A set of statues in its headquarters illustrated its global dreams: five men, each from a different continent, each chiseled with stereotypes.[12] The North American was a cowboy with a pistol in one hand and a locomotive in the other. The African and Australian figures were dark-skinned warriors, brandishing weapons and wearing loincloths. The European was a noble-looking knight. (The ponytailed Asian just looked confused.)

When Hitler took power in 1933, the bank was transformed into a financing source for the Nazi military machine. Decades later, historians hired by the bank would explain its actions as the inevitable result of operating under a fascist regime. They would note, accurately, that most large German companies helped the Nazis and would distance the bank's management from the criminal behavior of local lenders that Deutsche took over. "He was at worst an opportunist, at best a man of character who had to practice his profession in a human system," one academic wrote of the bank's leader at the time, Hermann Abs.[13] That sanitizes a basic fact: Deutsche Bank and its executives were parties to genocide. World War II and the Holocaust would have happened without the bank, but its participation allowed the Nazis to improve the ruthless efficiency of their military campaign and their quest to cleanse Europe of Jews. And it was not an accident. Deutsche was involved because of decisions made by the bank's leaders for reasons of expedience, if not ideology.

Once Hitler ascended, the Jewish members of the bank's board were forced to resign. The resignations had been suggested by Germany's central bank, and though some Deutsche executives worried about setting a bad precedent, they were overruled by colleagues who were inclined to remain in the good graces of the Nazis.[14] At the bank's annual employee meeting in 1933, Nazi flags hung on the walls and podium, and the gathering began with a parade of the company's SS members. Deutsche soon started pressuring its clients to remove Jews from their boards of directors. By 1938, the bank had conducted hundreds of "Aryanizations"—taking over Jewish businesses or assets and handing them over to Aryans.[15] In the 1940s, the bank's annual reports were adorned with swastikas in lieu of a corporate logo.[16]

As Germany steamrolled across Europe, Deutsche took over conquered countries' local banks and dutifully completed the Aryanization process with those banks' clients. Deutsche sold more than 1,600 pounds of gold the Nazis had stolen from Holocaust victims—some of it extracted from Jews' teeth and then melted down—and the proceeds provided Hitler's regime with desperately needed hard currency to buy weapons and raw materials.[17] Deutsche financed the construction of the Auschwitz death camp and a new factory nearby, which was run using Auschwitz's slave labor and which manufactured Zyklon B, the chemical used in Auschwitz's gas chambers. The Auschwitz loans were closely reviewed by bank managers, who received regular updates on the progress of the camp's construction.[18]

There is no proof that Hermann Abs knew exactly what was going on inside the death camp his bank was financing. He wasn't a member of the Nazi Party. But it is inconceivable that he was completely in the dark. In addition to his role at Deutsche, he sat on the board of I. G. Farben, the chemical company that was building the factory alongside Auschwitz. At best, there is no record of Abs raising any questions or concerns about the bank's complicity in mass murder.[19]

So synonymous was Deutsche with German military aggression that the bank earned a cameo in the 1942 movie *Casablanca*. In a scene at Rick's Café, a German, later identified as a representative of Deutsche Bank, tries to get into the gambling room. The bouncer refuses him entry, as does Humphrey Bogart's Rick Blaine. "Your cash is good at the bar," he says.

"What! Do you know who I am?" the banker demands.

"I do," Rick responds coolly. "You're lucky the bar's open to you."

After Germany surrendered in 1945, Berlin was divvied up among the Allied powers. The ruins of the bank's headquarters happened to fall in the British quadrant. That proved fortuitous. Germany still owed England reparations from World War I. If the British had any hope of recouping that money, a strong German bank would be necessary to bring the country's economy back from the dead. Hermann Abs had fled Berlin in the back of a delivery truck on the eve of the Allied invasion, and he was now wanted as a war criminal. When he was later tried in absentia and sentenced to a decade of hard labor, the British came to his aid; Abs ended up working the fields at an upscale prison camp for a few months and then was released.

The American military did not feel as kindly. It concluded in a report that Deutsche Bank had been "a participant in the execution of the criminal policies of the Nazi regime in the economic field." The report recommended that the bank "be liquidated" and that top executives be barred from holding positions of power as Germany was rebuilt.

The United States didn't get what it wanted. As part of a compromise with Britain, Deutsche was split into ten regional institutions, forbidden from operating under the name Deutsche Bank. But this was a decentralization, not a demolition. The bank's legal structure was left basically intact, with no restrictions on the ten institutions interacting with each other. Unsurprisingly, it didn't take long for the bank's supporters—including Abs—to start campaigning for Deutsche to be resuscitated so that it could serve as an engine of European economic recovery and ward off the communist menace.[20] Slowly but surely, the ten ostensibly independent banks were fused back together. By 1956, they published an annual report under the umbrella name

Deutsche Bank Group. Soon after that, the ten banks were legally reunited, operating out of a three-story stone building in Frankfurt. The name *Deutsche Bank* was hung from the top of the building in large bold lettering. The bank's directors unanimously elected Abs—the convicted war criminal—to be their leader.[21]

What followed was an extraordinary era of growth and rebuilding in which West Germany and its leading bank (and some of its other large corporations) quickly returned to international prominence.

In the late 1950s, Deutsche again spread its wings internationally, doing business in South Africa, Mexico, Hong Kong, and Egypt. It lent money to companies all over Western Europe—and even in the USSR, where it led a group of banks that financed a natural gas pipeline for the communist government. (Ironically, the bank was helping the country at the same time that it had regained international acceptance partly because of the need to fend off the Reds.) Abs, a master of financial minutiae, was a workaholic, often surviving for months on four hours of sleep a night. With much of the West focused on the threat of communism, the war-criminal taint faded. In 1957, Abs and his wife were invited to attend Dwight D. Eisenhower's second inaugural.[22]

By Deutsche's centenary in 1970, it had more than a thousand branches in Germany and dozens of outposts around the world. It was one of Europe's leading banks, an extraordinary achievement for the flagship lender of a country defeated in back-to-back world wars. In 1984, the bank moved into a pair of gleaming 500-foot glass towers that dominated the Frankfurt skyline. Locals nicknamed the skyscrapers Debit and Credit.

Despite its international expansion, the bank was German

through and through. It took ownership stakes in some of the country's leading businesses: the automaker Daimler-Benz, the insurer Allianz, the airline Lufthansa. Its directors sat on the boards of other big German concerns. This was a bank that held corporate retreats and invited, for entertainment, leading German actresses to recite German poetry.[23] But that wouldn't last much longer. In 1987, a man named Alfred Herrhausen took over as the top executive, and he was determined to drag Deutsche Bank into what he saw as the promise of the modern capitalist age.

Herrhausen had grown up in a downtrodden industrial part of Germany and attended a school the Nazis had set up for gifted children. His goal was to one day be a philosopher or a teacher. When he couldn't get into a university philosophy program, he decided to study economics. In the 1960s, he worked in the finance department of a German utility company. He joined Deutsche in 1970, and he eventually gained responsibility for much of its international business before becoming its highest-ranking executive.[24]

Herrhausen believed that if Germany were to fully return to the international stage, it needed a bank with global ambitions—not just geographically, but also in terms of the types of products and services it offered to the modern corporation. With trade barriers falling and telecommunications making the world smaller, this was the moment to pounce. Herrhausen bought banks in Spain, Portugal, Italy, and the Netherlands, and he accelerated lending in the Soviet Union, transforming his institution into Europe's only pancontinental lender. He also acquired banks in Asia. "As the world becomes our marketplace, we must be present in the world," Herrhausen told an interviewer in March 1989.[25]

Herrhausen looked like a statesman and often acted like one, too. He had a long pointy nose and wore his fine brown hair short, parted neatly on the left, with no trace of sideburns. His skin was tan and so clean-shaven that it seemed to shine. He was a leading German voice for the economic integration of Europe and an advocate for forgiving the debts of third-world countries. He became a confidant of Helmut Kohl, the German chancellor, he dined with Mikhail Gorbachev, and he was a guest in the Connecticut home of Henry Kissinger.[26]

Perched on the thirtieth floor of one of Deutsche's skyscrapers, the fifty-nine-year-old Herrhausen looked down on the rest of the German financial capital. In November 1989, a week after the fall of the Berlin Wall appeared to vindicate much of Herrhausen's liberal free-market ideology, a leading German newspaper, *Der Spiegel*, gushed: "Hardly ever before has one person ruled the economic scene the way Deutsche Bank chief executive Alfred Herrhausen does at the present time. The banker is all-powerful."[27]

Herrhausen then made a play for even more power. Back in 1984, Deutsche had purchased a 5 percent stake in a venerable British investment bank, Morgan Grenfell. It was an opportune time to dive into the investment-banking business in London, where Margaret Thatcher's deregulation of the finance industry—the so-called Big Bang—had sparked an epic boom. In the fall of 1989, though, a French company made a hostile bid to buy Morgan Grenfell. Herrhausen decided to thwart the French and buy Morgan outright, an acquisition that would catapult the German company onto a global stage like never before. On Monday, November 27, 1989, he flew to London to unveil the $1.5 billion purchase of Morgan Grenfell. "We're trying to strengthen ourselves to become a real European bank," he told reporters.[28] It was the largest-ever acquisition of an investment bank. Deutsche Bank had become a true colossus, its shadow darkening much of the earth.

Four days later, on a chilly Friday morning, a convoy of three silver Mercedes-Benz sedans pulled up outside Herrhausen's home in the suburb of Bad Homburg to drive him the twelve miles into Frankfurt. Deutsche took security seriously, and his house, behind a white stucco wall, was under round-the-clock police protection. At 8:30 A.M., Herrhausen climbed into the middle car, with bulletproof windows and armored side panels. In front of and behind him were vehicles filled with his bodyguards. The convoy cruised along the suburb's tree-lined streets and, as was the practice, followed a different route than it had taken the day before.

A bicycle was parked on the side of the road. A satchel was strapped to the bike. Inside the satchel was a homemade bomb: forty pounds of explosives, shrapnel, and a large copper plate. An infrared beam, set up by terrorists posing as workmen, intersected the street.

At 8:34, the convoy breached the beam, and the bomb exploded. Shrapnel and the copper plate streaked into the street, scoring a direct hit on the rear half of Herrhausen's car, where he was seated. The impact threw the car several yards into the air, smashing its windows, and blasting off its doors, trunk, and hood. The copper projectile severed Herrhausen's legs. Before fire trucks or ambulances arrived, he bled to death in the backseat.[29]

The assassination shocked Germany, which had been in a celebratory mood following the fall of the Berlin Wall. Chancellor Kohl, visiting a Düsseldorf trade fair, cried. "It is a threat to our democracy," the future finance minister Wolfgang Schäuble told the German parliament. Some 10,000 business and government leaders from around the world showed up for Herrhausen's funeral. The site of the bombing became a shrine of flowers and burning candles.

The murder was the work of the Red Army Faction, a group of Marxist terrorists. They released a communiqué explaining the attack: Deutsche Bank "has cast its net over all of West Europe and stands at the head of the fascistic capitalist structure, against which everyone has to assert themselves."[30]

If the attack was intended to decapitate Deutsche, it was an unmitigated failure. At an even faster clip, the bank would soon grow bigger, more ambitious, and much more aggressive.

CHAPTER 2

EDSON AND BILL

O ne day in the future, Edson Mitchell would change Wall Street. For now, he was stuck on an egg farm.

The sprawling DeCoster farm in Maine was home to more than 2.8 million chickens in the 1970s. The place reeked, partly from all the birds and partly from the fumes emitted by the long-haul trucks that transported the eggs all over the country. If the smell wasn't bad enough, the farm's owner and operator, Jack DeCoster, had a history of mistreating his workers—many of them Vietnamese immigrants—and flouting workplace safety rules. By the time Edson started working there in 1975, DeCoster was on his way to earning the title of "Maine's most infamous businessman,"[1] a designation that would be cemented years later when his salmonella-infested eggs poisoned thousands of Americans and he and his son were sent to prison.

Mitchell, having just graduated from nearby Colby College with an economics degree, worked in the farm's accounting department. He didn't like the stench or the feeling of working for a bad man. Yet he didn't know what else to do with his life. He'd been raised in a fading Maine mill town; his father had been a janitor. There had been long stretches between jobs, and those

periods were awful for young Edson—he could feel his parents'
anxiety about how long they could survive without another pay-
check. He was determined not to follow a similar path of financial insecurity, and he already had a young family to support. He
and his high school girlfriend, Suzan, had married during their
sophomore year at Colby and, living in a trailer off-campus, had
a baby. Another would be on its way soon.

Finally the day came when Mitchell could no longer bear
working among the chickens. He quit and enrolled in business
school at Dartmouth. It was a big gamble, but he considered himself a born risk-taker and was brimming with confidence and
impulsivity.[2]

Students at Dartmouth's Tuck School of Business gravitated
toward jobs in finance, and the best place to land—the destination
that virtually ensured that you would quickly amass a small
fortune—was Wall Street. Positions with firms like Goldman
Sachs and Morgan Stanley were the real prizes, but even the scrap-
pier, lower-tier investment banks were rolling in money in the
1980s. Edson didn't make the cut. Instead, he became a so-called
commercial banker—making loans to companies—in Bank of
America's Chicago office. His clients included the likes of Beatrice
Foods, a huge chemical and food-processing company. It was a respectable gig, but Mitchell soon grew disenchanted. He yearned
for more than a respectable life—he wanted to be extraordinary.

An opportunity soon presented itself at Merrill Lynch, known
for its "Thundering Herd" of stockbrokers, so numerous that they
routinely moved markets. Merrill had ambitions of becoming a
well-rounded Wall Street bank, of earning the respect associated
with being a player in banking's big leagues. That meant it
needed to move beyond simply advising mom-and-pop clients on
which stocks they should buy in exchange for peanut-sized commissions. It needed to get into the more lucrative but much risk-

ier business of actually buying and selling bonds and other securities.

Mitchell was hired as a vice president in Merrill's Chicago offices to help with the bond-trading business. Within a year, he was promoted to a leadership role that required him to relocate to New York, where Merrill was based. He and Suzan, happy to leave Chicago, moved to a wealthy New Jersey suburb.

A short, wiry redhead, Mitchell was ferociously competitive and imbued with a frenetic energy that made him resemble a human whirlwind. He also was a charming, relentless salesman, the type of guy who could convince a vegetarian to order a steak through sheer optimistic persuasion. He took Merrill's headquarters by storm.

Mitchell had a big idea: Merrill should dive into the fledgling business of derivatives. Derivatives are products whose values are derived from something else. If you are an ice-cream maker, you might purchase derivatives whose value rises along with the price of milk. That way, as higher dairy prices eat into your ice-cream profits, your profits from the rising value of the derivatives will make up the difference.

In their simplest form, derivatives have been around for centuries, their values rising and falling along with the actual or expected prices of commodities such as tulip bulbs, oil, or pork bellies. But in the 1980s, they underwent a revolution, mutating from simple structures—tracking dairy prices, for example—to complex new breeds that, say, tracked the price of a particular type of milk in Vermont in certain months and that would gain or lose value based partly on the performance of another dairy product, in another state, in a different time period. In theory, anything could be linked—milk with car parts, orders for silicon chips with the price of peanut butter—as long as you could find parties willing to bet on both sides.

As banking became increasingly commoditized, specializing in derivatives was a way to stand out—a corner of the banking business not yet dominated by any of the established powers. Mitchell's hunch was that derivatives were the future—and if his company moved fast and decisively, Merrill had a rare chance to bust in and overtake some of the Street's biggest bond-trading houses, firms like the mighty Salomon Brothers. "I began to realize that this was an instrument that could pervade all aspects of what we did as a financial intermediary," he would explain more than a decade later, at his induction into the Derivatives Hall of Fame (sponsored, appropriately enough, by Arthur Andersen).[3]

This was Merrill's destiny, he argued to his superiors, and they should help him fulfill it. They bought the pitch, and Edson Mitchell soon set out on a hiring spree. To help lead his charge, he looked to another young man working as a Chicago banker. His name was Bill Broeksmit.

Jack Broeksmit had graduated from Yale and then served as a lieutenant in the Navy during World War II. After the war, he married Jane, a librarian and amateur artist. They had six children; William Shaw Broeksmit, born on November 5, 1955, was the fourth. The year after Bill's birth, Jack was ordained into the ministry by the United Church of Christ, and for the next decade he was minister of the First Congregational Church in Galva, Illinois, some 150 miles west of Chicago. Reverend Jack's sermons were filled with fables about the importance of understanding other people. The key, he preached, was to try to see things from other people's vantage points. Avoid casting judgment. Ask questions. Recognize and then try to put aside your biases. Congregants would come up to Reverend Jack after his sermons or stop him on the streets of Galva and solicit his advice. Bill would later tell people that his father had instilled in him the notion that over the long term, it paid dividends to do right by other people.[4]

The Broeksmits weren't poor, but they definitely weren't rich. "There was a certain amount of education pedigree, but there wasn't any money," the youngest child, Bob, would say.[5] Bill was slim and had dark brown hair so thick that it was hard to comb. His bushy eyebrows cast shadows over his brown eyes. He excelled at math and had a mischievous entrepreneurial streak. He had a newspaper route and enlisted his two younger brothers to wrap up and then deliver the Sunday papers. Bill paid them less than he was earning, pocketed the difference, and eventually used the proceeds to buy a television set that his father had been unwilling to purchase. Bill's business career was under way.

He received a scholarship to Claremont Men's College, a small liberal arts school in the Los Angeles suburbs.* Finance fascinated him. He talked his roommates' ears off about the markets. Even as an undergrad, he had a knack and an appetite for complex financial instruments, seeming to have an intuitive grasp of the relationships between things like interest rates and stocks— how rising rates might lead a particular company's shares to lose value. Bill, who had a facility for writing and enjoyed it, bankrolled his occasional market bets by churning out term papers for some of his wealthier classmates.

After graduating, Bill moved to Chicago. By day, he was hardworking, quiet, and introspective. When a colleague's wife died, Bill sent a sympathy card, something that would never have occurred to the group of new graduates. "I asked him why, and he said because it's what is done, it is the right thing to do," says his

---

* It admitted its first class of women in 1976, the start of Bill's senior year, and was renamed Claremont McKenna College. Twenty-five years later, I graduated from CMC.

girlfriend at the time, Liz Miles. "Compared to most of us, Bill was self-sufficient and responsible."

But his demons tended to come out at night—heavy drinking, hard drugs, prostitutes. Bill was the guy who, when others were ready to head home in the wee hours of the morning, would push everyone to have one more round. "He just didn't know how to turn it off," one of his best friends, Jon Schink, recalls. Friends could tell something—they couldn't ever put their finger on *what*—haunted him. "Bill was wonderfully brilliant, but deeply troubled," remembers Tom Marks, who was Bill's roommate in a rented Chicago brownstone. "He did things by night that were in sharp contrast to his daytime behavior."

Once, in the early 1980s, Broeksmit went to Las Vegas with Schink. After a night of drinking and gambling, the two men walked down the mostly deserted Strip toward their hotel. Two prostitutes approached Bill and started fondling him a little. As they walked away, Bill realized that the rollick had been a ruse: One of the women had stolen a wad of hundreds of dollars out of his pocket. He hollered at them, gave chase, and tackled the thief. They rolled around, fighting, on the dirty sidewalk until a pair of cops came to break it up and returned the money to Bill.

Bill got an MBA at Northwestern University and then a job at Continental Illinois, one of the country's largest and fastest-growing banks. He set out to master derivatives, tinkering with the structures of the fledgling products and conjuring new uses by mushing together different types of derivatives. Colleagues hailed him as a financial innovator—and that reputation soon spread.

Derivatives would later become a dirty word—wreaking havoc across the financial industry and the broader economy—but when Broeksmit joined Continental Illinois, he and his peers saw them as a powerful way for businesses to operate better. Companies could insulate themselves from risks in ways never before thought of. That allowed them to produce a greater number of widgets at a lower price, and those savings would be passed on to their customers while maintaining profits for the companies. Here was a rare financial invention—right up there with cash machines and credit cards and thirty-year mortgages—that was truly helpful for a great many people and institutions.

Wall Street, of course, had plans for derivatives far removed from the original mission of helping ice-cream companies protect against rising dairy prices. Derivatives would no longer be used mainly as mechanisms for companies to play defense; now they would be vehicles for banks and others to engage in financial speculation—essentially the spinning ball on the roulette wheel. This was about to become a hugely profitable, mostly unregulated corner of the global financial system. And that meant that people with expertise in derivatives—the more complex, the better—suddenly became coveted.

In May 1984, Continental Illinois was overpowered by a tidal wave of bad real estate loans. It was the largest bank ever to fail in the United States, a record it would hold for nearly a quarter of a century.

Broeksmit, not quite thirty, narrowly escaped the sinking ship. Edson Mitchell had come knocking just as the bank was taking on a fatal amount of water, and earlier in 1984, he accepted a job as one of Mitchell's lieutenants, charged with leading Merrill into the brave new world of derivatives. Bill and his young wife—a Ukrainian divorcée named Alla—relocated to Short Hills, a New Jersey suburb filled with palatial homes. The Broeksmits couldn't afford one of those—yet. They moved into a tidy colonial-style house that was a quick walk from the commuter rail station that would shuttle Broeksmit into Manhattan every day to work alongside Mitchell.

Merrill Lynch was cleaner than the DeCoster egg farm, but just barely. The place was the embodiment of Wall Street's unbridled id in the middle of a go-go decade: cocaine in the bathrooms and strippers on the trading floor.[6]

At the time, the list of derivatives available to Merrill's clients was limited. Bill and Edson expanded the menu. Bill started dreaming up new types of a popular derivative known as *swaps* that were designed to help institutions protect themselves from changes in things like interest rates. He combined different types of swaps into mutant instruments with names like *callable interest rate swaps* and *yield curve swaps* and *swaptions*.

This was good news for clients and great news for Merrill. Each time Merrill sold a swap to a client, it pocketed a fee. What's more, Broeksmit devised clever new ways for Merrill to protect *itself* by using derivatives when it bought assets from customers. Because the derivatives were reducing the risks Merrill faced on various transactions, the firm now had a greater capacity to do more of those transactions—which meant more revenue for Merrill.

All these new types of derivatives made corporate clients more willing to issue debt. After all, if they could protect themselves, or hedge, against volatile interest rates, that effectively lowered the cost of borrowing money. Fannie Mae, the government-controlled company that was the biggest financer of mortgages in America, was one example. Because so much of Fannie's business revolved around interest rates—it was buying boatloads of mortgages, with all sorts of different interest rates and repayment terms—it had a big appetite for sophisticated products to insulate itself from future changes in rates. Broeksmit concocted a complex solution for Fannie, and Merrill became the company's go-to bank. Soon scores of blue-chip companies were flocking to Merrill not only for the swaps but also to handle their sale of the bonds. Billions of dollars in new business poured in. Merrill suddenly was a formidable player. Mitchell got most of the credit—he was quickly becoming one of the rising stars of Wall Street—but it was thanks in large part to Broeksmit.

Decades later, grizzled veterans would look back on the changes that had transformed the banking industry and would pinpoint two catalysts. One was technology and the internet, which accelerated the business and made it more efficient. The other was the modern swaps market. Broeksmit was largely responsible for animating the latter into something resembling a living organism in its complexity. "Because of people like Bill, but maybe none more so than Bill, the derivatives business went mainstream in usage for investors as well as corporations, financial institutions, and government agencies," explains a former colleague who would rise to the top of Wall Street.

Edson's goal was to position the bank at the crossroads of so many different transactions that it could make tons of money by skimming tiny amounts off each. This required the bank to amass enormous positions in multiple vast markets—a risky endeavor. Edson and Bill took to describing this special place in the middle of all these flows as "the whitewater"—the place where the money moved so rapidly that it churned everything into a froth. As they saw it, at the vortex of this whitewater were derivatives—and Merrill would be right there, floating on the turbulent waters, slurping up the profits.[7]

On the seventh floor of the northernmost building in the World Financial Center complex, Mitchell occupied a corner office with nice views of New York Harbor and the Hudson River. Broeksmit's office was about half the size, but it was just a few paces away from Mitchell's. Colleagues noted that the hallway carpet between their two offices was literally worn thin—that's how much they and other colleagues were shuttling back and forth.

The partnership worked, and in the process the two men became friends. They bonded over their large families: Bill, one of six children; Edson, with his own five kids. They bonded over their rural roots: Bill from small-town Illinois, Edson from Maine. They bonded over the fact that they hadn't been raised in privilege, that they were both outsiders.

Edson and Bill discussed everything: their colleagues, their strategies, their clients, their futures. Mitchell didn't always agree with Broeksmit, but he sought his advice, and Bill felt comfortable giving his unvarnished opinion. They complemented each other, one man's excesses filling in the other man's voids. Mitchell was overflowing with nervous energy, unable to sit still. Some colleagues called him Fast Eddie because you rarely had time to explain anything to him in detail. Waiting for an elevator, he would repeatedly push the button—and once the elevator came, he would keep pushing the button for whatever floor he was going to, trying to speed things up. Broeksmit liked to tell stories about how small airports all over the Midwest were littered with rental cars that Mitchell had deserted outside the terminals, too rushed to return them properly.

His eternal optimism—everything was doable!—and his burning desire to prove that the janitor's son could surmount long odds and exceed expectations fostered a competitiveness that seeped into almost everything Mitchell did. He went ballistic when his employees got poached and, as a result, became very skilled at preventing them from leaving. (Once he flew to Tokyo to persuade a mid-level trader to stay put.) Unlike other executives who would outsource the job of hiring young finance nerds, Edson frequented business-school campuses, interviewing promising students and hiring them on the spot. He even pressured colleagues to buy extra Girl Scout cookies from his kids so they could earn more badges.[8]

Where Mitchell was loud, brash, and impulsive, Broeksmit was quiet, cerebral, and thoughtful. By Merrill's frat-boy standards, Bill—with wavy jet-black hair pushed back from his forehead, rimless glasses with thick lenses, and a way of pursing his lips and narrowing his dark eyes when he listened that, if you didn't know him well, could come across as a smirk—was a nerd. He was flabby and unathletic. He was comfortable staying silent. When he was deep in thought, he tugged his bushy right eyebrow—a tic so common that it became a family joke. (It was less endearing when his hand went to his eyebrow while he was driving. "Dad!" one of his three kids would holler from the backseat. "Both hands on the wheel!") When he spoke, it was in a way that made clear he was really hearing what others were saying. His manner in questioning wasn't aggressive; he wasn't trying to catch you or trick you. He didn't need to show off. Indeed, on more than one occasion, he turned up to interview a job candidate in clothes that were ripped—and then, while chain-smoking cigarettes, overwhelmed the bemused prospective employee with his intellect to such a degree that the person was *dying* to work with him. He also wasn't very ambitious; he preferred to manage only a few people and didn't want to climb the corporate ladder. He stood out in an industry brimming with socially maladroit math whizzes and slightly sociopathic type A personalities.

Broeksmit frequently repeated the mantra "How does that help the client?"—a well-worn cliché on Wall Street, but he actually believed it. It was always tempting to make a killing by scamming customers, but the better long-term strategy, he advised colleagues, was to structure things in a way that your clients would prosper. "Everyone in banking wants to make money," one of his colleagues and friends would explain. "But there are different degrees of avarice." Bill was on the low end of that spectrum.

For that reason, he became an important counterweight to Mitchell. When risk managers rejected a transaction pitched by one of Edson's guys and Mitchell inevitably wanted to skin the risk manager alive, Broeksmit would intervene. John Breit, a particle physicist hired to rein in some of the traders, many years later would credit Bill with having saved his job from an angry Edson on multiple occasions.

By the early 1990s, Merrill's board of directors was getting nervous about the bank's expanding portfolio of derivatives. The imprudent use of derivatives had caused violent explosions inside some proud American companies, such as Procter & Gamble, which lost $157 million on a batch of interest-rate swaps it had purchased with borrowed money. ("Derivatives such as these are dangerous," P&G's chairman lamented.[9]) Such blowups had damaged the reputations of the banks that had sold the soon-to-be-toxic instruments. Merrill's board wanted to avoid their bank stumbling into a similar trap.

One source of the bank's anxiety was that by the early 1990s, swaps and other derivatives had changed dramatically—and, more important, were being used very differently. What had not long ago been a device designed for institutions to shield themselves from fluctuating interest rates or dairy prices or whatever had become a vehicle for speculation. Wall Street banks, including Merrill, were cashing in on such gambling. But many less sophisticated companies and pension plans and university endowments and local governments were yearning for a piece of the action, too. Why confine yourself to putting money in some staid company's stock when you could potentially hit the jackpot betting on swings in interest rates in one country compared to interest rates in another country? The possibilities seemed endless—and banks like Merrill encouraged such dreaming, ready to take advantage of their clueless clients.

One day in 1993, Mitchell, Broeksmit, and Breit went upstairs to deliver a presentation to the bank's board about why derivatives were not intrinsically dangerous. Breit droned on and on. At least two board members nodded off. Afterward, the men rode the elevator downstairs together, and Mitchell congratulated Breit on his presentation.

"What do you mean, Edson?" Breit asked. "They literally fell asleep."

Edson guffawed. "That's what we want!"

As years passed, Bill and Edson became inseparable, even outside the office. They frequented the century-old Russian and Turkish Baths in the East Village. Sometimes Bill's oldest child, Val, was allowed to tag along, watching as the men melted in the 190-degree sauna and had contests about who could stay in the longest. (A bright yellow sign warned against remaining more than thirty minutes at a time, but such rules were meant to be broken.) They'd sit in there, clad in the green shorts that the baths provided to people who didn't want to be naked, the hot air singeing their lungs, gossiping about work and their families.

The Broeksmit and Mitchell families started vacationing together in Maine. Bill and Alla had a summer home in the rustic seaside town of Brooklin, with a tennis court and a pond, a long stone's throw from the ocean. Mitchell, who already had a souped-up log cabin in Rangeley, bought a grand place down the road from the Broeksmit house. Edson and Bill would face off in intense tennis matches, followed by plunges into the frigid Atlantic. Mitchell's five kids, accustomed to a procession of bankers stopping by their homes to suck up to their dad, could tell the relationship with Broeksmit was special.

It was thanks to Merrill that Robert Citron, the treasurer of Orange County in Southern California, ended up using taxpayers' money to dabble in derivatives. The bank's salesmen in California had spent years wooing this quirky man (Citron liked to wear turquoise jewelry and loud ties and he regularly consulted astrology charts) because they could tell he was a "pigeon"—an easy mark.[10] Sure enough, Citron soon started gorging on the tasty new interest-rate swaps that Merrill was cooking up. Orange County placed an astronomical wager that interest rates in the United States and in Switzerland would move in different directions.[11] Citron's municipality even agreed to buy the derivatives with money it borrowed from Merrill, fattening the bank's profits. By 1993, the county had amassed a $2.8 billion portfolio of the derivatives—and had become Merrill's biggest single client. For a while, Orange County's investments performed perfectly. Everyone was happy.[12]

Broeksmit realized that if Orange County ran into trouble because of the derivatives, that trouble would likely boomerang back at the bank. Even if Merrill didn't directly lose money on the transactions—in fact, *especially* if it didn't lose money—the reputational damage associated with appearing to rip off California taxpayers would be severe. Already, risk managers like Breit had been whispering to Broeksmit that Orange County—and therefore Merrill—was on shaky ground. Bill in turn had been whispering to others, but the warnings weren't being heeded. (This was making the bank's board of directors antsy, too—part of the reason Mitchell, Broeksmit, and Breit had been summoned to the boardroom for Breit's sleep-inducing presentation.) So not long into 1993, Broeksmit typed up a memo giving voice to his anxieties. He went through a number of drafts, agonizing over the details and sharing versions with friends and Merrill confidants. He wanted to make sure he got it right; it was almost as if he knew he was writing for posterity.

On February 24, 1993, Broeksmit presented the finished three-page memo to Mitchell, who signed it, too, and then it was sent to senior Merrill executives in New York and California. The memo noted that Orange County's investment so far "has experienced fantastic appreciation." But, Broeksmit warned, if market conditions changed, things could get ugly fast. "The potential adverse consequences for Orange County in the event of a substantial increase in interest rates and the flight of hot money . . . compel us to be more forceful," he wrote. "I believe we should go on record recommending the sale of the entire portfolio" of derivatives. At the very least, he argued, Merrill should not sell the county any more derivatives.[13]

The missive didn't work. There is no evidence that Merrill did anything to stop Orange County from continuing to feast on the derivatives. For the next twenty months, tens of millions of dollars in fees and commissions continued to fill Merrill's coffers.[14]

Then, just as Bill had worried, the Federal Reserve started increasing interest rates. By the end of 1994, rates had nearly doubled from a year earlier. Orange County's derivatives began losing money—and then more and more and more. By December, the losses were $1.7 billion. The county filed for bankruptcy—and then filed a lawsuit seeking $2.5 billion in damages from Merrill for "wantonly and callously" selling the county inappropriate financial instruments. The state senate started investigating. Before long, Bill's memo was unearthed and made public. The *Los Angeles Times* noted the "uncanny accuracy" of his predictions in a front-page story in May 1995.[15] *The Wall Street Journal* ran a long page-one article about the dissenter inside Merrill who had prophesied the coming mess. Bill Broeksmit's legend was born.

CHAPTER 3

WALL STREET'S
GREAT MIGRATION

More than five years had passed since the murder of Alfred Herrhausen. Deutsche Bank had bounced back, as it would in the future after the sudden downfalls of important executives. Three months after the assassination, the bank's shares were up by 30 percent, a resounding vote of confidence in the company's future.[1]

Herrhausen's successor was Hilmar Kopper. Like Herrhausen, Kopper believed that the bank's future lay outside Germany. (He referred disparagingly to German bankers as "chaste souls."[2]) With the crumbling of the Berlin Wall, Deutsche opened branches in East Germany and then Warsaw, Budapest, and Prague. Within a few years, it had half a dozen outposts in the former Soviet Union.[3]

That was all well and good, but the Morgan Grenfell acquisition had proved underwhelming. Its architects had hoped it would launch Deutsche Bank into the Wall Street elite; that hadn't happened. One problem was that senior bankers from Morgan kept quitting, not interested in working with a bunch of provincial Germans. And Deutsche remained too conservative to go toe-to-toe with Wall Street. In most of the bank, for example, derivatives were considered dirty, needlessly complex instruments that had a nasty tendency to spread risk rather than contain it. A top executive warned that the bank should never be permitted to become a "Deutsche Sachs or a Deutsche Lynch"—in other words, to lose its identity to Wall Street.[4] While the bank had several hundred employees in the United States, it was an afterthought in the country's booming capital markets, surpassed not only by American banks but also by second-tier competitors from Japan, Britain, and France.

In 1994, Deutsche's top executives gathered in Madrid to talk strategy. Kopper declared that the bank's weak standing was an embarrassment not only to Deutsche but to all of Germany. Two recent events had made that plain. First, one of the bank's biggest customers, the German real estate developer Jürgen Schneider, had been revealed as a fraud. Deutsche had been his largest lender, financing flashy shopping-mall projects, including one practically next door to the bank's Frankfurt headquarters, and it now was staring at losses approaching $1 billion. The bank had put so much faith in this single client because its run-of-the-mill lending businesses were not very lucrative; making enormous loans to a guy whose financial statements Deutsche hadn't even bothered to review seemed like an enticing shortcut.[5]

And then, in another humiliation, Goldman Sachs had landed a coveted job helping to privatize Deutsche Telekom, the state-owed phone monopoly. Goldman—with its global presence and wealth of stock-issuing experience—had the ability to sell DT's shares worldwide and to trade them once they were public, and that had landed the American bank one of the all-time plum German banking assignments.[6] Wall Street was coming to Germany. Should Germany go to Wall Street?

It was time, Kopper argued in Madrid, to get serious about investment banking. Deutsche needed a big hire—a charismatic rainmaker who could lead the bank into the promised land.[7]

Just before Christmas in 1994, Bob Flohr had received a phone call from Edson Mitchell. A trim, polished man with a self-confidence derived from being an alum of both Princeton and the elite consultancy McKinsey, Flohr was a recruiter who had been working closely with Mitchell for a decade. His job was to find good people for Edson to hire and to serve as an informal adviser and source of industry intelligence. Now Edson told Flohr that they needed to get together as soon as possible. In the first days of 1995, they met for breakfast at the Princeton Club on West 43rd Street in Manhattan. Along with requiring jackets for gentlemen, the club had a policy against talking about work in the dining room. But that was all Mitchell wanted to discuss. He had become a minor industry legend for slingshotting Merrill into the big leagues, and now he wanted to capitalize on that success. After more than a decade at Merrill, he told Flohr, he was ready to build something new.

Flohr, as it turned out, had recently heard that Deutsche was planning an investment-banking blitz. Intrigued, Mitchell authorized him to go talk with his contacts at Deutsche on his behalf. Flohr flew to London to meet with Michael Dobson, an erudite Brit who was running Deutsche's investment-banking arm.[8] Would he be interested in hiring Edson? Yes.

A month or two later, Mitchell embarked on a top secret mission to Germany. He met with Deutsche's brass about moving to London to lead the bank's push to be a big player in financial markets worldwide. The job interviews went well. Usually the key sticking point in such negotiations is money, but Edson didn't drive a hard bargain on his own pay—he agreed to about $5 million a year for his first two years, roughly what he'd been making at Merrill. His main condition was that he be allowed to hire absolutely anyone he wanted to. Deutsche agreed.

Merrill soon got wind of what was happening. The firm offered Edson more money, more autonomy, more employees. But he was restless and ready for his next adventure. He stopped answering the plaintive phone calls from his Merrill higher-ups. The Monday after Easter, Edson boarded a helicopter from New York City to Princeton, New Jersey, where Merrill executives were gathering for a summit. He broke the news that he was leaving, that it wasn't up for negotiation, and that he would like their helicopter to take him back to the city.

Dobson and Flohr had flown in together from London that morning on the Concorde, with Dobson panicking the whole way that Mitchell might get cold feet at the last minute. The two men were scheduled to meet him at the Princeton Club at eleven A.M. to seal the deal. Mitchell was running late but eventually strode into the club's 1950s-era pinewood dining room, grinning. "It's done," he announced. A relieved Dobson—he no longer looked like he might faint—summoned the waiter and ordered a round of gin and tonics.

In the summer of 1995, the Mitchell family moved to England. Edson bought a brick mansion—known as Tall Trees, because it was surrounded by tall trees—in a leafy commuter town southwest of London. His title at Deutsche was head of global markets. As he had at Merrill, Mitchell saw derivatives as the key to becoming a big player in the most important markets.[9] Since Deutsche had been effectively sitting that game out, he was starting from scratch. Walking into the bank's London offices, housed in an ugly black cubical building on Leadenhall Street, felt like being transported back to another age. The walls were decorated with dark oil paintings of royals on horseback. Men wore waistcoats. Frilly maids and tuxedoed butlers scurried along the dimly lit hallways. Deutsche had hired sporadically in random areas on multiple continents, but neither technology systems nor trading desks nor corporate strategies were integrated. The place was a bunch of fiefdoms. There were no computer models to figure out how to value derivatives, even simple ones like stock options.

For Edson, the key first step was to assemble a team of loyal lieutenants. His former employer became his poaching ground. His first recruit was Michael Philipp. Philipp had started off as a professional potter, making ceramic mugs and plates. He baked them in a kiln in his backyard and sold them at local markets. He was earning about $12,000 a year, and he and his wife, a teacher, had three kids. Wanting more money, in 1980 he enrolled in business school at the University of Massachusetts. He got a job interview at Goldman with Robert Rubin, the future Treasury secretary. When Rubin learned that the bushy-bearded Philipp could convince people to shell out $5 for a homemade mug when the mass-produced version cost only $1.75 at a store, he got excited: "You'll be great in this business!" Philipp got the job and never made another mug. In 1990, he joined Merrill Lynch and met Edson.

Now the two were at Deutsche, trying to figure out how to assemble an army. They flew to Frankfurt and, meeting with the bank's top executives, outlined two options for vaulting the company into Wall Street's top tier. One approach was to buy an investment-banking power like Salomon Brothers, which would cost at least $5 billion, perhaps much more. Or they could construct an investment bank by hiring lots of people, which they estimated would require only $2 billion. The two Americans figured the frugal Germans would go for the cheaper option, which is what they wanted to do anyway. They were right—and now they had a $2 billion war chest at their disposal.

Mitchell and Philipp's recruitment pitch was simple: Deutsche was a superstar in the making. "It's a sixteen-cylinder engine running with four cylinders firing," Mitchell argued to one Merrill executive, Kassy Kebede, a native of Ethiopia who later married the supermodel Liya. He agreed to join his former boss.

Next up was another Merrill executive, Anshu Jain. He'd been two years behind Philipp at UMass. When Philipp landed at Goldman, Jain had used that connection to help secure a job interview there. He didn't get the gig—he was perceived as a little too much of a geek—but he was soon hired by Merrill. There he had to contend with the largely Irish Catholic sales force repeatedly mistaking him for an IT guy and asking him to fix their computers. Now, nearly a decade later, Anshu was a managing director—among the youngest ever at Merrill—and had matured into one of the firm's best derivatives salesmen. But he was only thirty-two, and he worried that he would squander his hard-won reputation by starting over at Deutsche. Philipp gave a pep talk to Jain's wife, Geetika, arguing that this was an unmissable opportunity to get in on the ground floor of something special. Anshu took the leap.

One other coveted Merrill recruit was Grant Kvalheim. Desperate to stop the exodus to Deutsche, Merrill offered Kvalheim a bigger job and promised to match whatever astronomical sum Mitchell was dangling, and Merrill's leaders thought they had warded off the predator. Edson, however, didn't like to lose. He took the Concorde to New York and then drove his black BMW 8 Series coupe, which he kept at the ready in New Jersey, out to Kvalheim's home in Princeton. Mitchell upped his offer one last time, pushing it well into the millions per year—the latest example of him doling out "NFL-type salaries,"[10] a Merrill

executive grumbled. Kvalheim finally relented—on one condition: He wanted Mitchell's BMW. Edson reached into his pocket
and tossed Grant the car keys. "I left for a genuine opportunity,
the feeling of exhilaration and accomplishment when you're
pulling together an organization," Kvalheim explained to a reporter at the time.[11]

Mitchell instructed his first round of recruits to each find the
best five people they knew in their respective areas, hire them,
and then have those five people each hire the best five people,
and so on. Thus began an epic spasm of hiring. There were non-
stop job interviews—in the office, at pubs, in hotels. One favorite
spot was London's five-star Lanesborough hotel. In the middle of
interviewing candidates in the lounge, Kassy Kebede would often look around and see Edson or Anshu a few tables down, also
grilling applicants. Soon Deutsche's stuffy offices were overflowing, more people than there were desks.

When Mitchell arrived, his markets business had about 2,000
employees.[12] Within eighteen months, he and his crew would
hire another 2,500 people—including several hundred from
Merrill. It was one of the greatest migrations in Wall Street
history. And there was no question about the driving force: Edson.
He had a magnetic personality and a reputation as a gifted manager. He was like a beloved football coach, someone who wasn't
the best athlete but had a unique ability to inspire others to perform beyond their natural limits. "He was the rainmaker, the
energizer," one of his recruits raved. Some of his mesmerized
troops referred to him as the Wizard of Oz.

There was one crucial person left out of this exodus: Bill
Broeksmit. It wasn't that Mitchell didn't want him. He did. In
fact, Bill had been the first person Edson tried to recruit when he
knew he was going to Deutsche. But Bill wouldn't budge. (Mitch-

ell, not missing a beat after being rebuffed, enlisted him to inter-view some candidates for senior Deutsche jobs, even though Broeksmit was now technically his competitor.)

Part of it was that Broeksmit was conservative, and it seemed like Mitchell and the others were taking a flier. Another factor was that the Orange County debacle was still playing out, in the legal system and in the press, and Broeksmit felt duty-bound to help tidy up the mess. His colleagues thought he was crazy; what kind of man was so loyal to a faceless institution that he would pass up untold riches to do the right thing? It didn't hurt that Merrill applied a full-court press to keep him. Stan O'Neal, one of the firm's top executives (and later its CEO), led the charge. Broeksmit sat silently while O'Neal presented all the reasons he shouldn't bolt, and O'Neal came away with the impression that he had sold him on the merits. But the biggest reason Broeksmit didn't take Mitchell's bait was that he was tired—not a quality that many forty-year-old investment bankers admit to. But you can pull only so many fourteen-hour days, for so many years, without it taking a toll. He didn't want to rise to the next level of management, and he worried that his two young daughters were growing up without a father.

In March 1996, Broeksmit announced that he was retiring. When a Merrill spokesman told *The Wall Street Journal* that Broeksmit was leaving "to spend more time with his family"—a common euphemism meaning someone got fired or was resign-ing in disgrace—it was actually true.[13] A top executive was quoted saying that Bill needed time to recharge. "We would love to have him back," the executive said.[14]

A couple of months later, Broeksmit and his family were up in Maine when Mitchell paid a visit. He still wanted Bill to join him at Deutsche. By now they had assembled a pretty strong suite of traders and sales guys, but they were missing a premier

expert in understanding and managing risk. Bill acknowledged
to Edson that he missed Wall Street's adrenaline, but said he
didn't feel ready to return.

Edson, however, let it be known just how much money Bill
could expect to make. It was a very large seven-figure number
per year, considerably more than he'd been earning at Merrill.
Bill soon agreed to take the job. He would be the bank's co-head
of proprietary trading—in other words, of making wagers with
the bank's own money—with a focus on derivatives, reporting to
Mitchell.

Even after signing on, Broeksmit wasn't sure the effort to
rocket Deutsche to the top of Wall Street would actually work. "I
thought it would be an adventure," he told a colleague years later.
In November 1996, Bill, Alla, and their two daughters moved to
London. (Val stayed in the States, attending Albright College.)
Edson and Suzan hosted the new expatriates for a welcome dinner soon after their arrival.

All of their lives—and the very essence of Deutsche Bank—
were about to change.

CHAPTER 4

FORCES OF DARKNESS

One day a sign appeared in the lobby of Deutsche Bank's London headquarters. It spelled out the bank's name phonetically: *DOY-chuh*. This was an important corrective: Many of the American newcomers had been telling people that they worked at "Douche Bank."[1]

Slowly, but not that slowly, the influx of Americans began changing Deutsche's culture. The newbies didn't know the first thing about the bank or Germany. All they knew was that their mandate was to drag this tradition-bound institution into modernity. The way Mitchell and his entourage saw it, the place's stubborn Germanness was the main impediment to unleashing its full animal spirits. Before Edson's arrival, most of Deutsche's prosperous business clients had been borrowing money from or issuing bonds via the bank—and then going to a rival, often JPMorgan, to purchase the accompanying derivatives to protect against fluctuating interest rates or other economic forces. Mitchell's goal was for Deutsche to offer all of those products in-house. He positioned his new derivatives team—led by Broeksmit—at the very center of the bank's London trading floor, so they were within earshot of as many traders and salesmen as possible. Now they just needed the Germans, with their deep distrust of cavalier Anglo-American investment bankers and derivatives, to unshackle them.

Part of the problem was that the bank had a hierarchy baffling to the Americans. There was a board of directors charged with supervising the company and its executives, but beneath that was another board called the *vorstand*. It consisted of eight top executives who each had responsibility for a particular part of the bank—investment banking, retail banking, wealth management, legal affairs, technology, and so on. The vorstand operated by consensus and resisted change. Mitchell wasn't even on the vorstand; no American ever had been. Further complicating things, there was no CEO at the bank. Instead, one of the vorstand's members was elected as "speaker," and that man (it was always a man) was in charge, but only so long as he retained the support of his colleagues and of the supervisory board. The Germans saw the overlapping boards and consensus-driven leadership system as a source of strength and stability, preserving the fundamental nature of a proud German institution and, by design, making it hard to change things quickly.

Mitchell couldn't stand the slow pace and all the pomp. He found it ridiculous that the vorstand had its own floor in Tower A of the Frankfurt skyscrapers, accessible only by a special elevator. Before anyone—visitor, government dignitary, employee—could board the elevator, they had to walk through metal detectors and be frisked by heavily armed security men. It seemed crazy that each office on the floor was palatial and decorated by the bank's in-house curators with museum-caliber German artwork. The fact that vorstand members traveled with a squadron of motorcycle cops in a convoy of bombproof Mercedes S-class limousines—the reinforced doors so heavy that men had to strain with both hands to open and close them—struck Edson's crew as completely over the top.

Quite a few members of the two boards didn't have the faintest idea about how these Americans thought a global bank was supposed to operate, much less one that was trying to secure a foothold on Wall Street. They knew nothing about investment banking or trading or derivatives, other than that they instinctively distrusted these American exports. That wasn't necessarily a defect—it can be good to have skeptical board members asking rudimentary questions—but guys like Mitchell had extremely limited patience for people who needed things explained twice. What's more, Mitchell and his colleagues got the distinct impression that the Germans, especially those on the vorstand, were trying to foil them by vetoing transactions and slow-walking decision-making. "They want us dead," Edson told Anshu. Mitchell nicknamed his German overseers the Forces of Darkness, and the moniker stuck among his troops.

The Germans, for their part, thought the growing pile of derivatives accumulating on Deutsche's books was a cause for concern—a fear that would eventually prove well founded. "At almost every executive meeting, we talked about the ever-increasing balance sheet size brought about by the ever-increasing volume of derivatives," Hilmar Kopper, the bank's leader, would recall. It "was nothing we were proud of."[2] The Germans looked at Edson's ilk with a combination of disdain and fear. They referred to the Americans as bandits and anarchists. "We can't control them," a vorstand member lamented.

Mitchell seemed to relish his reputation as a powerful outlaw. Once, in Frankfurt, an employee didn't recognize him and asked who he was. "I'm God," Edson replied.[3] He realized that the vorstand's dearth of investment-banking knowledge could play into his team's hands: What the vorstand didn't know, the vorstand couldn't stop. Mitchell demanded that control of the entire markets business be consolidated in London. At the time, several German cities—not just Frankfurt and Berlin but also places like Stuttgart and Mannheim—had their own bond-trading outposts. Broeksmit was put in charge of wresting all this power away from Germany. The situation, explained in his technocratic manner, "was the sort of thing that produced duplication of effort and dissipation of energies." It did not endear him to the German workforce, but that didn't much bother Bill, because he believed it was the best thing for Edson and for the bank.

By the end of his first year at Deutsche, Broeksmit was feeling good about his decision to reenter the industry. He was proud of the bank's progress. Customers were responding well to changes that he and the team had implemented, and the profits were beginning to rush in. "That was really the moment for me when the bank's natural strengths, its reach, and the new technology and capabilities it had imported began to work together," he would explain in 2005, as part of an oral history project that the bank commissioned. "There was a lot of talk that [Deutsche] would pull back into becoming a German commercial bank and that this extension . . . into investment banking was an adventure that could be called off," he continued. "There was no turning back."

Mitchell had figured out a particularly aggressive trick to get his way with his tightfisted Frankfurt superiors: If they wouldn't fork out enough cash to keep hiring at a rapid clip, he would threaten to quit. At one point, he went so far as to inform his colleagues and bosses that he had accepted an offer to join the Swiss bank UBS. "It's Team UBS, boys," Edson told Bill and Anshu, urging them to join him. Other members of Mitchell's inner circle were pretty sure he was bluffing, but in any case more money for his team came through quickly after that, and he stayed put. The boards that were supposed to be overseeing Mitchell lacked a sufficient understanding of the markets to be able to figure out what he was doing, much less to rein him in, but they knew that losing him would be a disaster.[4]

One night in 1997, Edson and Suzan hosted dinner for about twenty top executives and their wives. The dinner was at the Mitchells' sixty-acre estate at Fox Chase Farm in New Jersey, and the whole crew flew in for the occasion. Edson's son Scott was the valet, parking the Porsches and BMWs in the farm's horse-riding ring. Suzan served homemade lobster salad. After dinner, everyone retreated to the house's lower level to play pool and Ping-Pong, which Michael Philipp dominated. Bill sat on a sofa chatting quietly. As everyone got drunk, the men looked around at one another and thought: *We are building something special.*

In the eyes of his underlings, Mitchell had many great qualities. One was that he would go to bat for you. If risk managers nixed a proposed transaction, he would try to cow them into quiescence. Even during money-losing spells, Edson browbeat his Frankfurt superiors into keeping the bonus pot flush. This was the only way, he lectured, to assemble a world-class team capable of taking on the titans of Wall Street. For bankers all over London and New York, this was fantastic news. The necessity of competing for talent with Deutsche quickly ignited a compensation arms race across the industry. Bob Flohr, the headhunter working for Edson, received congratulatory *attaboy* phone calls from his peers, who were themselves getting enriched through the spiraling payouts (the headhunters pocketed a percentage of whatever their clients got).

But the simpler things were important, too. If you had a meeting in Deutsche's New York offices, you could order bottles of Beck's—Deutsche's "official" beer—to be there waiting for you and your clients.[5] Another nice perk was the muscle-bound shoeshine guy who roamed the London trading floor, peddling services that included coke and women. Most of all, there were the parties. Technically, they were called "off-site retreats," lavish team-building junkets every few months in sunny cities like Barcelona. Mitchell framed them to his superiors as an essential way for people to get to know one another—after all, Deutsche was growing so fast that it risked being filled with strangers.

As much as some of the new recruits talked about the ideal of an entrepreneurial ethos, of constructing something big from scratch, Deutsche's culture was being built on a far less communal foundation of individuals racing to amass personal fortunes. That was fine as long as you had a strong counterbalancing system for managing risks and looking out for clients and making sure that young, ambitious, greedy bankers and traders did what was right for the institution, not just what was right for themselves. But if that culture was missing or weak or inconsistently applied, or if the person who assembled the team and was the spiritual leader and held everything together suddenly wasn't there any longer—well, watch out.

Mitchell surrounded himself with aggressive executives who were programmed to push the envelope. One colleague described them as "bloodthirsty piranhas." Edson liked swimming with these fish. And as generous as he was with bonuses and junkets, he could be plenty brusque himself. Striding across the trading floor, he would ask employees how their days had been. When one admitted that he'd had a lousy day financially, Mitchell barked: "I can hire chimps that lose money!" The threat was hardly disguised. Another time he was trying to recruit a star trader from a rival bank. He invited the man to his home in Rangeley. The guy kept saying no, and after hours of trying, late at night, Edson finally gave up. He asked his driver to take the man to the Rangeley bus station; the failed recruit would have to spend the night outside, waiting for a ride.

One of Edson's piranhas was Anshu, who in early 1997 was put in charge of running the entire sales force of the markets business. Born in Jaipur, India, in 1963, he was a member of the Jains, an ascetic religion that rejects the caste system and preaches nonviolence. When Anshu was in college in India, he fell in love with a smart, beautiful, extroverted classmate: Geetika Rana. When her family moved to the United States shortly after their graduation, Anshu followed her. He enrolled in the MBA program at UMass, where he met Michael Philipp.[6]

A cricket fanatic and cigarette smoker (until, after a successful bout of hypnotherapy, he quit in 1999), Jain was the type of guy who would ask you roughly a million questions when you brought a problem to him and would erupt if you couldn't answer every single one. He was intensely competitive. Once he, his cousin, and their wives traveled back to India to search for tigers in a national park. Just when they were about to give up, they spotted one. Anshu and his cousin hopped on top of the car with their video cameras. Anshu was so excited, so determined to get the best footage of the tiger, that he jumped down from the roof and started running toward the animal, his camcorder still pressed to his eye.[7]

Edson trained Anshu to have a certain amount of disregard for the rules. On one occasion, Jain was hoping to do a derivatives transaction with a giant hedge fund, Tiger Management. The bank's risk managers in Germany balked. "This is highly irregular," a German executive informed him regarding his plans to do a large, complicated trade with a ferocious-sounding American hedge fund. The German told Jain that the deal would have to be considered at the next vorstand meeting. Anshu complained to Edson; if they waited that long, the opportunity would vanish. Edson told Anshu to go ahead and do the trade.[8]

While Mitchell was swimming with piranhas, his closest colleague and friend remained Broeksmit, and he was not a predator. His grasp of complex finance and his proximity to Edson, and the fact that everyone knew that Edson trusted him more than anyone else, served as a potent defense system. Settling into Deutsche, Mitchell and his crew had realized that the German bosses were so clueless that his group could finance itself by borrowing money in the markets without going through traditional approval channels to get their budgets increased. Of course, the more they borrowed and the more they then placed on the roulette table, the greater the losses would be when the ball took an unfortunate bounce. Early on, Broeksmit saw this and put the brakes on everyone's risk-taking.

Broeksmit's partner at the bank—the other top trading executive—was Martin Loat. Martin looked up to Bill, partly because of his tight relationship with Edson, and often turned to Bill for counsel on tricky client situations. Broeksmit's advice tended to be simple: Be honest. Once a corporate client of the bank bought an enormous quantity of derivatives from Loat's team. Martin knew it was imprudent and sought Bill's opinion. Soon he, Loat, and an executive at the company that bought the derivatives were all on the phone together. It turned out the client didn't quite understand what it had just purchased. Normally in the banking industry, that would be a jackpot—few things cause traders to crack a bigger smile than an ignorant client. But Broeksmit recommended that they cancel the transaction, at no cost to the client. So that's what they did. Don't do deals that are "intellectually immoral," Bill told Martin, who never forgot that wisdom.

Such counsel reflected Broeksmit's evolving role within the bank—a shift that would leave him feeling responsible on the many future occasions when Deutsche would stray from the ethical path. He was still the derivatives whiz and risk expert. But more than that, he was becoming the superego of the investment bank, the guy whom everyone looked to as a restraining influence and, when that failed, to help sort things out when they went wrong. When assessing the merits of a potential trade, he didn't want to hear the marketing spiel about how great the transaction was. He wanted to understand its essence. "Let's get down to first principles," he'd say cheerfully. When a financial crisis erupted in Asia in the late 1990s, he went to Hong Kong to help the bank's team there get everything under control—assessing the assets Deutsche was holding, deciding which clients it was safe to keep doing business with, and figuring out how to extricate the bank from everything else. He reminded some colleagues of Harvey Keitel's Wolf character in *Pulp Fiction*, parachuting into messy situations and coolly, professionally, authoritatively issuing orders to mop things up.

In stressful times, Broeksmit was a calming presence. In euphoric moments, he was a dampening presence. He leveled everyone's mood and drained the emotions out of volatile situations. In an industry prone to explosions, his moderation served the bank—and Mitchell—well.

Edson and Suzan drifted apart, and in 1997, after two years in England, she and the kids moved back to the United States. The declared reason was that she didn't want to play the role of a corporate wife, traveling around with her husband and making small talk with strangers. At first Edson traveled frequently back to see his family. He'd jet in for one of Scott's basketball games or Ellen's horse shows and then spend the weekend. First thing Monday morning, he'd be back on a plane to Europe. But more weeks started to pass between each visit.

With his family gone and spare time on the weekends, Mitchell joined an exclusive golf club, the Wisley, south of London. Week after week, he and his inner circle at Deutsche would golf thirty-six holes on Saturday and then come back for another thirty-six on Sunday. "This was when we'd figure stuff out," one participant recalls. Mitchell wasn't good at golf, but he was a contagious gambler. The bets would start off manageable— maybe $100 on someone's putt—but they would increase at an exponential rate. Double or nothing was so common it became boring; Edson would arrange subgames within subgames, each with a bet attached to it. By the thirty-sixth hole, it wasn't unusual for $10,000 or a BMW to be on the line.

Edson was a master of the universe, but he also was lonely. One Saturday evening, Bob Flohr was preparing to host a fiftieth birthday party for himself. An hour before it started, the doorbell rang. Caterers were scampering about, and Flohr hadn't showered yet. Mitchell was at the door, looking like "a sad little boy on my doorstep," Flohr thought to himself. Mitchell spent the next hour hanging out in Flohr's backyard, sipping wine and chatting with Flohr's chauffeur. Edson seemed happy to just have someone to talk to.

On a warm evening in November 1997, Edson and Michael Philipp went out for drinks. Afterward, they decided to stop by Kassy Kebede's home in London's ritzy Knightsbridge neighborhood. Kassy's flat was in the midst of an extensive overhaul, and his interior designer, a twenty-seven-year-old Frenchwoman named Estelle, was there when the bankers arrived. Estelle was staying with Kassy, and they were in the kitchen, in their pajamas, eating leftovers.

Making himself at home, Mitchell sent his driver to a nearby Lebanese restaurant to fetch food, and they all sat in the kitchen eating and drinking together. Mitchell struck up a conversation with Estelle, a pretty brunette with sparkling eyes. "Where do you see yourself in five years?" he inquired. She stammered something; Edson thought her accent was irresistibly sexy. The next day, he called Estelle at Kassy's flat and invited her out to dinner. Estelle knew he was married and had kids and was a lot older and was her employer's boss. She politely said no. Always the salesman, Mitchell eventually persuaded her to let him take her and her sister out to dinner at an Italian restaurant in Chelsea.

Mitchell's life soon underwent a makeover. He started smoking and dressing in fashionable tailored suits. He stopped shaving and let his hair grow out. He suddenly wasn't around for weekends—the Wisley golf outings became rare—and he would show up at work a little later in the mornings. His crew gossiped that something was up with Edson, but they didn't know what.

A month later, Mitchell pulled Kebede aside at work. "I have to tell you something," he confided. "I'm seeing Estelle."

"What?" Kassy asked.

"She's my girlfriend," Edson said. Word dribbled out to his colleagues, and before long, Mitchell was bringing Estelle along to spend time with his work family. Early in 1998, they moved into a brick cottage that Estelle found on a quiet street in Chelsea. A riotous garden shielded the front of the house from passersby. Estelle decorated the interior, crafting it into what she called "a perfect nest."

Mitchell remained married, and his family would dismiss Estelle as a gold digger. But she loved Edson and sensed his vulnerabilities. Aside from Bill and Alla, he didn't have friends—only colleagues. It was a paradox for a man with such power over people—a reflection, perhaps, of Edson viewing the world primarily through a competitive, professional prism.

Edson's relationship with Estelle went from casual to intense to long-term. They rented a sailboat in Norway. They barbecued on the beach. They rode bikes in bathing suits on a Mediterranean island. On their first anniversary, they flew to Venice and stayed in a five-star hotel overlooking the Grand Canal. The first morning there, Edson walked onto their balcony and admired the splendid view. "I never realized how great it was to have money," he sighed. For Estelle's thirtieth birthday, they went to the South of France. Broeksmit and Loat came down for the festivities. Mitchell, his nose bright red from the sun, got drunk and put a ring on Estelle's finger. Afterward, Bill and Martin pulled their boss aside. "Mate, you can't do that," Loat scolded. "She'll take it the wrong way."

Mitchell—the human whirlwind, the restless, irrepressible force of nature—had dumped his family for a new, French-accented adventure. It was impulsive and reckless and destructive. He was about to act similarly with Deutsche.

CHAPTER 5

PROJECT OSPREY

Mitchell had been at Deutsche Bank for two years, long enough to know the place and its limitations. He concluded that no matter how many people he hired and how much money he extracted from Frankfurt, there was no way he was going to be able to build a Wall Street–caliber franchise on his own. In the spring of 1997, he hosted a summit of his top thirty or so lieutenants in an old Italian castle that had been converted into a hotel. The group had a frank discussion about where they stood. Purchasing another investment bank, the men concluded, was the only way forward. It turned out that Edson's initial proposal to his German superiors—either spend $5 billion on an acquisition or $2 billion on a hiring spree—hadn't been quite right. It would be better to do both, except with a much bigger price tag.

What to buy? Edson, Anshu Jain, and Michael Philipp spent the coming months running the numbers on some of Wall Street's biggest investment banks: Lehman Brothers, Bankers Trust, even Merrill Lynch. In the spring of 1998, Mitchell broached the idea of splurging on a big Wall Street bank with Deutsche's new leader, a tanned, polished German named Rolf-

Ernst Breuer. Breuer eventually assented, and the hunt accelerated. Mitchell's team code-named their mission Project Osprey,
after the hawk that plucks fish from the water with its razor-
sharp talons. Deutsche would catch its prey, but the quarry would
prove poisonous.[1]

Bankers Trust had been around since 1906. For most of its existence, it had been a trusty servant to rich families and companies, squirreling their money away and structuring transactions
for them in ways that exploited wrinkles in the tax code. In the
1980s, though, Bankers Trust had developed a taste for Wall
Street. It dabbled in leveraged buyouts, the fad of the day, and
then plowed into risky real estate lending, at one point making a
$100 million loan to Donald Trump. The loan was unsecured:
Bankers Trust had no claim to any collateral if Trump stopped
paying the money back, which is exactly what he did. "We were
brain dead when we made that loan," Charles Sanford, the bank's
chairman, groaned in 1992.[2] Before long, Bankers Trust moved
on to derivatives. *The Wall Street Journal* described the bank's
strategy as "trolling the fringes of banking," targeting low-end
clients and selling them complex instruments.[3] In a sign of the
industry mores at the time, Bankers Trust became a media darling, lavished with awards for innovative, aggressive investment
banking.

By design, Bankers Trust pushed the envelope. Soon it pushed
too far. Derivatives it had sold to some big companies, including
Procter & Gamble, blew up. The resulting litigation exposed
what everyone suspected but no outsiders had known for sure:
Bankers Trust was flagrantly ripping off its clients. The incrimi-
nating evidence was in the form of audiotapes of phone calls that
surfaced in litigation brought by P&G.[4] The P&G executives,
bank employees sneered, were "like farm boys at a country car-

nival." Other executives were asleep. The risks the clients were piling on were perilous, but the "gravy train" could not be derailed. And on and on.

Bankers Trust's next bright idea was to focus on investments in the "emerging markets"—countries with hot economies but few safeguards against fraud and financial implosions. That strategy worked for a year or two, and then in 1997 a crisis emanating from Asia bulldozed the markets that Bankers Trust had just entered.

By the fall of 1998, Bankers Trust was the eighth-largest U.S. bank, with $133 billion in assets and more than 20,000 employees in dozens of countries, and it was falling apart.[5] Bankers Trust was the very embodiment of a "too big to fail" institution. Worried officials at the Federal Reserve, charged with safeguarding the American financial system, knew that Deutsche had been sniffing around for a big U.S. acquisition. If the Fed could get the Germans to take Bankers Trust off their hands, well, it wouldn't be an American problem anymore—or so the central bankers figured. A call was placed to Deutsche: You'll be in our good graces if you solve this problem for us. In October, Breuer flew to Washington and met in a hotel room with the CEO of Bankers Trust to discuss a possible deal.[6]

Deutsche should have seen the problems ahead. As negotiations progressed, a senior Bankers Trust executive boasted to Joe Ackermann, a top Deutsche executive and Edson's boss, that "we don't need clients anymore." His point was that the Bankers Trust traders were such stars that they could make buckets of money by betting on the market with the bank's own money, that there was no need to get their hands dirty with the old-fashioned business of earning slender margins from executing transactions on behalf of clients. This was manifestly untrue—Bankers Trust was in dire shape largely because its traders kept messing up—

but even if the statement wasn't false, it wasn't a safe or sustainable way to run a bank. Ackermann would come to rue having missed that bright red flag.

Inside Deutsche, some senior executives, including Jain, warned Mitchell that Bankers Trust was a third-rate institution with a lot of third-rate employees and a deep well of managerial, financial, and accounting problems. Jain expressed his preference to acquire a more conservative and well-respected firm like Lehman Brothers.

Rumors of the Bankers Trust acquisition talks spread, and two weeks after Breuer's hotel meeting in Washington, the *Financial Times* reported that negotiations were under way. The article sparked a rally in Bankers Trust's publicly traded shares—bad news for Deutsche because it made the prospective acquisition more expensive. But when a German reporter a few days later asked Breuer whether the bank was involved in takeover talks—*übernahmegespräche*—he denied that anything was afoot: "In this industry everybody speaks with everybody. But there were no takeover talks," he lied.[7] The remarks sent Bankers Trust's stock tumbling. And so even before the deal was consummated, Deutsche's history with Bankers Trust was built on deceit.

The week after Thanksgiving—nine years after the purchase of Morgan Grenfell and the assassination of Alfred Herrhausen— Deutsche agreed to acquire Bankers Trust for about $10 billion.

First, though, there was some historical reckoning that needed to take place. More than five decades had passed since World War II, and Deutsche still had not come clean about its role financing the Holocaust. It continued to argue that it was basically a victim, exploited by the Nazis. In New York City, the comptroller, Alan Hevesi, threatened to block the Bankers Trust acquisition unless Deutsche confessed its sins.[8] That threat was enough to pry open the bank's vast archives, which covered six miles of shelf space. Secrets poured forth, obliterating the myth that Deutsche was an innocent bystander. It had financed Auschwitz. It had serviced the Gestapo. It had sold the Nazis' stolen gold. Breuer apologized: "I would like to reiterate that we deeply regret the misery and injustice suffered and that we acknowledge the bank's ethical and moral responsibility."

That was good enough to get the deal approved, and it radically reshaped the German bank. Prior to the merger, Deutsche's markets- and investment-banking arm had generated 29 percent of Deutsche's total profits.[9] A year later, the share was 85 percent.[10] Much of those profits were now derived from derivatives, a defining feature of Bankers Trust and now of Deutsche. No longer was Deutsche a predominantly German institution catering mainly to European clients. Once and for all, the power had shifted to the investment bank; there would be no more existential debates among top executives about whether the bank should continue its pursuit of Wall Street.

CHAPTER 6

TRUMP'S BANKERS

Many years later, as Deutsche Bank executives surveyed the wreckage, they would look back, trying to figure out how they had gotten into this mess. The Bankers Trust deal would turn out to be a big blunder, saddling the bank with mountains of derivatives and a reckless, amoral culture. The relationship with Donald Trump looked like another huge error. Deutsche executives would quip that whoever initiated the Trump relationship must have had some sort of head injury.

It was kind of a joke. It was also kind of true.

Mike Offit grew up in New York City surrounded by smart, ambitious winners. His father, Sidney, was a prominent author who was tight with Kurt Vonnegut and other literary titans. His mother, Avodah, was a high-profile psychiatrist and sex therapist. His grandfather was a Baltimore bookie of national notoriety; his grandmother owned an apartment building on the Upper East Side, and his father sometimes took Offit along to deal with tenants and oversee repairs. His brother, Kenneth, would go on to become a world-renowned oncologist and geneticist.[1]

After graduating from Brown University, Mike Offit ended up in a $300-a-week gig at an advertising agency owned by one of his mother's patients. It was not what he had imagined for himself. One day a friend who worked as a commodities trader at the New York Mercantile Exchange called Offit. Did he want to make some quick money? The trader had an inkling of what platinum prices were about to do. All Offit had to do was say the word, and his buddy would hook him up. Offit said the word: yes. Minutes later, the friend called back. The trade had already generated $900 in profits—the equivalent of three weeks' pay for Offit.

Offit, twenty-one at the time, decided he wanted to work at the exchange, known as NYMEX. It turned out anyone could do it—all you needed to do was shell out a few hundred dollars to "lease" a membership, which is what Offit did. The trading pits were chaotic. A slight man, Offit got trampled. Twice his instep was crushed in a scrum; another time he fractured his jaw. But Offit found the trading itself to be pretty simple. Buy low, sell high. "It was an elemental world of bids and offers, winners and losers," Offit would write about the NYMEX decades later.[2] Offit was a winner, and the money made the physical toll worthwhile.

In the early 1980s, Offit enrolled in Columbia's business school. His new ambition was to become a trader at an established Wall Street firm. His cousin Morris Offit was a prominent New York banker who was friends with Goldman Sachs's Robert Rubin. Morris pulled some strings and got his cousin an interview. Offit sat in a Goldman anteroom for hours waiting for Rubin to show up. When he finally appeared, Rubin greeted Offit with a blunt question, apparently designed to throw him off-balance: "What do you want?" Offit was hot-tempered (he once threatened to smash a colleague's head with a wooden chair) and irritated at having wasted his day waiting for Rubin. He pondered the question for a moment, then declared: "I want to leave." He marched out of the building.

Offit instead got a job at the investment bank First Boston in 1983, where his specialty was the nascent business of trading bonds made up of mortgages. After a few years he took over First Boston's team of mortgage-bond traders. In 1993, he was hired by Goldman, where his brusqueness with Rubin apparently had been forgiven. Offit kept trading mortgage-backed securities. One of his Goldman bosses was a nerdy fellow named Steven Mnuchin, who struck Offit as being in over his head. Mnuchin soon hired a new guy, a real estate whiz from California. His name was Justin Kennedy.

Kennedy had jumped into the commercial real estate business straight out of Stanford, where he'd earned an economics degree. The market was brimming with opportunities, and Kennedy gorged on properties in the western United States. His forte was large community developments in California and Colorado; at one point, he would boast that he'd managed to acquire a substantial portion of all the commercial real estate available in the city of Colorado Springs. Things went well for a while, but Kennedy overextended himself, and then the onset of the Gulf War caused markets to tank, and he realized that he was in too deep. His investors got their money back, but that was about it. Kennedy needed a real job.

Even after the failure of his real estate venture, he had at least one powerful asset: his family. His father was Anthony Kennedy, who had joined the Supreme Court in 1988. That opened lots of doors for Justin. Skiing in Aspen, the young Kennedy would mingle with billionaires and wannabe billionaires, men like Donald Trump. Kennedy secured a job interview with Mnuchin and landed on Offit's team at Goldman. "I believed he had the arrogance and brains to be a good trader," Offit would recall. Offit struck Kennedy as a quirky but brilliant man. They devised little games to play on the trading floor to flaunt their intelligence. In one, Offit or Kennedy would come up with an obscure word or phrase, and whoever guessed its meaning won a bundle of cash.

Such contests were fun, but they weren't as adrenaline-pumping as surfing the wildly undulating markets of the mid-1990s. Offit and Kennedy's team was making money, though the hours were long and the stress levels, off the charts. Sometimes Offit wondered if he was working himself to death. In January 1996, the worst blizzard in half a century buried New York City in three feet of snow.[3] Offit came down with a bad head cold, but he didn't slow down at work—he still was out the door, tromping through the snow, every morning at six A.M. His cold became an ear infection. Offit persevered, too proud to succumb to a minor bug. A few weeks after the blizzard, he was on Goldman's trading floor. One moment he was trading, the next he was lying on his back. He could hardly open his eyes, much less get to his feet, and the room felt like it was spinning. Colleagues and an ambulance crew crowded over him. "You're having a heart attack," a paramedic whispered into his ear. He told Offit that he was about to inject a shot of adrenaline directly into his heart. No way, said Offit. "Then you'll die," the EMT said. Offit was stubborn and a trained gambler. He bet the paramedic was wrong.

At the hospital later, alive but still unable to open his eyes because of debilitating dizziness, he learned that his heart was fine. The problem was that his out-of-control ear infection had resulted in his immune system's attacking and damaging his nervous system, which forced his brain into dangerous overdrive to compensate. (Kennedy, in Florida on vacation, got a call that his boss had nearly died and rushed back to New York.)

Offit spent months out on long-term disability. His short-term memory was shot. When he regained his sense of balance, he would venture out for a bagel and forget where he was going or where he had just been. He had to walk around with a piece of paper listing his home address and destination taped to his wrist. There was no way he could go to work, but he tried to stay involved. Lying in a darkened room in his apartment, he would call Kennedy on speakerphone to dictate trading instructions. Most of Offit's cognitive functions slowly returned, but he would never be the same. Decades later, he was still incapacitated by occasional dizzy spells, and his speech sometimes skidded into a stutter. Reading people was hard; detecting nuance and focusing on subtleties required painful amounts of concentration that he couldn't always muster. Dealing with the hubbub of Goldman's trading floor was too much. To make matters worse, the bank informed him in early 1997 that he would not be getting his full bonus because he'd missed so much work. Offit was furious, and he blamed one man. "Mnuchin fucked me," he would fume more than twenty years later.

Serendipity came in the form of Deutsche Bank, which hadn't yet inked the Bankers Trust deal. Edson Mitchell wanted to build an American business of creating, buying, and selling bonds, and he hired a handful of Goldman executives to lead the charge. One of them, Kevin Ingram, had essentially a blank check to expand the commercial real estate team.[4] Ingram approached Offit, who wasn't wild about starting over again at a new bank. But his Goldman career was obviously fizzling, and the cocky Ingram had a compelling pitch: "Let's kick Goldman's ass." Especially in the wake of Mnuchin's ingratitude, that sounded pretty good.

At Deutsche, Ingram put Offit in charge of commercial mortgages: making loans, bundling them into bonds, and then selling and trading those bonds. (These were huge mortgages to finance construction projects and purchases of buildings, not run-of-the-mill residential mortgages.) Deutsche had recently been scalded by its giant loans to Jürgen Schneider, the fraudulent German shopping-mall magnate, and so the overseers in Frankfurt—Mitchell's Forces of Darkness—weren't thrilled that Offit now wanted to stockpile large quantities of similar commercial real estate loans on the bank's balance sheet. One monocle-wearing executive admonished Offit for seeming to not understand that keeping mortgages on the bank's books, even for a short period of time, was risky and therefore a bad idea. Offit snapped that the entire point of a bank was to take risks—smart, quantifiable, manageable risks, but risks nonetheless—by lending money to customers.

One after another, the Goldman guys flamed out, unable to adapt from their freewheeling Wall Street experience to Deutsche's molasses-like checks and balances. Ingram's boss, Paul Jacobson, was gone by the end of 1997. The next year, markets were tanking, Ingram's desk was bleeding money, and Mitchell pushed him out.* That left Offit and Kennedy, whom Offit had recently lured, as the main ex-Goldman survivors. Now that they lacked a protector, the only thing between them and unemployment was ensuring that the money kept rolling in. And it did, tens of millions of dollars a month in revenue from the loan-securitizing machinery that Offit had built. He was promoted to managing director and head of the investment bank's commercial real estate group (and was upgraded to a vast two-

---

* Years later, Kevin Ingram was caught in a money-laundering and arms-dealing sting in Florida. He pleaded guilty to money laundering and was sentenced to eighteen months in prison.

floor office). Kennedy got a promotion, too. Sometimes Anthony Kennedy would stop by Deutsche's offices and give Offit a little hug to thank him for taking such good care of his son.

One key to Offit and Kennedy's success was that Deutsche was willing to finance projects that more established lenders refused to touch. Offit had great confidence in his ability to assess the merits of real estate deals, thanks in part to his childhood experience watching his father manage his grandmother's Upper East Side building. And there was lots of money to be made on the fringes.

One day in 1998, a real estate broker called Offit: "Would you make a loan to Donald Trump?" Trump at the time was a casino magnate known for his occasional showbiz hijinks and his on-and-off dealings with organized crime figures.[5] He also was a deadbeat, having defaulted on loans to finance his Atlantic City casinos and stiffing lenders, contractors, and business partners in other projects. Quite a few banks—including Citigroup, Manufacturers Hanover (a predecessor of JPMorgan), the British lender NatWest, and of course Bankers Trust—had endured hundreds of millions of losses at the hands of Trump. Established banks were wary of what was known on Wall Street as "Donald risk."[6] "There's some people in real estate that are extremely tough, but they still live up to the word of the contract. They'll do everything possible to maximize within the word of the contract," a senior Wall Street banker told the journalist William Cohan in 2013. "Donald doesn't necessarily live up to the word of the contract."[7]

Even Trump's friends would go to considerable lengths to avoid lending him money. Trump once approached a banker at Bear Stearns, seeking $150 million. The banker knew that Trump was pals with Ace Greenberg, one of the firm's top executives, and so he agreed to a meeting. Trump's pitch wasn't awful, but the idea of doing business with a default-prone circus barker was less than enticing. After the meeting, the banker stopped returning Trump's phone calls, figuring that he would get the message and go away. Trump didn't get the message. Instead, he took Greenberg out to breakfast and complained that he wasn't getting his calls answered. Greenberg arrived at the office that morning, rebuked the banker for ignoring Trump, and instructed him to solve the problem. "Well, Ace, it's easy to fix," the banker replied. "All we have to do is lend him $150 million!"

"We can't do that, it's Donald," Ace acknowledged. "Just make the problem go away." The banker thought about this for a while and came up with a plan. He called Trump. "Donald, I want to apologize for avoiding you," he began. "We can't do the deal." Trump asked why. "Because Ace doesn't want to," the banker answered. Trump protested that he was friends with Greenberg—in fact, they'd just had breakfast that morning.

"Donald, don't mistake this here," came the banker's rehearsed reply. "Ace loves you. The reason he doesn't want to do it is because he told me there's four guys in the world that he doesn't want to be on the other side of the table from—Bill Gates, Warren Buffett, Henry Kravis, and you." The ploy worked perfectly. "I can understand that," Trump allowed.

Virtually the only one who would provide money to Donald Trump at this point was his father, Fred, who had doled out tens of millions of dollars in loans to his favorite son, repeatedly rescuing his failing enterprises.[8]

None of this bothered Offit; big banks were often too conservative, he thought. He told the real estate broker, from the firm Cooper Horowitz, that if Trump had a viable project, Deutsche would be happy to consider it. (It didn't hurt that Kennedy had a casual relationship with Trump from mingling in social and real

estate circles over the years.) A few days after the call with Cooper Horowitz, Offit was in his office in Deutsche's midtown Manhattan building, across the street from the Museum of Modern
Art, when his secretary called. "Donald Trump is in the conference room," she whispered excitedly.

Offit hurried into the room, expecting an entourage. Trump
was alone. He had done his homework on Offit and his family,
including the fact that his brother was a star oncologist. "You've
got great genes," Trump brown-nosed. He explained what he was
after: a loan to finance renovations of 40 Wall Street, an art deco
masterpiece that, when it was built in 1930, was a contender to be
the world's tallest building. (New York's Chrysler Building ended
up taking the crown.) Trump had bought 40 Wall Street a few
years earlier, but the building, with its limestone facade and distinctive gothic spire, remained mostly empty and in a state of
upheaval due to previous renovations that had been abandoned
partway through.[9] Trump walked Offit through the proposed
project. He had mastered the details. Here's how much the windows will cost. Here's how much steel we will need. Offit was
impressed. Most real estate moguls delegated details to their subordinates; Trump, with his reputation as a blowhard and a failure, had memorized everything.

Offit agreed to lend Trump $125 million. Trump seemed giddy
with gratitude. He happily reported to Offit that other banks,
having heard that Deutsche was willing to do business with
Trump, now were contacting him, suffering from the dreaded
"fear of missing out" syndrome. Trump assured Offit that he was
rebuffing these suitors out of loyalty to his new friend. "We're
going to do lots of business together," Trump promised. Offit
hoped he was right.[10]

To seal their relationship, Offit commissioned a detailed scale
model of 40 Wall Street, complete with its ornamental green-

copper roof. A shiny plaque on the trophy's pedestal listed the details of the $125 million transaction, along with the names and logos of Deutsche Bank and the Trump Organization. The partnership between the two entities was now etched in gold, or at least a thin sheet of gold-colored metal. Offit gave one statue to Trump and kept another for himself.*[11]

The $125 million loan hadn't even been completed when Trump approached Offit with a pitch to borrow more. He wanted to build a 68-story residential skyscraper, clad in dark glass, across the street from the United Nations headquarters. This loan looked trickier. For starters, it was more than twice the size: Trump was seeking $300 million. It also was for ground-up construction, not renovations of an existing building. Because of the added risk such loans entail—construction projects can be delayed or derailed, leading the developer to default and leaving the lender empty-handed—bankers scrutinize them closely. Deutsche didn't have experience making construction loans, so Offit conceived a work-around in which Deutsche would partner with another German bank, one that did have the necessary experience, to help make the loan.

This deal was large and complex enough that it needed the blessing of Deutsche's vorstand, and Offit flew to Germany to make a presentation. He fumed to colleagues about what a waste of time and energy this was, how the Germans were just trying to show that they were in charge, how they were so unsophisticated that they wouldn't even grasp the merits of the transaction

---

* Trump soon rented a penthouse suite at 40 Wall Street to a Russia-born criminal named Felix Sater, who would spend the ensuing decades working closely with Trump's company, including trying to arrange for a Trump-branded tower to be built in Moscow in 2015 and 2016.

or the need for speed. "Mike *hated* Frankfurt," recalls Jon Vaccaro, a senior executive in the real estate division. It drove him crazy that "there was no such thing as a rubber stamp." To Offit's relief, the vorstand signed off on the loan. The only caveat was that the German bank that was partnering with Deutsche was concerned about the risk that any of the unions involved in the project might go on strike—not a rare occurrence in the construction world. Offit told Trump about the misgivings. A few days later, Trump returned to Offit's office with a letter, signed by all of the union leaders whose workers would be involved in the project, promising not to strike. Offit was taken aback; unions were not known for unilaterally relinquishing the right to strike.

"How did you do that?" he asked Trump.

"Don't ask," Trump advised, smirking. Offit wondered if perhaps Trump had bribed the union leaders. But he took Trump's advice and didn't ask; what he didn't know couldn't get in the way of the $7.5 million fee Deutsche stood to pocket on the transaction.

Trump was thrilled. He took Offit golfing and to Atlantic City, where they had dinner with Evander Holyfield. Offit arranged for his father to visit the bank's offices to meet Trump, and Sidney later gave him a signed copy of his memoir. Trump sent a thank-you note on his personal stationery. "By the way, you have a great son!" he gushed. Trump once called Offit's home and tried to persuade him and his wife, Dara Mitchell, a high-powered art saleswoman at Sotheby's, to fly to Atlantic City in Trump's helicopter with him. Dara nixed it. She had recently endured an evening seated next to Trump at a Manhattan fundraiser and was in no hurry to repeat the experience.

Trump soon sent Offit a photorealistic rendering of the planned Trump World Tower. Once built, the high-rise would be a dark monolith looming over the United Nations. In this image, though, it was bathed in golden sunlight, dwarfing every other midtown skyscraper. (For two years, the building would hold the title of the world's tallest residential building.) In the bottom right corner, Trump wrote with a black Sharpie: "To Mike—Thanks for all of your help—you are a <u>great</u> friend. –Donald"

More loans followed as Deutsche rushed headlong into a relationship that would have serious implications for the bank—and for the world. But even if Deutsche could have anticipated events to come, its hunger for growth and rich American clients probably would have, well, trumped any concerns.

Offit wouldn't be around much longer. He had been clashing with Mitchell, and that was not a recipe for longevity at Deutsche. Edson was getting grief from his bosses in Germany, who were antsy about Offit's ballooning portfolio of giant real estate loans, which had grown to about $7 billion. From Offit's perspective, nobody at Deutsche seemed to get that he had to make lots of these big loans so they could be packaged into securities that Deutsche could then sell to investors—basically, bunches of mortgages were lumped into one asset whose returns were based on borrowers repaying their loans. The very first step in that process was creating the mortgages, which was what Offit's team was doing, in large volumes. "I feel like I'm working in a furniture factory and the boss says, 'What are we doing with all this fucking wood?' " Offit sputtered to Mitchell.

On this rare occasion, Edson, so eager to embrace risk and so willing to disregard edicts issued from Germany, played the role of Boy Scout. He sifted through Offit's $7 billion portfolio and saw that Offit had informally pledged to make a $300 million loan to refinance the Trump Marina, a struggling Atlantic City casino. The paperwork looked complete, but Mitchell was suspicious. He had never respected Trump, telling his kids that he was a clown. Now Edson summoned the credit officer whose signature was affixed to the documentation. The credit officer said that he'd never approved the loan commitment, much less signed it.

Offit wasn't accused of faking the signature, but Mitchell wanted him out. After racking up losses later in 1998, amid a brief but acute crisis in the financial markets, he was let go. Offit perceived himself as a victim of Mitchell's towering ambitions. Regardless, Offit had constructed a sturdy relationship with Trump, and his departure wouldn't knock it down—in part because Justin Kennedy would stay at Deutsche for another decade.

CHAPTER 7

RIPTIDE

Around the time that he canned Mike Offit, Mitchell organized a corporate getaway for hundreds of employees. The retreat was in a luxury resort overlooking Lake Maggiore, in the foothills of the Italian Alps. The bankers flew into Milan, and a fleet of Mercedes sedans chauffeured them into the mountains.

The first night, there was a party in the hotel's event center. An executive, Mark Yallop, took the stage. "Ladies and gentlemen," he thundered, "I'd like to introduce you to Edson Mitchell!" Onto the stage strode a short black man with dreadlocks. It was a Caribbean reggae singer named . . . Edson Mitchell (stage name: Ajamu). Yallop had flown the performer to Europe. The crowd erupted. For once, Edson the banker seemed to be at a loss for words. He laughed. And they all partied as Edson the musician jammed.

For the next eighteen months, Deutsche Bank boomed—and Mitchell's crew, its collective id unleashed, celebrated its newfound clout.

Mitchell had always been an intense competitor, but colleagues started noticing him taking things to a new level. When he

learned that a large German bank, Commerzbank, was trying to
poach some of his employees, he retaliated by severing Deutsche's
trading lines with the smaller lender. That had the effect of cutting off Commerzbank from a significant portion of the global
financial system. It was the nuclear option, and it had the potential to destabilize an important bank. "That was a kindergarten-
like attitude and not worthy of a professional," Commerzbank's
chairman hissed.[1] Perhaps more revealing, at a company event in
Bermuda, he organized a staff sailboat race and hired a former
America's Cup sailor to captain his boat. When the sailor was too
drunk to take part and Edson's boat lagged behind, he powered
on its engine to beat the other crafts across the finish line.

On a Sunday night in February 2000, Mitchell got a phone call
from Breuer, the bank's de facto CEO. He had big news: Deutsche
planned to merge with Dresdner Bank, Germany's second-largest
lender. The deal, Breuer informed him, would be announced on
Tuesday. Mitchell didn't like being blindsided, and he and his
colleagues feared that an influx of German bankers would dilute
their power within the organization, especially since Dresdner
had a large investment-banking business that overlapped with
what Mitchell had built.

Two days later, Edson gathered his entourage at his Chelsea
cottage. He was scheduled to fly to Frankfurt the next morning
to attend a press conference about the deal, and his participation
would signal the buy-in of Deutsche's London-based investment
bankers. The men drained quite a few bottles of wine. The more
they drank, the angrier they became. They wanted no part in
this German deal.

Edson's boss, Joe Ackermann, had joined the bank in 1996. A
Swiss native, Ackermann spoke fluent German, but he was more
closely aligned with the American traders than he was with the
stuffy German overlords. That night, Mitchell reached Acker-

mann on his car phone. Edson said that he and his team were opposed to the Dresdner deal. "Please don't underestimate, Joe, how difficult this will be," he warned.[2] If the deal went through, Edson threatened, he'd quit. On the other hand, if Ackermann helped torpedo the deal, Mitchell said, he could count on the support of Edson's squad in his quest to become the bank's next chief. The next day, Edson skipped the Frankfurt press conference; the men instead golfed thirty-six holes at the Wisley.

Edson's message received, the Dresdner deal soon fell apart. When word reached Deutsche's London offices, a wave of cheering washed over the trading floor.[3] It was a crucial turning point. Breuer had lost the respect of his investment bankers, who realized that they could call the shots. A healthy fear, a sense of restraint, had been lost. Mitchell's crew was on top of the world, and they knew it.

Mitchell remained closer with the Broeksmits than anyone else, save Estelle. Some nights, Bill and Alla would be surprised by a knock on their door. Outside was Edson, his Porsche parked on the street, asking what was for dinner. After initially disapproving of his affair with Estelle, Alla had resigned herself to the situation. The two couples vacationed together, staying at a ski chalet that Edson and Estelle had purchased in the Swiss resort town of Gstaad.

For her part, Alla had enthusiastically ensconced herself in London's art scene and museums, taking classes and becoming obsessed with the works of Francis Bacon and Lucian Freud. She tried to figure out ways to incorporate their genius into her own painting. Bill, however, wasn't as energized. His job was simultaneously overwhelming and boring. Once again, he felt that he was neglecting his daughters and that he was burning out. He believed the bank was getting so big that it no longer mattered what he did. In August 2000, he decided to retire—for the second time in five years. Mitchell pleaded with him to stay, trying to impress upon him that he served as Deutsche's keel, preventing the huge ship from tipping too far in the wrong direction. Broeksmit equivocated, but eventually concluded that he needed to get out. He agreed to withdraw over several months. He told perplexed colleagues that he wanted to spend more time with his family and to study Shakespeare and to volunteer in a soup kitchen.

The fact that Broeksmit's retirements were becoming a pattern suggested to some of his peers that he had trouble coping with the pressure, that beneath the cool exterior was a fragile man. Before Christmas, Bill and Alla had packed up their stuff and moved back to New York.

Mitchell, by now one of the top executives at Deutsche, spent much of his time on the road, visiting outposts in Asia and Latin America, where derivatives trading was just getting off the ground. He had traveled a long, long way from being a janitor's son and working on the DeCoster egg farm. Over his five years at Deutsche, he had earned something in the vicinity of $50 million. American-style compensation had arrived on the shores of the River Thames, and bankers all over town were grateful for Edson's inflationary role. Now he was poised to become the highest-ranking American at any European bank, ever.

Yet for all his success, Mitchell constantly flirted with disaster. One afternoon in the summer of 2000, he and Estelle were picnicking on a Maine beach. Edson noticed that his little boat hadn't been properly moored to the nearby dock; the receding tide was sucking it out into the Atlantic. He jumped into the surf to retrieve the craft. He swam hard, but the boat was floating away faster. Never one to accept defeat, he swam harder still and was practically skimming through the chilly water. At some point, Edson realized that his considerable speed was not a product of his athleticism; he was caught in a riptide. A lobsterman spied the exhausted, flailing man out at sea and fished him out. Otherwise, Mitchell would have drowned.

When Edson had joined Deutsche in 1995, 70 percent of its investment-banking business came from within Germany. By 2000, that ratio had flipped.[4] That June, Mitchell and Philipp were promoted to become members of the vorstand—the first Americans to ever sit on the insular executive board. Setting out to modernize things, they changed the weekly meetings to weekly conference calls. The vorstand had a tradition of a different executive acting as secretary at each meeting, taking notes and typing them up into minutes. When it came Philipp's turn in the rotation, he made sure his notes were completely illegible. The vorstand hired a professional secretary to take notes going forward.[5]

More broadly, having transformed Deutsche into a Wall Street operator, Mitchell decided it was time to start focusing on other parts of the bank, where he could make his mark and expand his empire. Its retail-banking and wealth-management businesses, for example, were a mess. Philipp was dispatched to clean things up—a sign that the entirety of Deutsche was coming under Edson's spell. In September 2000, Ackermann was anointed as the incoming speaker of the vorstand—essentially the CEO—thanks in part to the support of Edson and his clique. Ackermann wouldn't take the job for another two years, but his ascent meant promotions for Mitchell's subordinates. He told his lieutenants that they all should expect to be elevated in the near future.

Throughout it all, Mitchell couldn't help flaunting his success. One day he bumped into Flavio Bartmann, a rare Merrill derivatives whiz whom Edson had failed to lure to Deutsche. Back then, Bartmann had warned Mitchell that there was no way he could turn the sleepy German bank into a Wall Street power. "Flavio, you were fucking wrong," Edson gloated now.

That was Mitchell in a nutshell. He viewed the bank as a means to an end, a vehicle to achieve his ambitions and prove that he could beat long odds. And now—with his mission arguably accomplished and his best friend quitting—he was growing restless again. A couple of weeks before Christmas in 2000, Edson invited Bob Flohr in for a meeting. The bank had recently moved into a modern sand-colored building decked out with modern art, the London headquarters to perhaps 10,000 employees. The two men sat in Edson's office, just off the trading floor. Family photos lined the walls, and smoke from Edson's Marlboros swirled in the winter sunlight. He alternated between puffing on his cigarette and eating a sandwich. Across the street were the ruins of the London Wall, built by ancient Romans—a centuries-old reminder of how seemingly invincible global empires, their leaders certain of their superiority, tend to overextend themselves and then disappear into history.

Mitchell told Flohr that he had heard that Stan O'Neal was next in line to become president of Merrill Lynch. "I'm better than Stan O'Neal," he asserted. "That should be me." Flohr was puzzled but remained quiet. Edson kept talking: "That's a job I would take. If you're any good at your job, you'll find a way to go to [David H.] Komansky," Merrill's chairman and CEO, who controlled the selection process. Flohr made plans to sit down with Komansky early in the new year.

CHAPTER 8

THE LAST DAY

O n the evening of December 21, 2000, Edson made the rounds at Deutsche Bank's Christmas party in London. The black-tie affair was held at the Grosvenor House hotel, across the street from Hyde Park. It promised to be a late, wild night.

Forty-seven years old, Mitchell had become an industry celebrity for many things: his motivational skills, his ambition, his recklessness, his willingness to spend ridiculous sums of money entertaining his staff. Each winter's Christmas bash needed to be more over the top than the last. The trend dated back to a subdued party a few years earlier, when Mitchell had commented that there weren't enough attractive young women in attendance. The following Christmas, someone hired dozens of attractive young women from a pair of "event agencies" to work the room. They wore little blue ribbons pinned to their little black dresses to make sure nobody confused them with female employees or wives.[1] (In an impressive twofer, that party made it onto a list of the all-time best London banking parties and also factored into a sexual discrimination lawsuit against the bank.[2,3]) This year, there were rumors of a VIP room stocked with escorts for the bank's managing directors.

Mitchell, clean-shaven, his rust-colored hair parted just so, looking sharp in a tuxedo, entered with Estelle, in a black halter-top gown, by his side—not for the first time at a semipublic event. They posed for a photo: Estelle draped one arm over his shoulder and placed her other hand affectionately on his chest, smiling warmly. As Mitchell strode onstage to address the more than 1,500 drunken bankers, the *Mission: Impossible* theme song blasted. He delivered one of his characteristic rally-the-troops speeches, pumping them up with talk of the great year they'd just wrapped up and the even greater year that was ahead.

The next morning, Edson caught the Concorde to New York. From there he boarded a quick flight to Boston. At Logan, his personal pilot, Stephen Bean, picked him up in a twin-engine propeller plane that Edson had bought years earlier. They flew to Portland, Maine, where Edson paid a quick visit to his parents to give them a Christmas present. He and Bean set off for Rangeley at 4:46 P.M. It was a route that the pair had flown countless times, sometimes with Deutsche colleagues like Broeksmit on board.

The sun had set, and faint stars were visible in the clear sky as the plane climbed to 11,000 feet. Twenty-nine miles out from Rangeley, the plane started its descent. Nine miles out, Bean could see the tiny airport's runway lights in the distance, and he prepared for the final approach. His wife was waiting at the airport, and Bean radioed to her that he would be landing soon. It was 5:15 P.M.[4]

Minutes passed. At the airport, there was no sign of the plane.

Bean's wife grew alarmed—she knew there were only a few possible explanations for why the plane hadn't landed yet, and none of them was good. She called her friends. Shortly after 5:30, one of them reported the plane missing to air traffic authorities in Boston. A search aircraft took off; volunteer firefighters climbed onto snowmobiles to scour the vicinity of where the plane had last appeared on radar—around Bear Mountain, a 3,125-foot heavily forested hump. In the dark, they found no trace. After several hours, the search was called off.

At dawn, search-and-rescue crews set out again. Around 7:40 A.M., a warden's plane spotted it: On the southwestern side of Bear Mountain, about 100 feet from the summit, was a broad, angry scar in the forest—broken branches, downed trees. And there, on a steep, rocky hillside, was the charred wreck. The plane had smashed into the mountain. Its cockpit, wings, and tail were shattered. Both men were dead.[5]

Estelle had flown to Switzerland to be with her family for the holidays. Mitchell was supposed to call her when he landed in Rangeley. She went to bed Friday night with her cell phone tucked under her pillow. She woke up the next morning, and the phone hadn't rung. She figured he had been too tired to call. Just then, her sister's phone buzzed. It was Edson's secretary. His plane had gone missing.

Estelle collapsed to the floor. "Edson is dead!" she shrieked. Her sister tried to calm her. It was possible the plane would turn up. But Estelle knew he was gone. Soon Joe Ackermann—who had been in bed in Zurich when the bank's security department phoned with news of the crash—called to offer his condolences.

Word spread through the bank. "Well, Edson's gone and done it this time," Michael Philipp told a colleague.

"What do you mean?"

"It looks like he's flown his plane into a mountain."

In New York, Kassy Kebede had been awoken by Estelle, so upset she could barely speak. Kassy called Bill and told him. Bill, who had loved Edson like no one else, was silent.

Later that day, Bill's son, Val, walked into the Broeksmit family's Park Avenue apartment. He could hear a Sinéad O'Connor song blaring in the living room. That was strange. His father hated Sinéad to the point of making fun of Edson for listening to her all the time. But now, clear as day, Sinéad's ballad, "The Last Day of Our Acquaintance," was being piped over the apartment's sound system. Val entered the living room. His father was sitting in an armchair, tears cascading down his face. He tried to compose himself when he saw Val. Mercifully, the song ended—only to start up again. Bill had it on repeat. Val sat down next to his father, and they listened over and over to the mournful music.

"Dad, you okay?" Val asked.

"Not really," Bill responded. "But I will be."

Deutsche, however, would not be. With his bottomless ambition and relentless pursuit of growth and profits, Edson Mitchell had planted the seeds of self-destruction at the bank. His fiery death acted as Miracle-Gro.

For all his flaws, Edson had been a unifying presence at the bank. He had an innate sense of how to prod people to perform better than they thought they could. And even as he pushed his subordinates for more, more, more; even as he shrugged off cautions from the bank's risk managers and accountants; even as he was hell-bent on world domination, he also was self-confident and self-aware enough to recognize some of his own weaknesses and blind spots. That was a big part of the reason that he'd kept Broeksmit by his side for all these years: Edson knew that Bill was a check on his worst impulses.

Now Bill was retired, and Edson was dead. Within hours, the race to fill the power vacuum was under way.

Justin Kennedy was on a golf course in Palm Beach, Florida, with his father, enjoying the balmy winter weather. The younger man's cell phone rang, and he answered the call and got the news: Mitchell was dead. "Oh my god, we're screwed," Kennedy blurted.* He knew Mitchell had been the one thing holding all of the competing personalities and factions in check. Now Kennedy's gut told him that all hell was about to break loose. He apologized to his father—he had to cut short their golf date and fly back to New York. Anthony Kennedy said he was very sorry to hear about Mitchell's death, but that Justin should probably relax. "I'm sure there's a succession plan in place," said the justice.

Justin shook his head. No, there wasn't.

Two days after Christmas, Joe Ackermann flew to London. He roamed the bank's trading floor, trying to calm the staff and to emphasize that Mitchell's death, tragic though it was, would not alter the bank's course. Ackermann's job now was to figure out how to replace Mitchell. Many of the thousands of people who had joined the bank in recent years had done so because they wanted to work with Edson the Sun God. Who would lead them now?

Anshu Jain, who had been in Delhi when he got word of Mitchell's death, had phoned Ackermann and said that Edson had promised him that he would soon be promoted to run the global markets business on his own. Ackermann doubted that, and Jain didn't force the issue. Regardless, he knew that while Jain was a salesman, and a good one, he wasn't a seasoned executive. He didn't know how to manage risks or balance competing budget demands or play the role of peacemaker—that was even the assessment of some of Anshu's deputies. Nor did he possess

---

* His former boss, Mike Offit, still seething about his forced departure, had a different take on Edson's death. "Karma is relentless," he told me, "and it caught up to Mr. Mitchell."

Edson's gravitas or charisma. One thing he did have was ambition. He very badly wanted to climb the ladder. "Get ready," Anshu warned a deputy shortly after Edson's death—the coming power struggle would be intense.

Ackermann decided to split Mitchell's job into pieces. Jain would run the biggest piece of the financial-markets operations, but smaller slices would go to executives including Grant Kvalheim, another of Edson's first recruits from Merrill. Kvalheim didn't like Jain, perceiving him as constantly trying to usurp his colleagues' power. Now he urged Ackermann not to reward Jain's bad behavior by handing him a bigger job. "Do you realize that nobody else on Edson's management team trusts Anshu?" Kvalheim asked. Ackermann replied that he was aware of that distrust, but he nonetheless was under the impression that Mitchell wanted Jain to have an enlarged role. "Joe," Kvalheim replied, "I loved Edson as much as anybody, but he's dead and the rest of us are still here." Ackermann didn't budge, and Kvalheim soon gave up on the possibility of working peacefully with Jain. He defected to the British bank Barclays.

Michael Cohrs, meanwhile, would be in charge of the global-banking division, which served the needs of corporations all over the world. Cohrs was an old-school investment banker, and the approach used by his team—spend years wooing clients and months working on a deal; collect a multimillion-dollar fee when the transaction gets completed—seemed quaint compared to the freewheeling money-minting machine overseen by Jain. Colleagues ribbed Cohrs that Anshu's traders generated in a couple of hours what Cohrs's bankers brought in over six months. On paper, Cohrs and Jain were on the same rung of the corporate ladder; in practice, Anshu made multiples more money and therefore wielded much more power. He moved into Edson's old office and hung a photo of his deceased mentor above the door.

Two years after Rolf Breuer's lie about not being engaged in *übernahmegespräche* with Bankers Trust, his deception threatened to come back to haunt the bank. The Securities and Exchange Commission opened an investigation, and by March 2001, its enforcement division had reached a preliminary conclusion: Deutsche and Breuer himself should be punished for misleading investors.

The SEC's head of enforcement at the time was Dick Walker, a permanently tanned, perfectly bald lawyer. A few months after his staff recommended taking action against Deutsche and Breuer, Walker made a surprising announcement: He was recusing himself from the case.[6] Two weeks after that, the SEC—seemingly out of nowhere—informed the bank that it had decided to close the investigation without any punishment. And three months after that, in October 2001, Walker announced that he was taking a job as a general counsel at Deutsche. "Dick Walker probably knows more than anyone about U.S. securities laws and regulations," a top Deutsche executive enthused.[7] Not long after, Walker hired Robert Khuzami, a federal prosecutor with a specialty in complex securities fraud cases, to join Deutsche and help shield it from government investigations.

Deutsche had discovered the power of the "revolving door"—the process of luring government watchdogs to the private sector—to neuter investigations.* With the SEC problem solved and a system now in mind for blunting future investigations, bank executives were feeling invincible.

---

* Walker maintains that his job discussions with Deutsche did not affect the SEC investigation.

Michael Philipp was on the thirty-first floor of Tower A of the Frankfurt skyscrapers, stuck in an interminable meeting with his fellow vorstand members. It was his first day back at work after a months-long leave while his wife successfully battled cancer. The date was September 11, 2001.

A young woman walked into the conference room and handed someone a note card. The executives passed it around the room: A plane had hit the World Trade Center in New York. People shrugged and the meeting resumed. About twenty minutes later, the woman returned with another note card. A second plane had smashed into the Twin Towers in New York. Executives gasped: This was terrorism, not an accident. Philipp looked out the window and, through the clouds, could see planes taking off and landing at Frankfurt's airport. He wasn't going to hang around in a skyscraper with planes whizzing by. "You guys are insane to be sitting at the top of the tallest building in Frankfurt," he told his colleagues.

He headed down to a pub and saw on the TV that a third plane had crashed into the Pentagon; another was down in Pennsylvania. He watched as Manhattan's two mightiest skyscrapers collapsed in an apocalyptic cloud of dust and debris. Upstairs, in the bank's own Twin Towers, the vorstand meeting dragged on for six hours.

That the meeting continued was all the more remarkable given that Deutsche's forty-floor Manhattan headquarters—which had been the offices of Bankers Trust—was right next to the World Trade Center. When the plane flew into the South Tower, some 1,500 windows were shattered in Deutsche's building. When the towers fell, flying metal and concrete ripped a deep, fifteen-story gash in the side of the building. What used to be its entrance was now a smoldering heap of wreckage, with shards of the World Trade Center's grill-like facade embedded in the walls. Miraculously, only one Deutsche employee died.

Ackermann decided that he needed to get to New York. American airspace was closed, so he and his wife took a private plane to Newfoundland. When the skies reopened, they boarded one of the first flights to New York. With its downtown offices wrecked, the bank had crammed extra employees into its building in midtown Manhattan. The place was overcrowded and decrepit—a number of employees had been hospitalized after contracting hantavirus from the enormous rodent population there. Ackermann strode in surrounded by an entourage of large men with earpieces and clad in all black; some traders assumed government agents were raiding the bank.[8] Ackermann thought his presence there showed his commitment to the American business.[9] But there was another reason he was in a hurry to get to New York: Deutsche was planning to list its shares on a U.S. stock exchange for the first time. Ackermann wanted to make sure the listing wasn't delayed. While the bank's shares had long been traded on the Frankfurt stock exchange, much was riding on them being easily tradable in America, too. In the privacy of his art-adorned fiftieth-floor condo in a skyscraper adjoining the Museum of Modern Art, Ackermann and his colleagues had secretly been plotting potential mergers with various U.S. banks, including JPMorgan, to transform Deutsche into a true global leviathan. To conserve cash, the proposed deals would take place mostly by swapping shares of Deutsche and its merger partner. That meant Deutsche's stock needed to be publicly listed in the United States.

The New York Stock Exchange reopened a week after 9/11, and on October 3, Deutsche's shares debuted, trading under the ticker symbol DB. It was the culmination of years of trying to break into the U.S. capital markets. Now the bank's executives

were on the dais at the stock exchange, perhaps the preeminent
icon of American capitalism, ringing the opening bell alongside
New York City mayor Rudy Giuliani. The bankers—one, from
Germany, wore a stars-and-stripes waistcoat and bow tie—
grinned and applauded as the bell gonged.[10]

It was a nice image (although Ackermann's merger fantasies
would never be realized). But a much more powerful symbol was
only a couple of blocks away.

Deutsche's downtown building was ruined. Executives from
Europe came to survey the wreckage and, wearing gas masks,
encountered a horrific scene. Human body parts—the mangled
remains of World Trade Center workers and first responders—
littered the basement. The building was beyond repair. But because it was filled with dangerous levels of mercury, asbestos,
toxic mold, and other nasty stuff, there was no way to dismantle
it without spreading more poison in Lower Manhattan. So the
shell of the doomed tower was draped in a veil of dark webbing,
an enormous tombstone towering over the hallowed Ground
Zero.[11] There it sat for years, a ghostly, impenetrable reminder
not only of 9/11 but also of the lethal mess that would soon lurk
within one of the world's biggest banks.

CHAPTER 9

ACKERMANN

J oe Ackermann was born in 1948, the son of a doctor, in the small Swiss town of Mels.[1] A strapping boy and a champion javelin thrower,[2] the young Ackermann had sometimes helped his father lift broken-legged skiers onto an operating table.[3] Ackermann's dad also treated lots of broke drunks, and he impressed on his son the importance of sobriety—in terms of both alcohol and money. Paradoxically, that focus on financial thrift also got Ackermann interested in the stock market. He took to finance, earning a PhD in economics—and henceforth would insist on being known, like his father, as Dr. Ackermann. (Later, as he racked up honorary professorships, he emblazoned his business cards with "Prof. Dr. Josef Ackermann.")

Ackermann first rose to banking prominence at Credit Suisse, the proud Zurich lender. He had eventually been a candidate to become CEO, but when he was passed over, that was the end of his time at Credit Suisse. He arrived at Deutsche in 1996, scarred by his experience in Zurich. Ackermann became keenly attuned to the internal power dynamics of big institutions and to the need to play politics in order to get ahead. And he had every intention of getting ahead at Deutsche.

Ackermann was a number cruncher with a photographic memory, the type who could recite a whole bunch of ratios that there had been no need to memorize in the first place.[4] That was both good and bad. His obsession with numbers—his theory that everything could be quantified and that those digits would tell the whole story—seemed dangerously one-dimensional, leaving no room to account for things like an institution's culture or a trader's behavior.

In 2002, Ackermann became the first non-German to be Deutsche's de facto CEO, the speaker of the vorstand. A skilled musician and opera devotee with a helmet of thick brown hair, he settled into the top executive's suite on the thirty-second floor of Deutsche's Tower A. It was a great moment for him, if not for Deutsche. With Germany mired in a recession, the bank's shares had declined that year by 17 percent—a cringeworthy performance, especially for someone like Ackermann, who kept close track of daily moves in the company's stock price. He had plans to reverse this slide—in fact, doing so was his primary mission. One easy step was to ditch the ownership stakes Deutsche had accumulated in Germany's leading companies. Ackermann saw those positions as relics of the bank's bygone days as a primarily German institution. He used the proceeds to pay dividends to shareholders and to expand the bank's most lucrative businesses.

Such was the mood of the moment, as expressed by impatient investors and Wall Street analysts: Banks should return excess capital to shareholders. Deep down, Ackermann knew he was gambling. If a financial crisis was to hit anytime in the next decade, it would be much safer for the bank to have that capital on hand, rather than in shareholders' pockets. But Ackermann's single-minded focus was goosing Deutsche's stock price, so he shunted those reservations aside.

Ackermann had surprisingly simple tastes. Visitors to his four-room rental apartment in Frankfurt were surprised to see that it looked barely lived in, devoid of personal touches. He kept his office similarly spare. Among the few custom items: a large crystal ashtray and a polished wooden cigar box. Smoking was forbidden in the skyscraper, but Ackermann's staff tinkered with the smoke detectors to make sure that the sprinklers wouldn't be set off when the boss sparked up.[5] Pleasing him was paramount.

Ackermann wanted more than to win. He wanted everyone to know he was winning. When Deutsche was named Bank of the Year by an industry magazine—a more or less meaningless honor—he crowed in the bank's annual report that "we accepted with pleasure." He later cited such awards as evidence that he had managed the institution well. A running joke inside the bank was that the most powerful person in Frankfurt was Joe's public relations man. Ackermann—ever drawn to numbers—had the bank commission quarterly opinion surveys to measure his standing with the German public. He had an unseemly tendency to boast—about how much Michael Bloomberg liked him or about how he'd received a standing ovation at a shareholder meeting or about how he had personal relationships with this prime minister or that king.[6] *Why*, colleagues wondered, *was this successful man so desperately insecure?* Some of his deputies believed he was a narcissist; more, though, felt he was propelled by personal feelings of inadequacy that he yearned to overcome but never could.

In September 2003, Ackermann kicked the bank into overdrive. He had become obsessed with a metric called *return on equity*—a measure, in percentage terms, of how much an investment in the company generated in profits over a given year. The figure obviously mattered to investors, and it mattered to Ackermann, partly because his compensation was contingent in part on how the bank performed for stockholders and partly because it was a yardstick that he could measure himself against. The objective, Ackermann declared publicly, was for the bank, by 2005, to achieve a return on equity of 25 percent; that meant that for every dollar invested, the bank was creating a new twenty-five cents of earnings. "Our targets are aggressive but realistic," he declared. That year, the bank's returns were on track to be 13 percent, so Ackermann was calling for them to nearly double within two years. But that understated the extent of his ambitions. Only a year earlier, the bank's returns had been a measly 4 percent.[7] Ackermann's 25 percent aim was stratospheric by comparison.

Into the 1990s, Deutsche executives had understood their mission as serving multiple constituencies: shareholders, employees, society. That was why leaders like Alfred Herrhausen had supported not only the integration of Europe, which was in the bank's financial interest, but also the cancellation of third-world debts, which was not. Now Ackermann was substantially narrowing Deutsche's conception of who it served—now it was shareholders, and shareholders alone, who really mattered.

Regardless of the wisdom or feasibility of achieving the return-on-equity milestone, Ackermann's staff was afraid to disappoint him. Employees dreaded his anger. "His signature youthful smile can suddenly freeze, his look and voice turn ice-cold," his former spokesman, Stefan Baron, wrote in an otherwise fawning 2014 biography.[8] When Ackermann set goals, they weren't suggestions—they were orders. "You had to meet them, no matter what," a top executive says.

Humans respond to incentives, and the incentives in this case were clear: The priority was to maximize short-term profits. If your division missed its quarterly financial targets, you would be lucky to get a stern dressing down in private—often Ackermann would jab at, undermine, and sideline underperforming colleagues. A saying became common among senior executives: "The current quarter is the most important quarter we're ever going to have." Do everything possible to make money now and to delay decisions that will reduce profits, even if doing so will mean larger losses down the road.

The bank's compensation systems were changed to reflect the new short-termism. Traders would now receive bonuses that were a percentage of whatever revenue they generated—without any way of recouping those bonuses if the traders' bets lost money in the future. Unsurprisingly, bankers not only strived for quick profits but tended to exaggerate how much money their projects were likely to bring in. Soon it was not unusual for elite traders to pocket an astonishing $30 million bonus at the end of the year.[9]

Some of Edson's longest-serving lieutenants were unnerved by Ackermann's leadership. Martin Loat—Bill's old partner, who had been dispatched to run Deutsche's Asian markets businesses—quit in frustration in 2003 and never worked for a bank again. Michael Philipp also resigned, exasperated, like many others, by what he saw as Ackermann's neglectful management approach. He was encouraging the investment bank to grow, which was fine, but it was becoming Deutsche's only source of profits. Philipp could see that with the entire bank's fortunes hinging on a single division, pressure was building for that division to take greater and greater risks, making the bank lopsided, deeply indebted, and overreliant on derivatives.

Traditionally, the first question a senior executive would ask about a proposed transaction was about how much risk was in-

volved. Now the first—and often last—query was about the potential for profit. In Deutsche's traditional German business, client
managers were told that they shouldn't bother to maintain relationships with German companies unless those relationships
would generate total returns for the bank—through fees or interest on loans—of at least 25 percent. Loan volumes shriveled as old
customers were tossed aside.[10] Previous plans to diversify the bank,
to wean it from relying on the investment bank as the main revenue producer, were shelved. Even to Loat and Philipp, who loved
debt and derivatives, this was starting to look like a time bomb.

Anshu Jain had set up his business to be aggressive. The way he
saw it, as much as he had admired Mitchell, the great man had
died with Deutsche a second-tier player. Jain's mission was to
vault it to the top. That meant revving up the sales engines across
the markets and investment-banking division—including parts
that traditionally had moved a little too slowly for his taste.

That included Michael Cohrs's banking group, which culti-
vated long-term client relationships. Jain authorized—even at
times encouraged—his sales-and-trading troops to pursue
revenue-generating relationships with large companies that had
traditionally been served by Cohrs's squad. Jain's term for it was
"monetizing corporate relationships." Soon his cadre stampeded
across relationships that the investment bankers had spent years
grooming. One example was the advertising company Publicis, a
long-standing client of Cohrs's team. The relationship had lasted
in part because it had been conservative. Investment bankers are
often disparaged for dispensing self-serving or destructive advice
to clients, but the best bankers' strategy is to earn money by earning trust. In the case of Deutsche's relationship with Publicis,
that approach struck Anshu's underlings as tedious; a team from
global markets looked for a shorter road to riches. They set up a

meeting with Publicis executives and persuaded them to buy a bunch of derivatives. Deutsche pocketed tens of millions in fees. As if on cue, the derivatives backfired for Publicis, causing significant losses. Its top executives complained to Deutsche officials about the hefty fees and asked for their money back. Jain's group said no. Publicis appealed to Cohrs's investment bankers. "Anshu, we've gotta give it back," Cohrs pleaded. Jain protested that Deutsche had adhered to the letter of its contract with Publicis. Cohrs tried to get Ackermann to intervene, but he refused. So Anshu's team made its money, but it cost Cohrs's team a long-time client. Cohrs would eventually resign, having concluded that his client-focused skill set was no longer valued.

Similar dramas were playing out across the bank. One reason Mitchell had been excited about buying Bankers Trust a few years earlier was that its Alex. Brown division in Baltimore, which focused on providing financial advice to rich families, was ripe for growth. Now Ackermann back-burnered those plans, preferring to plow resources into the securities sales-and-trading business—Jain's business.

Deutsche's embrace of a profits-at-any-price approach, its extreme tolerance for risks that were unbearable for most banks, had real-world consequences—such as when it helped funnel money into countries that were under economic sanctions for pursuing nuclear weapons or participating in genocides. Countries like Iran or Syria can print all the local currency they want, but to buy products—weapons, food, widgets—overseas, they need an international currency. The U.S. dollar is the closest thing to a globally accepted form of money—and Deutsche started helping the governments of sanctioned countries get access to gobs of American currency. When the Deutsche scheme got under way in 1999, it was unclear whether employees realized they were violating international laws. By 2003, there was no such ambiguity. Because the transactions were done in dollars, they had to be routed through Deutsche's New York operations, and that risked attracting the scrutiny of American law enforcement. "Please note that while DB is prepared to do business with Syria, we obviously have sizable business interests in the U.S., too, which DB wants to protect," one employee cautioned a colleague. "So any Syrian transactions should be treated STRICTLY confidential and should involve any colleagues on a 'Must-Know' basis only! . . . We do not want to create any publicity or other 'noise' in the markets or media."

To maintain the secrecy of the sanctions-busting transactions, employees deployed countersurveillance measures. One was to strip out the codes that identified the country of origin of the entities for which the bank was transferring money. "IMPORTANT: NO IRANIAN NAMES TO BE MENTIONED WHEN MAKING PAYMENT TO NEW YORK," read one missive.[11]

By 2006, Deutsche had zapped nearly $11 billion into Iran, Burma, Syria, Libya, and the Sudan, providing desperately needed hard currency to the world's outlaw regimes and single-handedly eroding the effectiveness of peaceful efforts to defuse international crises.*

In the Middle East, Iran was trying to fill a power vacuum left by the demise of Saddam Hussein's Iraqi dictatorship. To do that, it needed to keep its neighbor's fledgling democracy unstable. What better way to accomplish that than by waging a relentless campaign of bloody violence? The hundreds of millions of dollars that Deutsche wired to Iranian banks provided vital funding for the sanctioned country to pay for its terrorism. Soon Iraq was being ripped apart by violence. Roadside bombs detonated all over

---

* Ackermann denies responsibility for this.

the country, targeting the country's fragile government and the U.S. military forces that were trying to keep the peace. Much of the violence was the work of a terrorist group, Jaysh al-Mahdi, which had been armed and trained by Hezbollah, which had been bankrolled by Iran's Revolutionary Guard, which had been financed by Deutsche.

In May 2007, Blake Stephens, a twenty-five-year-old Army sergeant, was killed by a Jaysh al-Mahdi bomb south of Baghdad. Two months later, Army Specialist Steven Davis was killed in western Baghdad by a grenade thrown by a member of Jaysh al-Mahdi. Two months after that, in August, Army Specialist Christopher Neiberger, a gunner on an armored Humvee, was killed. And in September, Joshua Reeves, a corporal in the Army Rangers, was killed by another Jaysh al-Mahdi bomb. Back in Tennessee, Reeves's first child had been born the day earlier. If it seemed like a stretch to attribute the deaths to Deutsche's sanctions-violating work with Iran, nobody told the families of Sergeant Stephens, Specialist Davis, Specialist Neiberger, and Corporal Reeves.*[12]

The sanctions violations weren't the work of an isolated crew of rogue Deutsche employees. Managers knew. Their bosses knew. American regulators would later find evidence that at least one member of the bank's vorstand—in other words, one of Deutsche's most senior executives—knew about and approved of the scheme.[13] After all, it was profitable, and Deutsche's priorities under Ackermann couldn't have been clearer.

Other consequences of Ackermann's 25 percent target were less deadly but still far-reaching. He and Jain were determined to

---

* In 2018, the four families would file a federal lawsuit alleging that Deutsche played an "integral role in helping Iran finance, orchestrate, and support terrorist attacks on U.S. peacekeeping forces in Iraq from 2004 to 2011."

poach the top talent from the top Wall Street firms, and they wanted to move quickly. Each time a new squad of traders arrived, instead of learning how the technology worked on Deutsche's trading floor, the teams were authorized to just install their own financial models and computer systems. Before long, a hodgepodge of hundreds of different systems polluted the bank's ecosystem. One implication was that there was no way for the bank to measure or understand what it was actually doing. When board members asked questions like *How big is our portfolio of interest-rate swaps?*, the answer came back: *We don't know.* This would have been funny if it hadn't been so scary. And by the time the problem was recognized, there was no way to fix it—"It's like changing an airplane engine midflight," one top executive would explain— and certainly not without a massive long-term investment in constructing entirely new technology that integrated all of the bank's disparate systems. That would squeeze the bank's profits, which nobody—certainly not Ackermann—wanted to do.*

Partly as a result, different teams within Deutsche were going around to the same clients, pitching them the same products but at different prices. Prices were determined by computer systems that calculated how much it would cost Deutsche to do a transaction. But those equations relied on inputs from across the bank— how high the bank's overall funding costs were, for example. The splintered IT systems meant there was no way to pinpoint those numbers. Competing Deutsche teams roamed the land, undermining one another and bewildering clients.

Ackermann's closest colleague was Hugo Bänziger, the bank's chief risk officer, who had also come to Deutsche from Credit

---

* Ackermann denies that the bank underinvested in technology on his watch.

Suisse. Bänziger had been a lieutenant colonel in the Swiss armed forces, at one point commanding a tank battalion,[14] which bonded him with Ackermann, himself a colonel in the Swiss military reserves.[15]

Bänziger was a risk expert, but he was out of control with his employees. Every executive who was in the running to become a managing director—a title awarded to thousands of employees—had to attend a weeklong Risk Academy, often held in dormitories in the German countryside. The goal was to instill military-style discipline and stamina in his staff, and it metastasized into a hazing ritual. Candidates had to complete impossible assignments—rework the bank's entire balance sheet, for example—in minutes. The hot water in the dorms was turned off. Attendees were subjected to sleep deprivation. Exercises were crafted to create *informationsflut*, or information overload, as Bänziger put it. One guest speaker arrived at a Risk Academy dinner expecting to encounter the testosterone-fueled antics of a typical banking retreat. Instead he saw row after row of sunken-eyed lawyers and risk managers. In many academy classes, pupils were reduced to tears. "We want people who can stand up and take abuse," Bänziger explained to a colleague.

Fear of Bänziger extended beyond the Risk Academy sessions. Multiple women inside the bank had complained to the HR department that Bänziger had acted improperly toward them in the office and at off-site retreats, according to six former executives. Once Bänziger visited a company that was a Deutsche client and made such a show of hitting on a secretary, badgering her to go out on a date with him that night, that she burst into tears. Her boss called a senior Deutsche executive in London to complain. Ackermann says he knew about the allegations—at one point an outside law firm was hired to investigate, but it didn't find hard evidence to prove the particular woman's claims. Bänziger retained both his job and Ackermann's trust.*

Deutsche had operated in Russia on and off since the late nineteenth century, and after the collapse of the Soviet Union, it was one of the first Western banks to open outposts there. Ackermann told German leaders that it was important for the country to embrace Russia for geopolitical reasons. "We have to build the House of Europe, and Russia is part of it," Ackermann cooed. Really, Russia's fast-growing and lightly regulated markets represented an enticing opportunity for unconstrained profits.

In 1994, an American named Charlie Ryan had started a Moscow-based bank called United Financial Group. As Westerners clambered for a piece of the newly accessible Russian economy, United Financial grew quickly. Before long, it had one of the biggest stock-trading businesses in all of Russia. Wanting to get in on this success story, in 2004 Deutsche struck a deal to buy 40 percent of United Financial, and two years later it acquired the remainder for $400 million. All of a sudden, Deutsche had become a leading player in the chaotic country, the top foreign bank for Russian IPOs and mergers, working for formerly state-owned enterprises that had fallen under the control of a new class of oligarchs. Charlie Ryan became Deutsche's CEO for Russia.[16] "It's obvious today that Russia is hot," he explained to a reporter in 2006. "Three years ago"—when Ackermann had stomped on the bank's gas pedal—"Deutsche Bank was the only one to see it."[17]

This did not strike everyone as smart. Some executives had reservations about doing business in Russia and, in particular, doing business with United Financial. Ryan was an enigma;

---

* Bänziger didn't respond to my requests for comment.

what was a boisterous American doing ensconced in the Moscow business scene? Executives, including one of the bank's highest-ranking internal lawyers, wondered aloud whether he was an undercover CIA agent. Was this really the kind of person the bank should be tethering its reputation to? Another concern was that Deutsche was pursuing business with Russian oligarchs, and that meant it was almost certainly getting its hands dirty with corrupt money. The only question was when, where, and how much—and whether the dirt would leave a permanent stain on the bank.

This, though, was what it took to achieve Ackermann's return-on-equity target—especially since Ackermann himself was an unabashed cheerleader of the bank's expansion into Russia. Just as Georg von Siemens's entrancement with the United States had led Deutsche into the Henry Villard swamp a century earlier, now Ackermann's fixation with Russia would spur Deutsche into a similar quagmire. Like Siemens in America, Ackermann was blinded by his fascination with Russian culture and had developed tastes for its theater, opera, and food (blini with caviar was among his favorite dishes). He visited the country as much as once a month, striking up what he described as friendships with some of the bankers in Vladimir Putin's inner circle. One of them, Andrey Kostin, was the chief executive of VTB Bank. VTB was a government-controlled lender that had financed Russian intelligence agencies and was suspected of conducting espionage via its archipelago of international outposts. (Two leaders of the FSB, the Kremlin's modern-day spy agency, sent their sons to work at VTB.[18]) None of this seemed to deter Ackermann. He signed off on a $1 billion credit line that Deutsche extended the Russian bank.[19] And at a cocktail party in Saint Petersburg, he suggested to Kostin that VTB should consider building its own investment bank to speed the development of Russia's capital markets. Kostin heeded the advice. In 2008, he hired a team of more than a hundred bankers from Deutsche to lead the effort. The defections, while irritating Ackermann and Charlie Ryan, cemented Deutsche's bonds to VTB—and to Putin's clique.

Further gluing the two banks together was the fact that Deutsche in 2000 had hired Kostin's son, Andrey Jr., in the bank's London office, straight out of university. He would spend most of the next decade with Deutsche, eventually becoming a senior investment banker. Kostin Jr.'s prominent role, Ackermann would explain to a Russian newspaper years later, "is testimony to our good relationship" with the Russian financial establishment.[20]

That good relationship extended to helping wealthy Russians launder money into the United States—a crucial service, since few American banks were willing to accept the legal risks associated with moving suspect funds into the country. Oligarchs would move money to banks in neighboring Latvia. Those Latvian banks had "correspondent" relationships with Deutsche that allowed them to transfer money directly into American accounts set up in the names of innocuous-sounding shell companies. In 2004, a newly arrived compliance executive started testing Deutsche's anti-money-laundering systems and was stunned by what he found. Money was pouring into one of the bank's main U.S. legal entities—Deutsche Bank Trust Company Americas—from banks in Estonia, Lithuania, Cyprus, and most of all, Latvia. Deutsche hadn't batted an eye at the flood of transactions. All that business was lucrative for Deutsche, which pocketed fees on each transaction, but it spelled trouble with regulators. "You've got a big problem in Eastern Europe," the new compliance executive warned his boss. "Dude, you have no idea," came the unsettling reply.

Unlike Deutsche, the Federal Reserve had sophisticated software to track suspicious money flows, and it had been watching the Russian cash going to Latvia and then to the United States, where it soon disappeared into the luxury real estate market. In 2005, a team of regulators walked from the New York Fed around the corner to Deutsche's Wall Street offices, where they laced into executives for their Latvian lapses. The executives braced for a large penalty—something in the $100 million range seemed likely—and were pleasantly surprised when the Fed, along with New York's banking regulator, simply issued a written order requiring the bank to improve its anti-money-laundering systems. The caveat was that the next time similar problems cropped up, Deutsche wouldn't get off so lightly.

CHAPTER 10

THE MAR-A-LAGO PRIZE

n 1905, a German immigrant living in the Bronx set up a small barbershop on the ground floor of a newly constructed building at 60 Wall Street, in the heart of Manhattan's booming financial district. In an era before skyscrapers, the twenty-five-story, L-shaped tower was a landmark, its gargoyle-guarded roof visible from the nearby waterfront. The barbershop thrived, offering shaves and trims to a procession of bankers, stock exchange traders, lawyers, and office workers. The barber's name was Friedrich Trump. The same year that he opened the shop, his wife gave birth to a boy named Fred.[1]

Many years passed, the barbershop closed, and the old 60 Wall Street gave way in 1989 to a new 60 Wall Street, a forty-seven-story tower topped with a distinctive pyramid roof. For a time, it was home to J.P. Morgan & Co. Then that bank left, and in 2005, Deutsche Bank started relocating its American staff—displaced ever since 9/11—to its new home at 60 Wall Street.[2] And so Friedrich Trump's grandson—born to Fred's wife in 1946—became an occasional visitor to the site of his grandfather's old barbershop.

Deutsche's relationship with Donald Trump had only deepened since Mike Offit left. Justin Kennedy, now a managing director, had become a key point of contact for Trump and helped chaperone large real estate loans for him through the bank. Kennedy's role was to find customers to buy portions of loans after Deutsche dispensed the money, a process that allowed Deutsche to make larger loans than it otherwise could have. Kennedy sometimes sat with Trump in his luxury box at the US Open tennis tournament or at Manhattan nightclubs, where Trump would park himself at a table in the corner, facing outward, holding court like a Mafia don. Now, with Kennedy's encouragement, Deutsche hurried along a Henry Villard–like path.

In 2000, the bank had plunked down another $150 million to be used for the renovations of Trump's building at 40 Wall Street. The next year, Deutsche agreed to extend Trump a mortgage worth more than $900 million—at the time, the largest ever on a single property—so he could buy the General Motors Building on the southeastern corner of New York's Central Park. (Trump already owned half of the fifty-story building; he wanted the rest.)[3] And in 2002, Deutsche agreed to refinance about $70 million that he owed on some of his Atlantic City casinos.[4] Those loans came out of Deutsche's commercial real estate division, which Kennedy was helping to run.

Not everyone was enamored with Trump. Seth Waugh, one of Edson's many Merrill Lynch recruits and the head of Deutsche's American operations, learned around 2001 that the bank was planning to lend Trump about $500 million to use as he wished— basically an unrestricted cash infusion to stabilize the developer's flagging finances. Waugh had previously witnessed up close the carnage that Trump could inflict on imprudent financial institutions. At Merrill, Edson had assigned him the task of mopping up after Trump defaulted on nearly $700 million of bonds that Merrill had helped sell for his Taj Mahal casino in Atlantic City.

Waugh was in no hurry to repeat the experience at Deutsche. He voiced strong objections to the proposed new loan, in which Trump would not have had to put up any hard assets as collateral, and the deal soon died.

Yet Deutsche's broader Trump relationship rumbled on. In 2003, another arm of Deutsche, focused on helping companies raise money by selling stocks and bonds to investors, agreed to work with Trump. The point man on this part of the relationship was Richard Byrne—another Merrill veteran who had been involved in the Taj Mahal debacle. (Byrne had helped sell the ill-fated Taj bonds to investors.) Now Trump hired Byrne's group at Deutsche to issue bonds for his troubled Trump Hotels & Casino Resorts. Byrne knew this would be an uphill battle; not only had Trump defaulted in the past, but he also had recently been taunting investors that he might stop paying back other outstanding bonds.[5] Waugh didn't warn Byrne about the recently rejected $500 million loan, and Byrne organized a "road show" for Trump to meet with and try to win over big institutional investors. He escorted Trump to meetings all over New York and Boston. At every stop, boardrooms and auditoriums were jammed with traders, fund managers, senior executives, and secretaries curious to see The Donald Show, and Trump didn't disappoint. He rocked, he rolled, and he delivered wildly optimistic and inconsistent financial projections.

Afterward, Trump called Byrne to ask how much money they had raised. The answer, alas, was virtually zero. Byrne braced for an explosion as he explained to Trump that even though he'd been treated like a celebrity, nobody trusted him with their money. Trump took the rejection in stride. "Let me talk to your salespeople," he requested. Byrne agreed, and Trump came to deliver a pep talk. "Fellas, I know this isn't the easiest thing you've had to sell," he acknowledged. "But if you get this done, you'll all be my guests at Mar-a-Lago." Trump was always good at pushing an audience's buttons—a weekend with Trump at Mar-a-Lago: bragging rights that not even money could buy— and this new incentive did the trick. The salesmen worked the phones, cast a wider net for more clients, and managed to sell an impressive $485 million of junk bonds (albeit at a high interest rate that reflected investors' fears that Trump might default).

When the sale was complete, Byrne delivered the good news to Trump, who was pumped. "Don't forget what you promised our guys," Byrne nudged his happy client.

"What's that?" Trump asked. Byrne reminded him about the Mar-a-Lago trip. "No way they'll remember that," Trump weaseled.

"That's all they've talked about the past week," Byrne responded. Trump ultimately dispatched his private Boeing 727 to fly fifteen salesmen down to Palm Beach, Florida. During the day, they golfed. Trump, decked out in white polyester, impressed the bankers with his brazen cheating. At night, they dined at Mar-a-Lago, and Trump regaled them with story after preposterous story about his hijinks with casinos, real estate, Wall Street, and women.[6]

The following year, with his casinos on the rocks, Trump's company stopped paying interest on the bonds and filed for bankruptcy protection.[7] ("I don't think it's a failure; it's a success," Trump spun.) Deutsche's clients, the ones who had recently bought the junk bonds, suffered painful losses. Going forward, Trump would be off-limits for Byrne's division.

The excommunication, however, didn't apply to the whole bank. Trump soon went back to Justin Kennedy's commercial real estate group, seeking another enormous loan. This one was to build a ninety-two-story skyscraper in Chicago, which Trump planned to name the Trump International Hotel & Tower. It was going to be one of the tallest buildings in America, a glittering riverfront high-rise that included a hotel, a spa, restaurants, and nearly 500 condominium units.[8] Trump seduced the Deutsche bankers with flights on the same 727 that had recently brought Byrne's team to Florida.[9] He invited Kennedy to Trump Tower, six blocks away from Henry Villard's garish Madison Avenue mansion. Trump lavished him and his colleagues with praise and explained that his daughter, Ivanka, would be in charge of the proposed Chicago development—that's how important this project was to the Trump Organization, as his company was called.

Just as Waugh hadn't warned Byrne about the rejected Trump loan, now Byrne didn't warn Kennedy's crew about the bank's recent bad Trump experience. ("We just looked the other way," explains an executive in Byrne's division. "That was the Deutsche Bank culture.") Even so, the Chicago loan had all the hallmarks of trouble. Not only had Trump defaulted over and over again, but before extending another loan, Deutsche conducted an informal audit of Trump's finances. He had declared to the bank that he was worth roughly $3 billion. But when Deutsche crunched the numbers that his accountants had compiled, they concluded that the real number was about $788 million.[10] In other words, Trump had been saying his net worth was almost four times larger than it really was. For most banks, this would have been the final straw; how could you trust a guy to repay a huge loan if he was lying about how much money he had?

Deutsche, though, was undeterred. Executives were so eager for growth and big deals, so convinced of their own intelligence, that they managed to look past the obvious red flags. (Plus, Trump hadn't defaulted on the loans that the commercial real estate group had made dating back to the Mike Offit era.) In February 2005, Deutsche agreed to lend him $640 million for the Chicago project. The actual recipients were limited liability companies that the Trump Organization had created specifically for this occasion to shield its owner if the project went bust. But Trump also agreed to provide an "unconditional payment guaranty" of $40 million—that was what Trump personally would owe if his LLCs defaulted. (Trump also paid Deutsche a $12.5 million fee in connection with the loan.) Deutsche sold off pieces of the loan to other banks and investors, but it kept plenty of it on its own books, too. It was a fateful transaction, one that would shape Deutsche's relationship with Trump for years into the future.[11]

Around this time, and out of public view, Deutsche provided a series of other services to Trump. For starters, it created numerous "special purpose vehicles" to make it easier for him quietly to buy properties internationally. Thanks to the magic of derivatives, the vehicles—with obscure names that hid their connection to Trump—enabled Trump to do real estate deals in places like Eastern Europe and South America without putting any of his own money on the line; not only was he taking out loans to finance the deals, but he was also using other people's money to cover the small "equity" portion of the purchases. For a fee, Deutsche and investors bore the risk, over many years, that the projects would fail. This sort of structure was not unheard-of for major real estate developers. "It's a well-seasoned financing technique," explains Mark Ritter, a Deutsche executive who worked on the transactions at the time. But it added to the bank's already deep exposure to Trump—and helped the mogul strike under-the-radar deals in far-flung locales, including those that were popular destinations for people looking to hide assets.

At the same time, Deutsche also helped Trump find people to buy condos in his properties. When he partnered in 2006 with a

Los Angeles developer to build a Trump-branded resort in Hawaii, Deutsche organized get-togethers in London and elsewhere to connect Trump and his partners with wealthy clients who used anonymous shell companies to buy blocks of units in the sprawling Waikiki hotel complex. The bank played the same behind-the-scenes matchmaking role when Trump sought to drum up interest in a planned resort in Baja, Mexico. (That project collapsed.) In both cases, Deutsche steered very rich Russians into the Trump ventures, according to people who were involved in the deals—just a couple of years after American regulators had punished the bank for whisking Russian money into the U.S. financial system via Latvia.

Some members of Jain's inner circle had discussed the potential pitfalls of the Trump relationship, and they were worried. It wasn't only the not-insignificant risk that Trump would default on loans. The bankers also knew how filthy the New York real estate industry could be. They talked about Trump's well-documented ties to the organized crime world, and the possibility that Trump's real estate projects were Laundromats for illicit funds from countries like Russia, where oligarchs were trying to get money out of the country. "Everyone in the real estate business was involved in 'flight capital,' " one of Anshu's lieutenants would explain years later.

There was more to Trump's relationship with Deutsche than money. The bank was still trying to establish its brand in the United States, and despite his financial woes, Trump—whose hit TV show *The Apprentice* had debuted in 2004 on NBC—provided splashy publicity for the bank. With this in mind, executives cozied up to him and his family. They threw client parties at Mar-a-Lago.[12] They invited him to high-profile events. Every Labor Day weekend, for example, Deutsche hosted a pro-am golf event at the Tournament Players Club of Boston, featuring the best professional golfers and a smattering of celebrities and business leaders. Trump was a regular, working the crowds and autographing the $100 bills that fans thrust at him. On the golf course, Deutsche sometimes paired Trump with a senior bank executive like Seth Waugh, who would woo Trump over eighteen holes.

The year after Byrne's team sold the junk bonds for Trump's casino company, Deutsche dispatched its public relations staff to the course's clubhouse to conduct video interviews with some of the marquee participants. Trump, never one to shy away from a TV camera, sat down for a promotional shoot. What's your experience with Deutsche been? asked the public relations staffer charged with conducting the interviews.

"It's great!" bellowed Trump, whose company would file for bankruptcy protection two months later. "They're really fast!" He meant the bank was fast at approving his loans. The staffer asking the questions grimaced; she wasn't sure this reflected very well on her employer.[13]

Lo and behold, Deutsche achieved Ackermann's goal of a 25 percent return on equity in 2005. "Credit for this success goes to more than 63,000 highly motivated staff," he cheered, adding that the new goal was to keep profits growing at a double-digit clip going forward. "Deutsche Bank," he said, "is exceptionally well equipped to face the future."[14]

You wouldn't have known it by looking at Deutsche's financial statements, practically glowing with the heat of profits and light-speed growth, but this was a dangerous period for the bank. Ackermann was shooting for the moon. Consultants were hired to study whether having the word *Deutsche* in the bank's name impeded its global ambitions.[15] In early 2004, Ackermann entertained merger discussions with a variety of giant banks, including

Citigroup—the logical next step after his stillborn talks with JPMorgan a few years earlier.[16] It was an act of extraordinary hubris. Deutsche and Citigroup were vying for the distinction of being the world's largest bank—Citigroup was ahead, with about $1.5 trillion in assets compared to Deutsche's roughly $1.2 trillion.[17] Merging them would have spawned a behemoth of unimaginable size.

By now Ackermann had become a deeply polarizing figure to the German public, maligned as the embodiment of Anglo-American corporate excess. In 2005, he stood criminal trial for violating securities laws by approving huge bonus payments as the chairman of a German industrial and telecommunications conglomerate, Mannesmann. The case had nothing to do with Deutsche, and Ackermann was eventually acquitted, but a photographer had captured the grinning defendant flashing the "V for victory" sign in the middle of the trial. The image became a symbol in Germany of Ackermann's arrogance. Only 5 percent of respondents in a German poll said they believed Ackermann was committed to the country's social welfare.[18] A member of Deutsche's supervisory board took the extraordinary step of resigning in protest—and publicly blasting Ackermann for jeopardizing the bank's stability, for becoming too dependent on investment banking, for selling out the institution's German identity.[19]

It was all a backlash against Ackermann's—and Deutsche's— unparalleled power. And yet even as the public outcry intensified, Ackermann was welcomed into the German establishment. He and Chancellor Gerhard Schröder regularly got together for a glass of Bordeaux. Ackermann appeared before TV studio audiences for interviews with Germany's leading journalists. When one asked him if he cared who was chancellor, Schröder or his rival, Angela Merkel, Ackermann shrugged and said that he got along well with both. "I'm a little bit of a politician."[20] He smiled. When Merkel became chancellor, she hosted a dinner in his honor.[21]

This go-go period was precisely when the bank most needed someone to step on the brakes, maybe gently, maybe firmly, but definitely to apply some pressure to slow down this vehicle that was losing its capacity to steer. The bank needed someone who wasn't worried about being unpopular, who wasn't afraid to deliver unwanted news to his superiors, who was willing to say no.

Bill Broeksmit was a phone call away. No one rang.

CHAPTER 11

DER INDER

n the months after Edson's death, Bill had been glad that he no longer worked in banking. The endless hours, the cutthroat environment, the dubious ethics—these things had not caused Edson's plane to go down, but in some ways, if you squinted hard enough, perhaps they had contributed to it. Maybe, if he hadn't worked so hard, his wife would have stayed in London, and Edson wouldn't have boarded that fateful flight to Rangeley. Maybe he wouldn't have owned his own plane and would have been forced to fly commercial. Or maybe not. Broeksmit told acquaintances that the sudden death of his best friend had validated his decision to change his life's course.

With time and money to kill, he took care of the heartbroken Estelle. When Bill and Alla's London flat caught on fire, Estelle was given the cushy assignment of overseeing the extensive repairs and renovations, a task that kept her busy—and compensated—for years. She spent those years grieving. "I have to let go, and for some reason it's hard," she wrote to Bill in 2004. "I have no idea what to do with my life, where to go." Estelle had friends in Croatia, and she dabbled in real estate there, trying to occupy her life and mind. Even Donald Trump was in Croatia, "investing like [a] maniac," she reported to Bill. "If you are interested . . . let me know. There are still great deals." No thanks, Broeksmit replied. He was a conservative investor; following Trump into deals was not for him. (Ever since he had caught a teenage Val with a copy of *The Art of the Deal*, Bill had been ranting to his family about how Trump was a con man.)

In theory, retirement should have been fun for Broeksmit. Money was no object. Fine artwork, including a Damien Hirst, soon graced his and Alla's Park Avenue apartment. And while Bill could be a penny pincher—he might have been the only multimillionaire banker flying economy on international flights—he was plenty generous when it mattered. It wasn't just with Estelle. When a family member needed an expensive medical procedure that wasn't covered by insurance, Bill announced that he would pay for it. When the beneficiary resisted, Bill threatened the left-leaning relative to instead donate the money to the Republican Party. That did the trick.

The problem was the monotony. He did some consulting work for his old firm, Merrill Lynch. "Nothing too strenuous, but it's fun to be near the game," he emailed Estelle.

He bought a fluffy white bichon frise and named her Daisy.

He sat around in the apartment, puffing on a tobacco pipe, watching old movies.

He wrote long letters to the editor about executive compensation and tax reform. They rarely got published.

He frequented the Russian and Turkish Baths that he used to go to with Edson, but now he sat alone.

Most of all, he drank. Late at night, he still could go a little wild, urging college buddies and ex-colleagues to have one more round at two A.M.—and then vomiting in the morning. He diagnosed himself as an alcoholic. "I am not at all depressed," he assured an old Deutsche colleague, Saman Majd, "just very lazy and sluggish."

Anshu Jain was on the march at Deutsche. His business was climbing up the all-important league tables, and it was responsible for the majority of the entire bank's profits. Jain made no secret of his ambitions to one day become CEO. But as much as he yearned for that job, that's how much the cards were stacked against him. His Indian heritage made him an outlier in an organization that was still struggling with its acceptance of outsiders. *The Economist* in 2004 had famously attacked Deutsche as a giant hedge fund and derided Anshu as an "Indian 'bond junkie,'"[1] a moniker that took hold in some corners of the bank. At a weekend retreat, a German banker joked to the crowd of five hundred that normally investment banks had too many chiefs and not enough Indians—but that in the case of Deutsche, the problem was reversed. As the Americans and Brits (and Indians) in the audience exchanged nervous glances, the Germans roared. Jain knew that, behind his back, plenty of his German colleagues referred to him as *Der Inder*—The Indian. (The German media did it in public, regularly introducing the banker as "The Indian Anshu Jain.") It reminded him of his early days at Merrill, when he kept getting mistaken for an IT guy.

Jain chafed that while he toiled in the shadows, Ackermann was enjoying all the public credit. And the CEO was not making things easier. Behind Jain's back, Ackermann derided him to colleagues, deliberately undercutting his subordinate's prospects for advancement. He and his secretary sometimes laughed at Anshu's cloying emails about how grateful he was that his boss had taken the time to meet with him or had supported him in a contentious meeting.

But even if Jain had been German and had had a supportive boss, he still lacked key leadership skills. He had been trained by Mitchell and then Ackermann to generate revenue, nothing more. He was not responsible for keeping the bank's technology up to snuff. He was not responsible for ensuring that employees complied with the law or the bank's rules. He was not responsible for accounting. He was not even responsible for getting along with his colleagues running other divisions of Deutsche. All that mattered was that the money kept streaming in. Jain's single-minded obsession was in line with Ackermann's, but his inability to glimpse the world beyond those blinders meant he was ill prepared to ever become the leader of the entire bank.

With Mitchell's portrait looking down on him, Jain mimicked his mentor and surrounded himself with a small band of trusted advisers. Edson, though, had encouraged a certain amount of dissent—and had had Broeksmit not only as counselor but also as someone who could facilitate such pushback. Ackermann, who remained quietly tormented by his own self-doubt, diagnosed Jain as suffering from chronic insecurity, which he seemed to overcompensate for by screaming at his subordinates and lashing out when people disagreed with him. The result was that when Jain gathered his senior team in his office, they would go around the circular table, and each executive would awkwardly pay tribute to Anshu's leadership. His deferential clique became known as "Anshu's Army." He and his troops spent enormous amounts of time debating whether this decision or that action was the right thing to do—not for Deutsche, but for Anshu's standing inside the bank. Unsurprisingly, Jain believed that the best way to improve his standing was to continue maximizing profits.

Some of his colleagues soon noticed troubling patterns. Jain was willing to indulge employees who were making tons of money, even if they were doing it in suspect ways. His rain-

makers seemed to enjoy protected status. Nobody had the appetite to ask uncomfortable questions. When robust financial data
poured in from formerly obscure divisions, some of Jain's deputies glanced at one another with arched eyebrows—and then, for
the most part, kept quiet. There was a sense that the ends justified the means; as long as you were pulling in big profits, it didn't
much matter how you were doing it.

Rajeev Misra was a quintessential example. Growing up in an
affluent family in Delhi, Misra had met Jain in school at age
fourteen and they became friends. Misra's father expected his
son to become a surgeon or an engineer, and Misra enrolled in an
elite Indian engineering school before transferring to the University of Pennsylvania. As a mechanical engineering student, he
nabbed a summer gig helping design satellites at the Los Alamos
National Laboratory in New Mexico, but he couldn't get a full-
time job. Instead, after an unsatisfying stint at a software start-
up, he went to business school. Wall Street—with its energy,
entrepreneurialism, and copious amounts of money—seemed
like the ideal destination.

Interviewing for a job at Merrill, Misra boasted that he had
placed 126th out of hundreds of thousands of candidates in the
entrance exam for India's engineering academy and had received
a full scholarship from Penn. (Decades later, he still was bragging about those glory days.) His cocky attitude didn't impress
his interviewers. Nor did his concession that he didn't know much
about finance. "You'll have to teach me," he blurted. Only one
Merrill executive had found something amusing in that candid
response: Bill Broeksmit. He agreed to take on Misra as a trainee.

Misra stumbled out of the gates. Three months in, he slouched
into Broeksmit's office and informed his boss that he had lost
$200,000. Misra expected to be canned. "Don't do it three times in

a row," Broeksmit advised. "Once is okay." After that, Misra's career took off. He moved to London with Merrill, and four years later, in 1997, Jain hired him at Deutsche to be a top sales executive.

Misra, with slicked-back hair and sad brown eyes, kept getting promoted, and he eventually became the bank's head of credit trading (bonds, currencies, interest rates, and the like). There he would make his mark in part by pushing his team into the nascent field of collateralized debt obligations. The essence of a CDO was that you smushed together a bunch of securities—often they were bonds made up of mortgages—and then carved that mass up into lots of slices, some riskier than others, which you would sell as new. Under Misra's leadership, Deutsche became one of the planet's most prolific peddlers of these suddenly hot instruments. Investors—many of them unsophisticated European banks, pension plans, and municipalities—took Deutsche's advice and bought truckloads of them. Before long, that one business was hauling in $1 billion a year in revenue.

Misra became a star. He adopted an all-black wardrobe and festooned his office with trophies commemorating the deals he had arranged and the industry awards he had won.[2] He would praise Edson Mitchell for having imbued him with the can-do attitude that made his success possible. But it was an open secret inside Deutsche that Misra was permitted to push the envelope—not only by selling clients shoddy securities but by exceeding the risk-taking limits that applied to most other trading desks at the bank.* In meetings of top executives, Misra—chomping on nicotine gum, loudly smacking his lips—would go into detailed explanations of the mechanics of a failproof trade: why it was

---

* Misra acknowledges that his group at times sold shoddy securities and had unusually high risk limits, but he notes that he acted within the bank's rules.

necessary to loosen the risk limits a bit and how this brilliant strategy resembled trades Anshu himself had orchestrated in the past. Jain generally took the bait and would start reminiscing about whatever trade Misra had been referring to. A smile would creep across Misra's face. When Anshu was done pontificating, Misra would ask, "So that's a yes?" It generally was.

Some of Jain's deputies feared the destructive power of Misra's financial instruments, but they were under the impression that he was untouchable—so much so that when Misra chain-smoked his beloved cigarillos indoors, his staff scrambled to remove smoke detectors, instead of suggesting that their boss partake in his stinky habit outside.[3] After all, Rajeev and Anshu had been pals for basically their entire lives—and for that matter, Ackermann was also known for tampering with the smoke detectors.

Boaz Weinstein was another of Jain's anointed. He was a brilliant, intense man—a chess master and poker partner to Warren Buffett—who would be polite or nasty depending on his level of respect for you. Boaz, in his early thirties, had a two-headed role. He was overseeing a proprietary trading group—making bets with the bank's own money—and also managing relationships with a bunch of clients. Deutsche managers and compliance officers had signed off on the setup, but it was a glaring conflict of interest, the type of arrangement that wouldn't have been acceptable at more established Wall Street firms and that even at Deutsche provoked considerable grumbling. If Boaz and his team knew what big institutional customers were about to do in the markets, what was to stop them from placing bets in advance? One of Anshu's underlings, Mark Ferron, started asking around about why this unusual arrangement was acceptable. Word soon traveled back to him that nobody appreciated his "dumb questions," so Ferron stopped asking them.

None of this compared to Christian Bittar, who was engaged in outright criminality. Growing up in Senegal, Bittar had been a star math pupil, earning a spot at an elite French university and then a job as a trader at the French bank Société Générale. Deutsche poached him in 1999. He was on the bank's interest-rate swaps desk—a group that Broeksmit years earlier had envisioned as a way to help clients shield themselves from future changes in interest rates and that, in normal times, should not have been a terrific profit center. But by the mid-2000s, Bittar and his colleagues were crushing it. Colleagues nicknamed Bittar "Mr. Basis Point," because of his aptitude for reaping huge profits out of tiny movements in interest rates.[4] (A basis point is a hundredth of a percentage point.)

Ferron, who was the chief operating officer of Jain's global markets business, sensed that something was amiss here, too. Bittar exhibited the classic warning signs: brainy, prickly, and all of a sudden, making buckets of money. Ferron voiced his misgivings on multiple occasions, but was told not to worry; the executive running that division, Alan Cloete, had it all under control. Ferron wasn't so sure—if ever there was a case for a proctologic examination of a business, this appeared to be it. "We don't need your help" was the final response—the end of the matter, at least for the time being.

Ferron, after all, was regarded as a second-class employee, not a star. "You spend too much time in the kitchen," Jain lectured him at one point. "You should come out and sit at the big table." The implication was that Ferron—and others in risk management, accounting, technology, and operations—was inferior to the revenue producers, a marginal employee who only sucked money away from the all-important bottom line.

During these flush years, Deutsche executives and traders reveled in their cleverness. They had concocted intricate structures designed to throw off big profits, and the structures were working as intended. Alarm bells didn't go off when proprietary trading went from representing 5 percent to 17 percent of the investment bank's profits, or when the amount of money at risk on a daily basis spiked higher. The vorstand certainly didn't try to rein things in. But this success didn't reflect the bankers' genius. Banks at the time were able to borrow virtually unlimited amounts of money from a variety of sources—central banks, depositors, the bond markets—at rock-bottom prices. When you are getting money for practically nothing, it is not that hard to turn a profit. All you have to do is find assets—stocks, bonds, mortgages, derivatives, whatever—that produce greater returns than the interest you have to pay to borrow money. That's a low hurdle to clear when your borrowing costs are near zero. Many big banks were taking advantage of this environment, but none more so than Deutsche. Its leverage ratio—the measure of how much of its money was borrowed, calculated by comparing the bank's assets to its capital—reached a stratospheric fifty-to-one.[5] (In other words, the overwhelming majority of its balance sheet was financed by debt.) By contrast, the big American banks averaged twenty-to-one ratios, which, though less than half of Deutsche's level, were themselves high by historical standards.

This business model, however, worked only as long as financial, economic, and political conditions remained favorable. Any number of variables—higher interest rates, a market crash, tougher regulations, new technology that altered the competitive landscape—could spoil the party. If that happened, the trading business would suddenly bring in much less revenue, but its high costs—not least, the gargantuan bonuses that Deutsche had promised many traders—wouldn't budge. Ackermann and Jain managed to push that asterisk out of their minds. They convinced themselves that they had perfected this moneymaking machine. They thought they were good, not lucky.

Arrogance bred mistakes. It wasn't just the bigger risks taken on the bank's trading floors. The company also was getting greedy and reckless when it came to acquisitions. There was Russia's United Financial Group, which would soon be a launching pad for all sorts of trouble. The bank made another ill-conceived acquisition that same summer of 2006: an American company called MortgageIT, which specialized in a risky type of home loan called Alt-A mortgages. This would prove to be just about the worst time imaginable to buy a producer of low-quality American mortgages, and there were plenty of red flags waving in Deutsche's face as it breezed through due diligence under the innocuous code name Project Maiden.[6] MortgageIT didn't have an anti-money-laundering program, for example. It had been under government scrutiny for predatory lending. And in Deutsche's own analysis, MortgageIT had "weak or limited" programs to ensure the loans it was making were likely to be paid back.

Here was an opportunity for Ackermann to exercise some leadership. When Jain called him from an airport lounge to discuss the planned transaction one final time before the paperwork was signed, Ackermann noted that this seemed like not a great time to buy a risky mortgage company.

"You don't like it?" Jain asked.

"No, I don't."

"Let's leave it then," Jain offered. That would have been the end of it, except that Ackermann lost his nerve. "No, do it if your team needs it," he backtracked. And so that's what Anshu did, rationalizing that Deutsche needed a steady supply of risky mortgages for Rajeev Misra's guys to package into securities. The bank's comically bad plan, as outlined in a presentation to its board, was to expand MortgageIT's range of products to include "near prime and subprime products" as well as Alt-A loans. Anshu's squad was confident it could navigate the risks. In July 2006, the $429 million purchase was announced. "We are extremely pleased to have them join our effort as we continue to expand our mortgage securitization platform in the U.S. and globally," Jain declared in a press release about the very sour lemon he had just acquired.

All this growth helped the company achieve a milestone that would have been unimaginable a decade earlier. In 2007, its balance sheet bulging with about $2 trillion in assets, Deutsche became the world's biggest bank.[7]

CHAPTER 12

FIREMAN

Dark smoke billowed out of the abandoned Bankers Trust headquarters in downtown Manhattan. It was a Saturday afternoon in August 2007, and the dark tower, cloaked in black mesh ever since 9/11, had caught fire after a construction worker dropped a lit cigarette. Hundreds of firefighters rushed to the scene, desperate to prevent the blaze from spreading and the poisons inside the structure from contaminating the surrounding area. The conflagration soon engulfed thirteen floors of the building. It took seven hours to extinguish. Two firemen perished.

Around the time that the building burned, Jain and his colleagues were in Barcelona for an annual conference the bank hosted for financial markets practitioners. The event took place at the Hotel Arts, a luxurious beachfront resort. By day, there were lots of presentations and one-on-one meetings. But the real action took place at night. One evening the Rolling Stones performed—Deutsche, with Anshu's grudging sign-off (he wasn't a big Stones fan; he would have preferred Dire Straits), had paid them more than $4 million to jam for an audience of a few hundred.[1] The crowd consisted almost entirely of men, and they weren't about to dance with each other, so they awkwardly tapped their feet and nodded their heads to the music as Mick Jagger pranced onstage.

At this year's event, the focus was the fast-approaching financial storm. Two hedge funds run by the investment bank Bear Stearns had just collapsed, early tremors in what would become a global financial earthquake. One hot night, Anshu and a few colleagues attended a dinner with a group of leading hedge fund managers and private equity executives. "The talk was all about how to avoid the oncoming train," a Deutsche executive would recount.[2] Jain knew things were bad, but the apocalyptic tone rattled him. Around 9:30 P.M., he summoned his top lieutenants to a windowless hotel conference room and issued an order: "Put the ship into complete reverse." The bank needed to accelerate the sales of its riskiest positions, especially anything tied to the U.S. housing market, and they needed to do it *now*. It was a bold, prescient move, one that arguably saved the bank, and it would prove to be Jain's finest hour.

The problem was that it was easier to order a fire sale than to actually ignite one. Much of the worst stuff sitting on Deutsche's books wasn't easily salable—not many people wanted to buy risky securities right then. And Deutsche's computer systems were so disjointed that it was hard to even figure out what the bank owned. On top of that, Rajeev Misra, who had the clearest insights into where all the land mines were likely to be buried in the suddenly explosive credit business, was plotting his exit from the bank. He was unhappy with the way Deutsche was being run, with Jain striking him as dangerously uninterested in monitoring risks. To Misra, it represented a fundamental breach of responsibilities—albeit a breach that many of Misra's colleagues would level right back at him. (Bankers: not always the best at introspection.) In early 2008, after pocketing a $50 million bonus and securing a commitment from Deutsche to seed his planned hedge fund with $350 million, Misra resigned. (Mark Ferron, Anshu's longtime lieutenant, also resigned in frustration around that time.)

With emergencies everywhere, Jain recognized that he needed help. He summoned a longtime colleague, Henry Ritchotte, back to London from Tokyo, where Ritchotte had been helping run Deutsche's Asian businesses. Jain gave Colin Fan, another loyalist from the Merrill days, a lofty title. And that August, around the time of the Bankers Trust fire and the Barcelona boondoggle, Anshu phoned Bill Broeksmit. He agreed to come aboard as a consultant, with the possibility of it evolving into a full-time gig.

Days later, Jain happened to have lunch with one of Edson's kids, Scott, and mentioned that Bill was returning to London. Scott joked that Anshu seemed to be getting the band back together. "There's one thing I learned from your dad," Jain replied. "When the shit hits the fan, there's one person you want standing beside you, and that's Bill Broeksmit."

Broeksmit was desperately needed at Deutsche. A parade of consultants and regulators recently had poked around and concluded that the bank wasn't properly measuring or controlling its risks, especially when those risks happened to emanate from lucrative businesses. Even Ackermann, happy to take credit for the profits that Jain's juggernaut threw off, doubted that his underling was keeping his feral traders on a sufficiently tight leash and therefore welcomed Broeksmit's return. Bill was soon given an obscure title—head of capital and risk optimization for the investment bank—that belied the extent of his firefighting mandate: to discover where the brush fires were and to squelch them before they turned into infernos. It was made clear to everyone that he reported directly to Jain, which gave him considerable clout.

Broeksmit not only possessed a skepticism of traders but also had the nerve to voice that skepticism to Anshu. He instituted weekly risk-assessment meetings within the investment bank—until then, such meetings hadn't occurred regularly—and took on the role of "bad cop," as two top executives would later put it. He became the guy shooting down proposed transactions, reining in unruly traders, and insisting that extra capital be allocated to cover risky trades, effectively making those trades a little less profitable, and therefore less attractive, for traders.

One of Broeksmit's first tasks was to advise Jain on what to do about MortgageIT, purchased barely a year earlier. Bill talked to some people and crunched some numbers and returned with a sobering conclusion: The company was worth zero. That was more than an embarrassment. It meant that, at the end of 2007, Deutsche would have to recognize a big loss in its annual results—the last thing the bank needed as it headed into a crisis. So Broeksmit suggested a work-around: MortgageIT should keep issuing mortgages, avoiding the risky stuff that had been its specialty and instead focusing on large loans to safe customers. This did nothing at all to deal with the awful loans MortgageIT had already made, but it would allow the company to hover in place, keeping alive the prospect of "a profitable exit in the future," Bill emailed Anshu in September 2007. "Even if the platform turns out not to be worth further investment, at least you get past year-end without having to write it off." It allowed Deutsche to avoid disclosing an unfixable problem in a business for which it had just paid nearly half a billion dollars, without lying to anyone about the terrible state of the business.

And so MortgageIT kept churning out mortgages, and Deutsche kept packaging them into securities, which it sold to investors. As prosecutors later found, the bank lied to clients that it was conducting rigorous due diligence when in fact Mort-gageIT had stopped doing any due diligence whatsoever.

Broeksmit was then dispatched to deal with Boaz Weinstein, who was losing senior executives' trust. It had dawned on them that Weinstein's role as proprietor of his own internal hedge fund meant he wouldn't necessarily be making decisions that were in the best interests of the bank, as opposed to the best interests of Boaz. After all, Weinstein was getting a cut of his hedge fund's profits, but he faced no downside risk—if his fund made $100 million, his personal cut might be $10 million, whereas if he lost $100 million, his cut would be zero. With that math, traders had a powerful incentive to swing for the fences.

By 2008, Weinstein was bucking orders to unwind his trading positions. Always cocky—Weinstein liked to boast that he was the "best credit trader in the world"[3]—he now protested that it was stupid to be selling in a moment of weakness. "I don't give a fuck," Jain retorted, demanding that his subordinate follow orders. Weinstein continued to drag his feet, losses mounted in his previously profitable fund, and Broeksmit was dispatched to coax the recalcitrant young trader to release his grip on his portfolio. The two men gradually sold off its contents. Ultimately it would incur $1.8 billion of losses, swamping Weinstein's profits from the prior two years. Bill's next assignment was even less pleasant: ushering Weinstein out of the bank.

Over the next year, the global financial system nearly collapsed. Hundreds of banks, large and small, capsized. So severe was the crisis that senior executives at more than a few banks collectively yanked millions out of their personal accounts and opted to stash the cash in their homes, fearful that the entire system could come crashing down at any moment. The United States and many other Western economies sank into deep recessions.

Deutsche racked up billions of dollars of losses. In any other period, it would have been a catastrophic, perhaps fatal, rout. Instead, as central bankers worldwide rushed to the rescue, dousing the financial fire with buckets of free money, Deutsche emerged as a winner. Its losses proved manageable. That was partly thanks to Anshu's 2007 order to start selling risky stuff. It was also partly because the bank had found ways to paper over some of its toxic investments, hiding what would turn out to be several billion dollars of losses from regulators and investors. And it was partly because some of the bank's most adrenaline-crazed traders had placed gargantuan bets that profited from the implosion of the U.S. housing market.

The leader of this pack was a fast-talking bond trader named Greg Lippmann.* By 2005, he'd concluded that the American real estate market was heading for a big fall, and he realized that the CDO business that Misra's guys had been pumping up could be used as a vehicle to bet on it. Misra signed off on using the bank's own money for the wager—and then sweet-talked Jain into increasing the normal risk limits so that Lippmann could supersize his bet. Teaming up with some big hedge funds, Lippmann created what one expert, Nicholas Dunbar, dubbed a "virtual CDO factory." But unlike a normal factory, this one churned out products that were designed to fail. Lippmann's team and a cluster of elite hedge funds selected mortgage securities made up of the worst, most likely to default home loans—some sourced from MortgageIT—and then used a type of derivative called credit default swaps to gamble that the instruments would lose money.[4] "I'm short your house!!!" was the slogan on the T-shirts that Lippmann's squad giddily handed out to folks who were in on the

---

* Lippmann inspired the character played by Ryan Gosling in the film version of Michael Lewis's *The Big Short*.

bet.[5] Sure enough, when the housing market cratered, Deutsche earned many hundreds of millions of dollars in profits. For his part, Lippmann pocketed a $50 million bonus in 2007.[6]

Of course, there was some collateral damage. For starters, many of Deutsche's less sophisticated clients—the dupes who had bought the garbage the bank was selling—were losers, but the bank justified this on the grounds that it was simply providing those clients what they wanted, and what they wanted, very unwisely, was additional exposure to the peaking U.S. housing market. Another not-inconsequential side effect of Lippmann's big bet—and a similar one orchestrated by traders at Goldman Sachs—was that it deepened the approaching financial crisis. Because these guys were stoking the CDO machine, the demand for mortgage-backed securities consisting of high-risk mortgages remained hearty, and that meant mortgage lenders—including MortgageIT—kept making those high-risk loans to people who couldn't afford them. Absent Lippmann and his ilk, fewer people (and institutions like Deutsche) would have made a killing, but fewer people with underwater mortgages would have lost their homes (and fewer banks probably would have collapsed).

Lippmann wasn't the only one inside Deutsche cashing in on the crisis. Justin Kennedy was, too. Back in 2005, he had been trying to figure out how to explain the commercial mortgage business to some outsiders. On the whiteboard on his office wall, he sketched out a diagram of how mortgages get packaged into securities, which get packaged into other securities, which get packaged into CDOs, and on and on. It dawned on Kennedy that this whole structure was pretty flimsy. All it took was a wave of people or companies falling behind on their mortgage payments for the dominoes to start toppling. Kennedy, whose father still popped by the office from time to time, invited some colleagues to admire his whiteboard handiwork. "This will for sure collapse,"

he predicted to them, and they started figuring out ways to profit
from—or at least not lose money on—that collapse. One of their
strategies was to bet against banks that owned lots of CDOs. The
fact that Deutsche had sold so many CDOs to banks helped Kennedy's crew figure out which banks were most likely to suffer. By
2008, their bet had swelled into the billions of dollars.

It was a proud moment for Deutsche. "After some initial criticism, Deutsche Bank is recognized as one of only a few global
financial institutions to master the crisis without direct government aid," the bank crowed in a corporate biography on its website.[7] This was at best misleading. The Federal Reserve alone
provided billions of dollars in loans to Deutsche, though a far cry
from the ownership stakes that the federal government took in
hundreds of American banks.[8] And Deutsche was indirectly
aided by governments that bailed out its trading partners. Without such assistance, it likely would have suffered fatal losses. But
Ackermann basked in the glory—and an $18 million payday.[9] He
bought properties in Switzerland and New York, where he already
had the fiftieth-floor condo in the Museum Tower. He won the
2008 European Banker of the Year award. *The New York Times*
hailed him as "the most powerful banker in Europe."[10]

Ackermann harnessed that momentum and seized more power.
He had been the speaker of the vorstand, but he wanted to be the
actual CEO, a role that Deutsche had never previously had. A
CEO wouldn't serve at the whims of his fellow executives; he
would be beholden only to the supervisory board. And the supervisory board, largely made up of employee representatives who
generally lacked nuanced understandings of the business, would
be much easier for Ackermann to steamroll. With the board's
acquiescence, he soon got his wish: Going forward, Deutsche
would be led by a CEO.

Ackermann and Jain saw the bank's avoidance of a direct tax-payer bailout as a vindication of their profits-at-any-price strategy, and investors tended to agree. While the bank had lost most of its market value over the past year—from about $70 billion to $21 billion—that constituted victory in the industry's gory war zone. "We are relatively strong today, precisely because we made such large profits," Ackermann preened in October 2008.[11] But that was a self-serving argument—one trotted out by bankers far and wide to justify their actions. It is true that, all else being equal, the more profitable a bank is, the less likely it is to be crippled in a crisis. But all else is rarely equal. The most profitable banks often are the ones taking the greatest risks. Those risks aren't always apparent in the moment. That is why, time and again, banks that have held themselves up as paragons of virtue often have their comeuppance.

Deutsche wouldn't have to wait long for its reckoning. Its balance sheet had quadrupled over the past decade, and its more than $2 trillion in assets made it nearly as large as the entire German economy. One of the craziest elements of this eye-popping statistic was that only about 15 percent of those assets were loans to businesses or households, which historically had been banks' bread and butter; three times as much was in the form of derivatives.[12] Those complicated gambles could go south at any moment. All it took was an unexpected event like a major corporate bankruptcy or a huge natural disaster or something being wrong in the equations underlying the derivatives. Indeed, many of these instruments were already worth far less than they had been; if Deutsche had assigned them honest values, the bank would have faced catastrophic losses. For now, executives lied about the derivatives' values, praying they would bounce back before anyone outside the company realized their diminished worth.

Unlike American banks, which had been forced by their government to fortify their balance sheets with billions of dollars of fresh capital in the crisis's immediate aftermath, Deutsche convinced itself that it was sitting pretty. It didn't need such fortification, because it knew what it was doing; after all, look at how well it had played this once-in-a-lifetime financial crisis that had felled so many of its peers. It was a profound miscalculation, a direct result of the hubris that had taken hold on the tightly guarded vorstand floor in the Frankfurt skyscraper.

Before he ascended to near the top of the bank, Jain had been able to look at a situation where Deutsche made money and see that luck had played a role. Now, though, he sat in his corner office, watched over by the portrait of Edson, and misinterpreted luck as skill. Alex Crossman, who had spent eight years as Anshu's chief strategist, could see the cocktail of arrogance and power changing the way top executives looked at the world—and themselves. The instinct to profit from the crisis, from people whose lives were being destroyed, struck him as immoral. Crossman had previously made it a point to occasionally pick a small fight with his boss—scolding Jain for his repeated phone calls at the crack of dawn on weekends, for example—just to remind him that he couldn't be pushed around. Anshu generally would apologize and back off. Over the years, though, as Jain's power grew, his tolerance for reprimands and dissent diminished. Throughout the business and political worlds, this is a classic warning sign: When a leader loses the ability or willingness to hear constructive criticism, his organization is in danger. In the moment this is often hard to see, because the institution's tangible successes—profits, awards, growth—act as lulling opiates for the leader, his employees, shareholders, journalists, even regulators. Crossman, however, could see the warning signs. He quit banking and became a teacher.

CHAPTER 13

"THIS GUY IS A DANGER"

A s the financial crisis reached full throttle in the fall of 2008, Donald Trump owed $334 million on Deutsche's 2005 loan for his Chicago skyscraper. The hotel, restaurants, and spas were open, but the condos were still under construction. ("I built a great monument to the city," Trump declared.[1]) With the economy sinking, nobody was buying his luxury apartments.[2]

The Trump loan had been diced into mortgage-backed bonds that Deutsche had sold to investors, while also keeping a portion for itself. The loan had been due in May 2008, but Deutsche, acting on behalf of itself and the bondholders, agreed to grant Trump a six-month extension. With the November due date approaching, Trump sought another extension. This time the bank said no.

Trump, however, had no intention of repaying the loan on time. He asked his lawyers to figure out a work-around. One of them dissected each of the loan documents and, on a conference call with his colleagues to brainstorm how their client could wriggle out of his obligations, mentioned the existence of a so-called force majeure—act of God—provision in the loan agreement. That meant that in the event of an unanticipatable catastrophe, like a natural disaster, the contract wasn't enforceable. A lawyer on the call piped up that Alan Greenspan had just called the financial crisis a "credit tsunami"—and what was a tsunami if not a natural disaster, an act of God? One lawyer, Steve Schlesinger, presented the idea to Trump. "It's brilliant!" he declared, and Schlesinger and his colleagues basked in the warmth of Trump's pleasure. He instructed his lawyers to execute the plan.

Three days before the loan was due, the lawyers wrote to Deutsche that Trump considered the financial crisis to represent a force majeure that allowed him to stop paying back his loan. Days later, Trump filed a lawsuit citing the provision and accusing Deutsche of engaging in "predatory lending practices"— toward him!—and of helping ignite the financial crisis. "Deutsche Bank is one of the banks primarily responsible for the economic dysfunction we are currently facing," Trump asserted. In an extraordinary act of chutzpah, he sought damages of $3 billion.

Deutsche filed its own suit, seeking the $40 million Trump had personally guaranteed back in 2005. The bank pointed out that the same day Trump had notified Deutsche that the financial crisis constituted a contract-voiding act of godly devastation, he was quoted in two newspapers boasting about how he was unscathed by that very crisis.[3] One of his deputies was quoted bragging that Trump's company had nearly $2 billion, ready to be deployed on a moment's notice.

In trying to get Trump to pay back the money he owed, the bank made a persuasive argument for why it should never have loaned him that money in the first place. Deutsche's lawsuit quoted from Trump's book, *Think Big and Kick Ass in Business and Life*, in which the future president explained how he had handled banks during a real estate downturn in the 1990s. "I turned it back on the banks and let them accept some of the blame," Trump wrote. "I figured it was the banks' problem, not mine. What the hell did I care? I actually told one bank, 'I told you you shouldn't have loaned me that money. I told you that goddamn deal was no good.' " Deutsche argued in the suit: "The fact that he is now resorting to the same tactics he has consistently employed throughout his career as a real estate magnate should surprise no one." Indeed.

Shortly after the suit was filed, Trump bumped into Justin Kennedy. "Nothing personal," Trump said. Kennedy replied that there were no hard feelings: Business was business. But when senior Deutsche executives learned about Trump's litigation, they were irate. "What the hell are we doing lending money to a guy like this?" Dick Walker, the bank's general counsel, asked his colleagues. "It's a bullshit claim, but we have to deal with it."

More than four years had passed since Trump's casino company had burned Deutsche and its clients by defaulting on the junk bonds. That had spelled the end of the Trump relationship for one wing of Deutsche's investment banking unit, but the alarm bells hadn't saved another wing from stumbling into its own bad deal. Now the time had come for the rest of the investment bank to wash its hands of Donald Trump. Going forward, he wouldn't even be permitted at the bank's golf tournament. "This guy is a danger, and we're done with him," one of Anshu's lieutenants said.

Kennedy, having made a killing off the financial crisis and now seeing an important client fall by the wayside, decided to leave the bank at the end of 2009.

CHAPTER 14

THE PENDULUM SWINGS

With astonishing speed, Deutsche Bank went from being the toast of the industry to arguably its leading problem child. What had once made it a darling of investors—its securities-selling and investment-banking juggernaut—now made the company a pariah among crisis-scarred shareholders. Regulators and investors worried that the bank—which had not strengthened itself with new capital from the government or private investors—didn't have enough of a financial cushion to absorb potential losses in the future. International groups like the Organisation for Economic Co-operation and Development were warning that Deutsche's ratio of assets to equity—its leverage ratio—was still nearly fifty-to-one.[1] No responsible business would operate like that—if the borrowed funds dried up, the company would be dead.

Because the bank had enjoyed a "good" crisis, it hadn't felt much pressure to shrink. Executives didn't realize that they had delayed, not avoided, their reckoning. Investors did, however, and the bank's share price reflected that lack of confidence. As the world emerged from the financial crisis and the resulting Great

Recession, the shares of Deutsche's closest rivals—companies like JPMorgan and Citigroup—rallied back to their pre-crisis levels and then scooted higher still. Not Deutsche. Its shares had peaked back in May 2007 above ninety-one euros apiece and then bottomed out in January 2009, just as Barack Obama was sworn in as president, at about thirteen euros. By the following May, they had rallied to nearly forty-seven euros. At this point, the shares were worth just over half of what they'd fetched three years earlier. It was the highest they would ever get.

It wasn't just the bank's shortage of capital that was unnerving investors. Deutsche's stockpile of derivatives had been growing ever since the arrival of Mitchell, Broeksmit, and Jain more than a decade earlier, swelling even more with the Bankers Trust acquisition. Investors—newly attuned to the potential perils of derivatives, given their pivotal role in the just-ended financial crisis—started running the numbers, and they realized Deutsche was sitting on trillions of dollars of these instruments. Deutsche expected the derivatives to make money over time, and it had booked the anticipated profits up front, even though many of the contracts extended for years, even decades, into the future. A dramatic change in the economy or regulations or laws or their trading partners had the potential to slam Deutsche with enormous losses. And since the bank had already reaped the profits, there was nothing but downside ahead. If Deutsche had to sell the derivatives, it would essentially have to give back those profits. Did the bank really have a handle on its exposure? What if its math were wrong?

Ackermann had an opportunity at this moment to take advantage of the bank's relative strength. He could have thickened the bank's capital buffers by selling new shares—a course supported by some of the bank's top executives. He could have moved expeditiously to scrub the bank of unwanted assets, which would have entailed some short-term financial pain but eased investors' anxiety about the company's long-term health. He could have invested in a massive overhaul of Deutsche's rat's nest of IT systems.

He did none of those things. Instead, Ackermann's biggest strategic move was to buy Germany's downtrodden post office bank. Ostensibly, the acquisition of Postbank was crafted to bolster Deutsche's presence in its home market. But the rationale never made much sense. Postbank was a colossal mess, its technology even more antiquated than Deutsche's. And serving Germany's notoriously frugal savers was far from a lucrative business. To finance the deal, shareholders had been asked to pony up $13 billion, and those who refused saw the values of their current investments diluted as Deutsche issued more than 300 million new shares—what it could have done to replenish its capital—to get the Postbank money anyway. Several senior executives had cautioned Ackermann against the deal, arguing that it was crazy to squander money at the precise moment that American banks were bolstering themselves with billions of dollars of fresh capital. Ackermann swatted away the concerns and noted that the purchase was the right thing, the patriotic thing, to do for Germany in the midst of the continent's economic crisis. (Quite a few executives believed Ackermann was more interested in burnishing his public image than in doing what was right for the bank.) But Deutsche's board sided with the CEO, and the deal got done.

It was one more abdication of leadership that the bank would come to rue, especially because Deutsche was about to face a new source of financial pressure. After years of laissez-faire regulation and law enforcement, the pendulum was swinging back toward intensive government oversight of an industry that, not for the first time, had demonstrated its propensity to shove the world into a deep economic pit. The conventional wisdom over the previous decade had been that banks could be trusted to basically police themselves—after all, they had a powerful interest in self-preservation. But their capacity to exercise restraint had proven woeful, and so a new period of government scrutiny got under way, with regulators devoting more resources to monitoring the inner workings of giant financial institutions and prosecutors on the prowl for serious misconduct.

Deutsche, propelled by a culture that rewarded aggression and having profited from its envelope-pushing and sometimes illegal behavior, had been a big winner in the hands-off period. It would be an even bigger loser in this new era, and the trouble would affect not only the bank but also its top executives—men like Bill Broeksmit.

Rod Stone's first real job was watching porn. It was the early 1980s, and Stone, who grew up in the hardscrabble London neighborhood of Brixton, worked for Her Majesty's Customs and Excise, a government agency whose main mission was combating the smuggling of goods into Britain. A brisk business had sprung up around secreting sex videos into the country, and when a truckload of videocassettes was intercepted, it was Stone's job to sit in a room and watch each one, logging the nature of the obscene acts. For a few years, he spent fifty hours a week watching and describing porn. In 1984, still working for the customs department, he graduated to more serious law enforcement. He helped chase down Gaddafi's London-based weapons trafficker. He busted tobacco- and alcohol-smuggling rings. He got a thrill out of navigating through labyrinths of tax and real estate records and going head-to-head with criminal masterminds. "It was the pitting of wits," he would explain.

The customs agency eventually gained responsibility for collecting taxes, and Stone, now in his forties, shifted gears, developing an expertise in a type of sales tax that was rife with fraud.

In theory, every time a company shipped products from, say, France to England, it had to pay an import tax when their goods crossed the border. But because the European Union was a free-trade zone, the importer could then apply for a government refund of whatever taxes had been paid. Criminal gangs around the EU had cooked up elaborate schemes in which they didn't pay the initial tax but still claimed the refund. The British government was losing billions of pounds to these fraudulent refunds, and Stone picked apart the international chains of shell companies that were shipping products, evading taxes, and claiming fake refunds.

In 2008, Stone noticed that some of those same fraudsters were getting into something called carbon-emissions permits, part of an EU program to reduce greenhouse gases. Sales taxes were due each time a permit changed hands, but as with any product sold within the EU, those taxes were eligible for refunds. In 2009, groups of fraudsters started claiming fake refunds from the British government. Stone was surprised to see that a few large banks were working with these gangs—and Deutsche, which had a team of London traders devoted to trading emissions permits, was leading the pack. Up until 2009, Deutsche had always been a net payer of sales taxes, known as VAT. Then that June, it claimed a refund of more than £15 million. That refund was processed and paid. Three months later, Deutsche submitted another refund request, this one for £48 million. Stone launched an investigation.[2]

Early on, he warned Deutsche in writing that its traders appeared to be partaking in tax fraud. But the Deutsche traders—one of the alleged participants was surnamed Lawless—kept doing it.[3] In November 2009, Stone marched into the bank's London offices and told its lawyers that Deutsche had already been put on written notice that it was likely engaged in fraud and that the consequences for the continued misbehavior could be severe. Stone paid another visit the following month and read the lawyers the riot act.

The British government eventually altered its tax rules to prevent the fraud, and Deutsche's London trading desk adapted—moving to claim refunds in Germany rather than Britain.

When a Deutsche employee asked a colleague why the bank was willing to take such a large legal risk, the response came back: "Because we're that greedy."[4] Stone helped his German counterparts figure out what was happening. In April 2010, police raided Deutsche's Frankfurt headquarters. Finally executives pulled the plug on the emissions-trading strategy,[5] which by then had generated nearly $250 million in illegal refunds.[6] A German judge would later find that the fraud was enabled by the "risk-affirming climate"[7] that dominated Deutsche. Internal safeguards, such as a tough compliance squad or rigorous know-your-customer rules, were strangely absent.

Just as Mark Ferron had suspected, Christian Bittar, the star trader and one of Anshu's anointed, had been cheating. The success or failure of many of his trades hinged on tiny movements in something known as Libor (an acronym for the London interbank offered rate). Each day the world's biggest banks estimated how much it would cost them to borrow money from other banks. Their estimates were averaged together, and the result was Libor. Libor served as the basis for trillions of dollars of interest-rate derivatives, which were the primary instruments that Bittar was using to make his market bets. Bittar had realized it was surprisingly easy to manipulate Libor. Since the benchmark was an average of banks' estimated borrowing costs, all you had to do was to get a few banks to move their estimates up or down. That's what Bittar did—and he soon became one of the entire company's most prolific profit engines. (Much of his success stemmed from a bet—apparently unrelated to his Libor manipulation—on where broader financial markets were heading.)

In 2009, Bittar was in line for a bonus of more than $100 million, thanks to an arrangement Jain had approved that awarded him a percentage of whatever revenue he generated for the bank.[8] There was no way to avoid scrutiny of such a monster payout, and Ackermann was appalled when he heard about it. Anshu phoned the CEO to defend the bonus and described Bittar and his colleagues as "the best people on the Street." These traders were making "mountains of money."[9] But before cutting Bittar his nine-figure check, the bank initiated a review of his desk's windfall. Did Bittar have a golden touch or was something else at play? The examination was conducted by the bank's "Business Integrity Review Group,"[10] and it was a farce: A single Deutsche employee was responsible for sifting through tens of thousands of internal documents and transcripts to see if Bittar was cheating. Many of the materials were in French, which that employee didn't speak. The review didn't find anything problematic. Bittar collected his money.

Word of the gigantic payout rippled through London's banking circles. As U.S. and British authorities started investigating Libor manipulation, Bittar's bonanza would serve as an extreme example of how traders were incentivized to engage in fraud.

Since the late 1990s, Deutsche had been peddling products to hedge funds, including the enormous Renaissance Technologies, that helped them avoid taxes. Founded by a former government code-breaker, Renaissance specialized in using computer programs to scout out tiny market inefficiencies that could be exploited. The firm recruited engineers and mathematicians, including an IBM programmer named Robert Mercer, a right-wing zealot who once noted that he enjoyed spending time with cats more than with people. Mercer eventually rose to the top of Renaissance, helping it become one of the world's most successful hedge funds.

Renaissance was always looking for a new, sharper edge, and that's where Deutsche came in. The bank hatched a plan in which Renaissance parked billions of dollars of securities and other assets with Deutsche. The bank legally owned the assets, but Renaissance handled the trading of them. Once a year, Renaissance could withdraw profits from the Deutsche account and get taxed at a long-term capital gains rate of 20 percent—about half what it would have faced without the Deutsche structure. The strategy generated billions of dollars in tax savings for Renaissance. Deutsche collected fees totaling $570 million from Renaissance and other hedge funds for setting up the structures.[11]

Unfortunately for Deutsche and Renaissance, the transactions caught the attention of Bob Roach.

Roach had grown up in Beacon, a factory town in New York's Hudson Valley whose main claim to fame was being home to Pete Seeger. Roach was a star wrestler, and after graduating from college, he continued wrestling—with big companies. He worked on environmental investigations for the Massachusetts government and then, in Washington, for Michigan representative John Dingell, holding dirty industries accountable for the messes they'd made. Roach was self-effacing, with an aw-shucks demeanor and a wide-mouthed, infectious laugh, and that served to disguise his doggedness; his motto was "be a grinder." He developed a knack for surfacing documents that proved corporate culpability. In 1998, he became a staffer on the Senate Permanent Subcommittee on Investigations. The committee's members, led by Senator Carl Levin, prided themselves on picking investigative targets based on merit, not politics. When the interests of Republican and Democratic panelists diverged, Republicans made a point of signing off on Democratic subpoenas, and vice versa.

More or less from the moment he joined the committee, Roach had been chasing Deutsche. The first time he came across the bank was in 1999, right after its acquisition of Bankers Trust. Roach was investigating how banks catered to dictators and their families, helping them keep their embezzled money secret. It turned out that Bankers Trust—through its private-banking division that served many of the world's richest people—was among the banks that moved money for Raúl Salinas, the corrupt brother of Mexico's former president.

A few years later, Deutsche popped up again. This time it was part of a Senate investigation into tax shelters arranged by accounting firms like KPMG. Deutsche had extended a huge credit line to KPMG to finance what appeared to be fraudulent financial structures. Roach and his team uncovered evidence that Deutsche executives in Frankfurt knew about the illicit practices. Next up, Roach dug into Deutsche's peddling of sure-to-lose CDOs to unsuspecting clients. Now Roach got wind of the bank's tax work with Renaissance, and it smelled foul. He convinced his boss, Senator Levin, that it was a worthy target of a major investigation.

The world's oldest bank was headquartered in the picturesque Tuscan hill town of Siena, best known for a raucous horse race, the Palio, around its central piazza. Banca Monte dei Paschi di Siena had been founded in 1472, two decades before Columbus sailed to America. The bank occupied an ancient stone palace, its walls bedecked with medieval and Renaissance masterpieces. For 530 years, it existed peacefully, becoming a pillar of the Tuscan community. Its charitable foundation doled out hundreds of millions of dollars a year to the local university, sports teams, museums, and the like—an amount larger than the city's annual budget.[12]

Then, in 2002, Paschi went to Deutsche to buy some derivatives. The goal was to free up cash so that it could participate in a wave of mergers remaking the Italian banking industry. Paschi had previously invested in another Italian bank, now known as Intesa Sanpaolo, and it wanted to liquidate that investment without forfeiting the right to future profits if the Intesa shares gained value in the future. For a steep fee, Deutsche set up a series of derivatives whose value would rise or fall along with Intesa's stock price.

For a few years, the transaction worked as planned. But when markets went haywire at the onset of the financial crisis, the derivatives racked up enormous losses. Paschi returned to Deutsche for help in 2008, and the German bank dished out . . . more derivatives.

It was a complex two-part deal. Boiled down to its essence, the first part of the transaction was guaranteed to make enough money for Paschi that it would paper over the hundreds of millions of dollars of losses it was facing on the 2002 transaction. The Italian bank could avoid disclosing crippling losses. The second part of the trade was a guaranteed moneymaker for Deutsche—and a money loser for the Italians—but the profits would accumulate over a period of several years. In theory, if Paschi earned enough money in the future, it could pay what it owed Deutsche without outsiders realizing what was happening. In short, Deutsche could notch big profits without taking much financial risk and the client could hide losses, at least until it had to pay back Deutsche.

The executive ultimately in charge of the group that devised this plan was Michele Faissola. A slim, well-dressed man with dark eyes and hair, Faissola had grown up in Italy; his uncle was one of the country's leading bankers. At Deutsche, Faissola had aligned himself with Anshu and had risen to be a leader of the derivatives team. By 2008, he was a top Deutsche executive. Colleagues reckoned that Deutsche had paid him tens of millions of dollars over the years; his Chelsea townhouse featured an indoor swimming pool. (Faissola and his wife, Maria, had become close friends with Bill and Alla Broeksmit.)

Late in 2008, Deutsche's committee of risk managers met to discuss the proposed Paschi arrangement. Faissola was one of the highest-ranking members of the committee, and his underlings happily pointed out that the proposed structure could be replicated for other clients, presumably those that also were looking to mask their financial problems. Deutsche could make money over and over again. "This is fantastic!" a senior executive exclaimed. The deal got approved, and the anticipated tens of millions of dollars in profits—including the fees that Paschi paid for the privilege of working with Deutsche—would be credited to Faissola's group for the purposes of tallying their year-end bonuses.[13, 14]

Behind the scenes, out of most of his colleagues' view, Bill Broeksmit had played a role in many of these soon-to-be scandals. He didn't cause them—in some cases, he tried to prevent them—but that was the sort of distinction that could easily get lost on government authorities looking for people to hold accountable for the banking industry's many sins. The consequences would be tragic.

CHAPTER 15

CLUELESS OLD MAN

Across Deutsche's cavernous trading floors in New York and London, recklessness and disregard for rules were the norm. This, of course, was nothing new: Edson Mitchell had encouraged a cavalier attitude from the get-go. But he had been restrained, at least sometimes, by rigorous, old-fashioned German overseers—not a profit-obsessed enabler like Ackermann. And of course Mitchell had Bill Broeksmit as his sidekick—and everyone, back then, listened to Bill. That was no longer the case today.

Troy Dixon was one of Deutsche's brash young traders, his unit specializing in bonds made up of home loans, an offshoot of Rajeev Misra's old group. Dixon was straight out of central casting (except that he was African American, and Hollywood generally didn't cast black men in movies about Wall Street). When things were going well, he would hoot and holler and everyone would know his team was on a roll. When things weren't looking good, he would slouch at his desk, glum and silent.

In the summer of 2009, Dixon's unit had made a massive wager that Americans with high-interest mortgages would *not* default—partly reversing the bank's earlier Big Short on the U.S.

housing market. Dixon's team amassed a gargantuan $14 billion position of these mortgage bonds.[1] At first the trades were making money, but risk managers worried that Dixon was cutting corners and that his bets were so massive that if they went wrong, it would present a very big problem for the entire company. The risk guys spent weeks compiling a dossier detailing how Dixon was on the verge of spinning out of control. They presented the materials to Broeksmit, who agreed that this didn't look safe. He set up a meeting with Dixon and urged him to rein things in. Dixon refused. A week or two later, Broeksmit returned to the risk managers, who looked up to him as a rare voice of reason and restraint in the bank's upper ranks. He said he had received "strong pushback" from above in his efforts to curtail Dixon.

Broeksmit kept noodging, though, and Dixon griped to his team that some nerd—a guy clearly lacking the killer instincts that propelled people to the top of Wall Street—was harassing him. Troy and his team were pretty sure Bill didn't grasp the nuances of their trade. It was too complex, they believed, for someone of his age and lack of sophistication to comprehend.

Broeksmit could tell he was pissing off Dixon, and he decided to try to smooth things over. Bill invited Troy and his team out to dinner at an Italian restaurant in Manhattan's Tribeca neighborhood. The men sat around a large candlelit table. Floral tapestries hung on exposed-brick walls. The dinner got off to an awkward start, with Broeksmit and Dixon continuing to bicker about the wisdom of the mortgage trades. Neither man would drop it. Across the table, some of the traders snickered to one another that Bill was out of his depth. The conversation eventually meandered to seemingly safer topics like Jerry Sandusky, the former college football coach who had just been sentenced to prison for child molestation. Broeksmit had never heard of him. When someone remarked that Sandusky was in for a tough time in prison, Bill asked why. The traders looked at each other—is this guy for real? Someone answered that it was because he molested boys. Bill asked, "So?" He didn't get it: Child molesters are the most reviled crooks in a prison. Broeksmit kept asking questions that betrayed his ignorance about college football and prison hierarchies. The traders started chuckling again. This old man was clueless. At the end of the meal, Bill picked up the tab and bolted for the subway, hardly bothering to say goodbye. Dixon and the other traders went off to a bar to laugh about him and kept mocking him at work for several days: "This guy is fucking weird."

Here was a powerful sign of the generational shift that had swept Wall Street and Deutsche in the decades since Broeksmit had been a pioneer of the derivatives market. Traders who had grown up viewing banks as casinos were replacing those who had conceived of derivatives as vehicles to make money by helping clients hedge their risks. The new breed of gamblers didn't realize that they didn't know everything. (Dixon's trades ultimately blew up, costing Deutsche $541 million and attracting the attention of federal regulators.[2]) Bill was astute and sensitive; surely he didn't miss the unsubtle cues. His time had passed.

In 2010, Deutsche hired a young man named Eric Ben-Artzi to work in its risk-management group, with a specific focus on its holdings of hard-to-value derivatives. Ben-Artzi had grown up in Israel in a family full of big, stubborn personalities. His grandfathers fought to secure Israel's independence. One of his uncles was a paratrooper killed in action. Another uncle was Benjamin Netanyahu, the once and future prime minister. Ben-Artzi's brother had become Israel's most famous, or infamous, refusenik—a conscientious objector who was locked up for shirking his mandatory conscription in Israel's armed forces.[3] Less dramatically, Eric became a mathematician and computer pro-grammer. Like so many others with those qualifications, he had drifted into banking, lured by the money and the challenges of solving complex financial riddles. But after a spell at Goldman Sachs, he discovered that he didn't have the right constitution for Wall Street. The way he saw it, he wasn't aggressive enough to be a salesman and wasn't greedy enough to be a banker. His goal was to ease into academia, and he figured the Deutsche gig— with a heavy emphasis on theoretical research about how to de-termine the value of derivatives—was a step in the right direction. He also figured a giant international bank knew what it was doing.

Ben-Artzi's job consisted in part of using Microsoft Excel to build models to check the valuation of derivatives and to see how they would fare in various scenarios, including once-in-a-millennium financial storms. Ben-Artzi quickly realized the bank's clunky systems produced fuzzy, imprecise results. One of the biggest problems was that the trades he was plugging into Excel were leveraged—meaning the traders had made them us-ing borrowed money, a tactic that could increase their profitabil-ity but also made them much riskier—but the numbers he had been given didn't account for the financial consequences of that leverage. In other words, they were greatly underestimating the risk involved in the transactions. At first Ben-Artzi gave the bank the benefit of the doubt—presumably this was the result of slop-piness, not fraud, and the bank's higher-ups didn't realize how inadequate their models were. Within a few weeks, though, he had asked enough questions and received enough stonewalling to conclude that executives didn't want to know why the models were wrong; they just wanted results that would confirm the wisdom of the present course. When he flagged the leverage problem to his superiors, he was told not to ask so many questions. When he persisted, a superior marched over to his desk and shouted at him to stop.

Like his relatives, Ben-Artzi was stubborn, and he didn't stop. The more he dug, the more concerned he became. Trades that the bank was valuing in the billions of dollars appeared to be basically worthless. This did not look like an accident. The bank appeared to have been systematically inflating the value of tens of billions of dollars of derivatives. This meant that Deutsche's much-touted resilience during the financial crisis had been illusory, the product of bogus accounting. That was so stunning that Ben-Artzi initially doubted it could be true.

Soon his doubts faded. The risk department at the time was run by Hugo Bänziger, the former tank commander. Shortly after Ben-Artzi joined Deutsche, Bänziger held a town hall meeting for employees in the basement of 60 Wall Street. When a senior risk manager asked about how well the bank was coping with all of the government authorities examining Deutsche, Bänziger derided the "fucking regulators." Ben-Artzi wondered whether this was a normal attitude at Deutsche—it certainly wasn't how Goldman had operated. The answer came a few months later, when Ben-Artzi attended a bank retreat at a hotel in Rome. This time another senior risk manager gave a talk about how employees should craft their explanations about risk to suit different audiences. If they were talking to a regulator, for example, they should play down the amount of risk involved. Sitting in the heavily air-conditioned conference room, Ben-Artzi and his colleagues exchanged nervous glances as the executive counseled them on how to pull the wool over the authorities' eyes. The executive wrapped up his presentation on an ominous note: If risk managers didn't let traders take chances, he warned, the bank would have to shrink, and that would mean fewer risk managers would have jobs. To Ben-Artzi and his dumbfounded colleagues, it sounded like a threat: Play ball, or risk losing your job.

Ben-Artzi had seen enough. It was time to follow his brother's lead; he had to stand up for his principles. He dialed an internal bank hotline to blow the whistle on what he regarded as serious misconduct involving how the bank was valuing its derivatives— the fraud was so vast, he and some colleagues believed, that Deutsche would have been insolvent during the financial crisis if it had come clean about its assets. Worried that Deutsche might point the finger at him for the wrongdoing he was revealing, he also lodged a complaint with the Securities and Exchange Commission. Soon Deutsche barred Ben-Artzi from any further examination of the bank's derivatives and, not long after, fired him. Another employee who similarly warned the SEC that Deutsche had hidden crippling losses was pushed aside, too. Deutsche was sweeping its plentiful problems under an enormous carpet.

Around lunchtime on Wednesday, December 7, 2011, employees in the basement mailroom of Deutsche's Twin Towers in Frankfurt noticed a bulky brown envelope addressed to Joe Ackermann. When they ran it through an X-ray machine, they spotted what looked like shrapnel. Police and a bomb squad rushed over, their sirens screaming. Inside the envelope was a small explosive device, sent by an Italian anarchist group.[4] An accompanying letter attacked "banks, bankers, fleas, and bloodsuckers."[5]

Like Abs and Herrhausen before him, Ackermann had assumed the mantle of statesman. He traveled the world on a private NetJets plane, dining with world leaders including Vladimir Putin and George W. Bush—not to mention a who's who of European politicians and royals.[6] With Europe now in its own financial crisis, and entire countries like Greece and Ireland falling apart, Ackermann had become a sort of shadow finance minister for the entire continent. Germany was Europe's most powerful country, dictating bailout terms for failing nations, and it was Ackermann to whom Germany's chancellor, Angela Merkel, regularly turned for financial advice.[7] But unlike the role that Herrhausen had played, such as urging the forgiveness of the debts of third-world countries, the advice Ackermann provided tended to benefit banks—and one bank in particular. Restructuring Greece's crushing debt in a way that would help that country recover but that would saddle its creditors with losses was dangerous, he warned. And indeed it was dangerous—for Deutsche, which owned boatloads of Greek government bonds. (Because of their riskiness, the bonds came with high interest rates, which had attracted profit-hungry institutions.) Ackermann got his way, and the Greek government, unable to dramatically reduce its public debts, needed to find other, draconian ways to come up with money, such as slashing budgets and selling prized public assets. The results were savage: Islands, marinas, and airports were put up for sale. Unemployment, homelessness, crime, and suicide rates soared.[8]

Ackermann's successful fearmongering didn't endear him to the public. In many parts of the world, he had become a villainous figure. A Berlin songwriter composed a satirical ditty that cheerfully called for his assassination. Several months before the letter bomb was sent, the International Monetary Fund's former chief economist branded Ackermann as "one of the most dangerous bankers in the world."[9]

In the United States, the Occupy Wall Street movement had taken hold in Lower Manhattan, with protesters brandishing placards, sleeping in tents—and transforming the public, tree-lined, and well-heated atrium of Deutsche's headquarters at 60 Wall Street into a locus for activists.[10] American regulators, too, had Deutsche in their sights. During the head-in-the-sand regulatory era of the Clinton and the second Bush administrations, Deutsche had housed its vast Wall Street business in a few shell companies that weren't subject to American oversight. At the time, the government's assumption had always been that American regulators didn't need to worry about a giant foreign bank's U.S. operations because the parent company would rescue them if they encountered trouble. But the financial crisis had shown that was wishful thinking; there were plenty of examples of frail banks leaving their foreign subsidiaries to die lonely deaths. And Deutsche's wobbly finances—in particular its bottomless pit of derivatives and its exposure to the European economic crisis—seemed to put the American outpost at risk of being abandoned in a pinch. So regulators in the United States introduced rules that required banks like Deutsche to buttress their American operations.

Deutsche's first response was to tinker with the legal structure of its main U.S. business entity to exploit a gap in the law (which initially didn't apply to certain types of holding companies) and evade the new rules. But when that plan came to light, angry lawmakers and regulators slammed the loophole shut. Deutsche shrieked in protest: Requiring more money to be kept in the United States meant less money being available elsewhere in the world, and that could hurt the global economy, Ackermann threatened. The claim was implausible, but he was well positioned to lean on regulators. He chaired a powerful lobbying organization called the Institute of International Finance. When policymakers—including senior U.S. officials like Treasury secretary Tim Geithner and Federal Reserve chairman Ben Bernanke—convened gatherings to hash out new rules, the IIF's representatives, often Ackermann himself, generally were in the room. (The IIF also was one of the most outspoken advocates against restructuring the debt of Greece and other stricken countries in southern Europe.)

At a time when regulators seemed to be gaining the upper hand, the reality was more complex. Different countries jealously guarded their authority over their domestic banks. Deutsche more than almost any other multinational financial institution deftly managed to exploit rivalries among regulators to shield itself from tougher rules or greater outside scrutiny. German regulators—in particular an agency called BaFin, which prided itself on protecting its local companies—rushed to circle the wagons. They pushed to water down proposed international rules that would cap how much risk banks like Deutsche were allowed to take. When foreign governments tried to investigate the bank, BaFin ran interference, insisting that any demands for information be diverted into a labyrinth of German bureaucracy.

Frustrated American and British regulators took to deriding their German counterparts as "the representatives of Deutsche Bank" because they were so clearly doing its bidding. For now, Deutsche executives sat back and enjoyed the regulatory turf war. Their amusement wouldn't last.

CHAPTER 16

ROSEMARY VRABLIC

n the final months of Joe Ackermann's reign as CEO, the bank—cocky, fractious, hungry for profits, indifferent to its clients' reputations—made three loans that would haunt Deutsche for years. They originated with a woman named Rosemary Vrablic.

Vrablic had grown up in the Bronx and then moved to the New York City suburb of Scarsdale when she was ten. Her sister, Margaret, was thirteen years older and helped raise young Rosemary. Vrablic attended the Ursuline School, a private Catholic girls school,[1] and then Fordham University. She commuted to the school's Bronx campus and apparently kept to herself. In her four years there, the only mention of her in Fordham's yearbooks or student newspaper was her black-and-white portrait in the senior yearbook. In 1982, she graduated with an economics degree into the teeth of a recession. The only job Vrablic could find was as a bank teller. Ambitious and eager to launch her career, she noticed that aside from the manager at her bank branch, there were approximately zero women in senior roles in the banking industry. "You need to be patient," the female branch manager cautioned her. Vrablic, trying to model herself on that manager, dressed in jackets with shoulder pads and wore blouses with floppy bows. "Be a lady," she always reminded herself.[2]

One day, after an unsuccessful job interview in Manhattan, the commuter train she was riding back to Scarsdale, where she was living with her parents, broke down. As other passengers grumped, Vrablic chatted with her seatmate, a man named Howard Ross. They both worked in banking, and Vrablic alternated between asking incisive questions and offering thoughtful insights about the industry. Two hours later, as she finally got off the train, Ross handed her his business card; he was a senior executive in the New York office of Israel's Bank Leumi. "You know, you just gave the best interview of your life," Ross said, inviting her to call him to talk jobs. Vrablic wasn't sure about his intentions—this was the banking industry in the mid-1980s, and sexual harassment was the rule, not the exception—so she waited six months to call him. When she did, Ross connected her with another guy who enrolled her in Bank Leumi's credit-training program. The bank—with a brisk business serving wealthy Russians—happened to be a hub for tax evasion and would be busted for not doing enough to combat money laundering.[3] This is where Vrablic would learn the ropes.

She eventually landed a job as an analyst at another bank, where—despite the demeaning nickname of "Little Rosemary"[4]—she found a mentor to help her prepare to climb the corporate ladder. In 1989, a headhunter recruited her for a job in Citicorp's private-banking arm, a division of the company whose sole purpose was servicing ultra-rich individuals and families. Historically, private banks acted as wealth managers and souped-up concierge services for their clients. But Citi was widening its suite of offerings, including by making loans to finance clients' big real estate projects. Vrablic started off as a junior banker, eager to make her mark, years of pent-up energy and ambition now un-

leashed. She quickly learned to take advantage of Citi's new lending service, which few other private banks were willing to match.
Before long, she was tantalizing would-be clients with enormous
loans to finance their construction and development projects.
From there, Vrablic watched her roster of clients expand via re-
ferrals. Within a few years she had become one of New York's
leading bankers to the super-rich.

After six years at Citi, she was hired by what would become
Bank of America, where she helped set up its new private-
banking business. Her group focused on clients with more than
$50 million to invest.[5] "They have a few assets and many homes,
ex-wives, and many children," she explained in 1999.[6] Vrablic
specialized in dealing with difficult men: "They're successful
and they've earned their money by being tough."

In the late 1990s, Vrablic's small circle of friends, who knew
her as Ro, consisted in part of hard-drinking gamblers. Tall and
slim, her brown hair cut short, Ro could hold her own, polishing
off round after round, bantering about sports, often wearing an
old New York Rangers jersey. Through the bank, she had easy
access to front-row Yankees and Rangers tickets, and when she
wasn't using them for clients, she sometimes sent her grateful
friends off to enjoy a little taste of her good life. They marveled
at how this unassuming woman—boozy and foul-mouthed and
sports-obsessed when they were hanging out in sticky-floored
Irish pubs on Manhattan's East Side—had a parallel life schmooz-
ing some of the world's richest people.

Before long, Vrablic owned a $4.4 million Park Avenue pent-
house apartment. She bought a sprawling Arts and Crafts–style
weekend house, with panoramic Hudson River views in virtually
every room, up near West Point. She endowed a scholarship at
the Ursuline School to honor "the memory of her parents and
their lessons on the value of hard work, independence and striv-

ing toward one's goals."[7] She donated money here and there to Democrats like Chuck Schumer.

One of her youngest clients was Jared Kushner, who was taking over his family's small real estate empire. (The Kushners happened to have a long-running relationship with Bank Leumi—the Israeli lender where Vrablic had her first big career break.)

Deutsche at the time was still on its never-ending quest to become a household name in America. Ackermann had been pushing to expand the company's small private-banking division, which had been inherited from Bankers Trust and then left in sleepy solitude. He envisioned a more robust business that also doled out big loans. Ackermann put a fellow Swiss German, Pierre de Weck, in charge of reinvigorating the business, and de Weck hired a small group of executives from Citi. One of them was Tom Bowers. He surveyed the New York banking and social scene, asking anyone he could find who the best private banker out there was. A single name kept popping up: Rosemary Vrablic. Her reputation for tending to clients, for knowing and meeting their every need, for making big loans, was sterling. Bowers met with Vrablic and was impressed. Her training over the years had left her with a keen grasp of how to structure loans to please clients while minimizing default risks. In the summer of 2006, Deutsche persuaded the forty-six-year-old Vrablic to defect from Bank of America. Part of the deal was that she would report exclusively to Bowers and that she was guaranteed to be paid about $3 million a year for multiple years, an unusual arrangement at the time. To celebrate her hiring as a managing director and "senior private banker," Deutsche took out an ad in *The New York Times*, listing her direct phone number and email address.[8] Elevating the private bank into a "dominant position . . . is a core strategic priority for Deutsche Bank," the company declared.

Bowers trumpeted that "Rosemary is widely recognized as one of the top private bankers to the U.S. ultra-high-net-worth community."

To differentiate itself from a crowded field of competitors, Deutsche planned to do deals that were too risky or too complicated for rival banks to stomach—the same strategy that Mike Offit had deployed a decade earlier when trying to get the commercial real estate business off the ground. "Deutsche needs damaged clients," one of Vrablic's former colleagues would explain. Financially healthy and uncontroversial billionaires could easily go to bigger, more prestigious American banks. Deutsche picked up the scraps, including clients with unusual needs. When the billionaire Stan Kroenke wanted a loan to buy the iconic British soccer club Arsenal, some large American banks balked. Vrablic, however, hammered out a transaction in which Deutsche would accept as collateral some of Kroenke's other professional sports teams in the United States. The deal got done, and Deutsche reaped millions of dollars in advisory fees and interest on the loan—and positioned itself for years of additional business with the mustachioed sports magnate.

"Rosemary saved the day again" became a common refrain inside the bank, which counted on her to rake in tens of millions of dollars in annual revenue. She was by far the top producer in the bank's New York offices. Vrablic, by now bestowed with the uncreative nickname RV, kept mementos from her loans—including a golden shovel, to commemorate a construction project she financed—on display in her office. She was known inside Deutsche as someone who would push hard to get deals done, earning her the fierce loyalty of her hard-to-impress clients. Once she led a small group of Deutsche's executives and investment bankers to a meeting with Steve Ross, the CEO of a major New York real estate company. Everyone filed into the boardroom, shaking Ross's hand, but Vrablic received a tender embrace from the billionaire. Ross sat down across the conference table from the investment bankers and invited Vrablic to sit right next to him. The effect—not lost on anyone in the room—was that Vrablic was on Ross's team as they squared off against the Deutsche investment bankers auditioning for work with Ross's company.

Despite, or perhaps partly because of, her prowess, Vrablic wasn't very popular inside Deutsche. Envious investment bankers perceived her as a threat to their own relationships with clients. She had a tendency to be brusque, refusing to collaborate with private-banking colleagues; on an annual performance review, she was told she needed to improve her teamwork. She stirred up even more resentment when Deutsche higher-ups trotted her out to regional offices to teach the bank's wealth managers how to boost their lending volumes. ("We felt disrespected," one sniffed.) Vrablic's deal to report directly and exclusively to Bowers, the head of U.S. wealth management, meant that she bypassed the CEO of the private bank, to whom all of her colleagues reported. The arrangement added to her colleagues' resentment of what looked like special treatment.

The litigation between Trump and Deutsche over his refusal to repay the loan on his Chicago skyscraper had dragged on for two years. It was finally settled in 2010 with the bank agreeing to give Trump two years to make good on his obligations, including the $40 million that he had personally guaranteed. That meant that Trump needed, by 2012, to come up with a bunch of money. And if he wanted to keep expanding his empire, he would need to identify a new source of credit. The trouble, as ever, was that serious banks wouldn't get anywhere near him; the risks, financially and reputationally, were far too great. Even Deutsche, it seemed, was now off-limits after the Chicago debacle, especially since it was the second time that a division of the bank had effectively banished him as a client.

Jared Kushner had married Ivanka Trump in 2009, and he was becoming familiar with the Trump family's finances. He knew his father-in-law was looking for cash. He regarded Vrablic as the single best banker he'd ever worked with; she had become a good friend of the Kushner clan. (When Jared threw a party in 2007 to celebrate his purchase of *The New York Observer*, Vrablic was there at the Four Seasons restaurant, mingling with guests like Tom Wolfe.[9]) So Jared in 2011 invited Vrablic over to Trump Tower to meet his wife and father-in-law. Trump explained his situation to the banker, and then he popped the big question: Would Deutsche's private bank be willing to lend him $40 or $50 million with Chicago's Trump International Hotel & Tower as collateral? That would allow him to repay what he still personally owed Deutsche for the Chicago loan.

Why on earth would one arm of Deutsche even consider lending money to pay off defaulted debts owed to another part of the company? The answer was that Vrablic was excited by the prospect of landing a major deal with a major new client. She brought the proposal to Tom Bowers, who agreed that it was worth considering. A small team sifted through Trump's personal and corporate financial records and tax returns. The first thing the bankers noticed was that Trump was assigning absurdly rich values to his real estate assets. In one especially egregious case, he claimed that an estate he'd purchased in New York's Westchester County for about $7 million was now worth $291 million. His stratospheric valuations "were extremely aggressive," recalls a person who reviewed the documents. "He used the most optimistic assumptions at all times."[10] The bank ended up reducing the assets' values by as much as 70 percent.

The funny thing was that, notwithstanding Trump's serial exaggerations, his underlying finances weren't all that bad. He had limited debt, at least compared to his fellow real estate magnates, and cash was pouring in from *The Apprentice* and from licensing deals he'd struck to put his name on properties he didn't own. Making the deal more palatable for Deutsche, Trump was willing to personally guarantee the loan, meaning that Deutsche in theory could seize his assets if he didn't pay it back. (The fact that a similar, albeit smaller, personal guarantee hadn't prevented him from defaulting on the original Chicago loan did not seem to bother the bank.) Aside from the minor detail that he was a recidivist defaulter, Trump looked like an attractive borrower. Vrablic and Bowers tentatively agreed to lend him $48 million.

Because this would be the first time the private-banking division had lent money to Trump, it had to go through a few committees inside the bank for final sign-off. And this is where things got rocky.

When top executives in Anshu's investment-banking unit heard that another division was about to rekindle the Trump relationship, they went ballistic. Jain made the case at a meeting of the bank's top executives: How on earth could Deutsche do business with this guy after he had so publicly burned the bank? What precedent would that set for other would-be deadbeats? If Trump defaulted yet again, which seemed entirely possible, how would Deutsche explain that to investors and regulators?

Bowers and Vrablic argued that from the private bank's standpoint, the loan was sound. What's more, Deutsche and Trump had settled their litigation back in 2010. They tried to pacify their colleagues by pointing out the surreal fact that the new loan from Deutsche's private-banking arm would allow Trump to repay what he owed the investment-banking division. Bowers and Vrablic grumbled that the investment bankers were just jealous that the private bankers had figured out how to structure a loan with Trump in a way that seemed virtually risk-free for Deutsche.

Bowers wasn't afraid of a fight. He'd earned a reputation for playing hardball with colleagues. Now he asked his boss, Pierre de Weck, for help pushing the loan through, and de Weck appealed to Joe Ackermann. Ackermann, in his final months as CEO, had embarked on a worldwide farewell tour and wasn't fully engaged. Having cruised through the financial crisis, he believed the bank had capital to spare—indeed, he viewed that as one of the bank's distinguishing advantages. He told de Weck that he didn't object to the Trump loan.*

The bank's lawyers reviewed the situation. In December 2011, one of them, Steven Haber, emailed Bowers to report that "this client is cleared." (Haber previously had clerked for Judge Maryanne Trump Barry, Donald's older sister.) Stuart Clarke, Deutsche's chief operating officer in the Americas, emailed Bowers a similar message, reflecting the sign-off from a Frankfurt committee charged with vetting transactions that posed risks to the bank's reputation: "There is no objection from the bank to proceed with the client." Attached to the email was a huge PDF file containing all of Trump's personal and corporate financials, to make clear that everyone who'd vetted the proposed transaction was fully aware of the new client's heavy baggage.

Around the same time, Trump announced plans to buy the Doral Resort & Spa in Miami. The property, spanning some 650 acres, featured a sprawling if run-down 700-room hotel and four separate golf courses, including the notoriously challenging Blue Monster. The resort was wending its way through bankruptcy,

---

* Ackermann and de Weck said they don't recall this conversation.

and Trump got the price down to $150 million, with the understanding that he would probably have to spend that amount again to upgrade the golf courses and the hotel. Golf insiders thought Trump was overpaying for a property that was in the flight path of Miami's busy international airport. But Trump had no intention of personally paying for the project.

One of his first phone calls was to Rich Byrne, who years earlier had helped Trump's casino company sell junk bonds and had been rewarded with the weekend trip to Mar-a-Lago. Trump's subsequent default on those bonds had ended his relationship with Deutsche's securities unit, which Byrne now ran, but the two men had stayed in touch. Now, in early 2012, Trump told Byrne he was preparing to buy the Doral and asked whether Deutsche would consider providing financing. Byrne agreed to take a look at the numbers, not bothering to tell Trump that there was zero chance Deutsche would actually help him.

Byrne, though, didn't know that the private-banking division was in the mix. Trump invited Vrablic to Florida to see the property. The day after she got back to New York, she walked into Bowers's office. "Trump wants to go buy Doral," she explained, and he wanted Deutsche to loan him the money for the purchase. For the second time in a matter of weeks, Bowers dispatched a team to study a possible Trump loan. The private bank already knew his finances; now they got to know the Doral's numbers. The conclusion was that Trump seemed to be getting the resort at a reasonable price. And Trump not only agreed to personally guarantee the loan, but he also vowed to add millions of dollars to his wealth-management account at Deutsche. The bank charged fees for managing those assets, and so the relationship with Trump would become a bit more lucrative.

The caveat, Trump and his daughter Ivanka warned Vrablic, was that if Deutsche couldn't get the loan approved quickly, they'd have to shop it to a rival bank. It was, of course, a bluff—no other bank was going to touch Trump—but it had its intended effect, kicking Deutsche's underwriting process into overdrive. The private bank was ready to pull the trigger, but once again the investment bankers in New York got wind of what was happening. Once again, Anshu's Army angrily protested. They warned that Trump—who at the time was spreading the lie that Barack Obama hadn't been born in the United States and therefore was an illegitimate president—wasn't the kind of client Deutsche should be doing business with. (This was a bit rich, coming from guys who had rarely batted an eye at a client's sketchy reputation.) The private bankers saw nothing but sour grapes. "They didn't want us to be winning," a private-banking executive would tell me.

The Doral loan went up through the chain of command, the investment bank's concerns were overruled, and the transaction got approved. A legal entity in the United States—Deutsche Bank Trust Company Americas, or DBTCA—wired two loans totaling $125 million to the Trump Organization. (One of them expired in about three years, at which point Deutsche would have the choice of whether or not to renew the loan.) Afterward, Trump called Byrne's office. Byrne had no idea that the private-banking group had agreed to make the loan, and he didn't want to pick up the phone because he figured Trump would just badger him for an answer on whether Deutsche would lend the money. Byrne's secretary reminded him that Trump would keep calling, getting angrier and angrier, so he might as well get it over with and take the call.

She patched him in. "Rich," Trump bellowed, "I'm just calling to thank you! I know you must've approved it, but Rosemary and her team gave me the money." Byrne, thinking on his feet and happy to take credit, pretended that he knew all about it. He congratulated Trump and then, as an aside, asked about the interest rate that Vrablic's squad was charging on the loan. Trump said it was well under 3 percent. Byrne couldn't believe that Deutsche—after its long, bitter history with Trump—was now extending him a nine-figure loan at such a low interest rate.

In public, Trump insisted to a journalist that he didn't really need Deutsche's money for the Doral acquisition, but he acknowledged that he was nonetheless grateful for the bank's help. "We have a great relationship," he said.[11, 12]

CHAPTER 17

ANSHU ASCENDANT

Kaiser Wilhelm II had opened the Festhalle event center in Frankfurt in 1909, and its pink colonnaded facade, cavernous main hall, and 120-foot-high cupola ceiling made it an instant landmark in the city's cultural scene. Over the decades the Festhalle was the venue for countless concerts, auto expos, sporting events, even magic shows. In the course of one week in spring 2012, two big events were scheduled to take place. One was a concert by Jay-Z and Kanye West. The other, on May 31, was Deutsche Bank's annual shareholder meeting. Normally the latter wouldn't have been a big deal, but this was an important occasion: It marked Joe Ackermann's final moment as CEO.

It was a sweltering day in Frankfurt, and municipal vehicles roamed the streets, spraying water to cool the asphalt.[1] More than 7,000 shareholders showed up at the Festhalle, the most ever at a Deutsche annual meeting.[2] Buffet tables were piled with sausages, potato salad, and more than 11,000 sandwiches.[3] A booth offered souvenir photos in case any shareholders wanted to take home a memory of their day with Deutsche. The bank had printed stacks of a glossy magazine to commemorate Ackermann's decade as CEO. It featured photos of him with world leaders—across a conference table from Vladimir Putin, dancing with Christine Lagarde, smiling at Angela Merkel, sitting with a stone-faced Mikhail Gorbachev—and quotes from academics, journalists, and international dignitaries. "His skillful leadership of Deutsche Bank through difficult economic times has been an inspiration for the world's financial community," Henry Kissinger cooed. "When Joe retires in May, he will leave with the knowledge that Deutsche Bank is well equipped to face the future with confidence."

These elites were out of touch with the seething anger that much of the public continued to feel toward banks and their leaders. Especially in Germany, Deutsche's increasingly severe problems were well known. Outside the Festhalle, suit-wearing protesters rapped about "fat pig bankers." Someone dumped sewage near the hall's entrance, hoping bank executives and shareholders would have to traipse through it on their way in.[4]

Their displeasure was warranted. The reckless mismanagement of Deutsche was bad for its shareholders, but it was dangerous for the world. And this was to say nothing of Deutsche's campaign to water down regulations and stiff-arm prosecutors, tactics that undermined the ability of financial watchdogs to police the banking system. If the problems at a bank of Deutsche's size escalated, the company wouldn't just collapse—it would drag down other big banks along with it. Only a few years removed from the global financial crisis, nobody needed to be reminded how such a chain of events would play out. Shock waves from the bank's implosion would ricochet around the world, causing great harm to national economies and personal pocketbooks.

When Ackermann took the Festhalle stage, he was greeted with scattered boos and shouted insults. Shareholders were unhappy about their decimated investments—down more than 75 percent from their peak five years earlier. (And of course they didn't know their bank was sitting on billions of dollars of hidden losses on derivatives, as Ben-Artzi and his colleagues had told the SEC.) Ackermann's face was projected on a giant video screen at the front of the Festhalle, along with the bank's official slogan: *Leistung aus Leidenschaft* ("Passion to Perform"). Ackermann— after a decade running the bank, his hair was gray, the rings under his eyes were dark—was unapologetic. "I have done my duty and served the company with all my strength," he intoned.[5]

Ackermann had spent a year campaigning to implant Axel Weber, the head of Germany's central bank and one of Deutsche's main regulators, as his successor as CEO. (Deutsche by now was expert in the benefits of the revolving door.) Weber seemed game, but after a pitched battle, the board rejected Ackermann's advice and selected Anshu Jain and Jürgen Fitschen, a longtime German banker, as the incoming leaders. (Anshu had cemented the outcome by making clear he would leave if he didn't get the job.) The pairing with Fitschen—and the fact that there would be two CEOs, not one—represented a compromise on the board between factions aligned with the investment-banking division and the German traditionalists.

Ackermann didn't hide the fact that he was less than thrilled with his successors. He worried that Jain lacked the charisma and international reputation to be able to play the diplomat role that Ackermann had so enjoyed. And he blamed Anshu for most of the bank's current problems, including the investment bank's unmistakable pattern of envelope-pushing misbehavior.[6] In his Festhalle speech, he hardly mentioned his two successors, only expressing his hope that they "can build on what we have achieved together."

As Ackermann droned on, Jain pulled an iPad out of his knapsack and appeared to tune out.[7] Nothing Ackermann said at this point could obstruct his ascent or change the fact that he would be the first non-European, the first nonwhite guy, to run this 142-year-old institution. It was the culmination of decades of ambition. He had helped build something from scratch, and now he was fulfilling Edson's destiny. The crown was his, or at least half of it was. And the way Anshu saw it, Jürgen would be the bank's public face in Germany, while he, Anshu, would be the one who actually controlled the daily operations. To celebrate, he bought his father a silver BMW X5.

Jain had every reason to feel proud of his ascent. He had traveled a long way from the rough young trader who was too geeky for a job at Goldman. He now possessed the polished, above-the-fray sheen of an accomplished politician. He spoke with confidence. His Hermès ties were always cinched in proud, bulbous knots. He moved into a luxurious apartment in an affluent Frankfurt neighborhood, a gold nameplate engraved with the letter *J* the only hint of its occupant.[8] He was now more than an individual; he was the face of an institution.

This metamorphosis had not occurred organically. He'd studied a book on German corporate governance. He had embarked on a campaign-style listening tour all over Germany. The bank's top executives each had been paired with a leadership coach who served as a personal counselor, and Jain's coach worked on teaching him the subtle art of carrying himself like a chief executive. (Some executives suspected that the coaches were acting as spies, reporting their secrets back to Anshu.)

But no amount of coaching could change the facts that Anshu didn't speak German (he'd taken lessons, without much effect) and that his skin was brown. Before he became CEO, Anshu consulted with a senior German politician. "I want you to do one thing, Mr. Jain," the politician said. "Learn German." Anshu

laughed it off, pointing out that everyone he knew in Frankfurt
and Berlin spoke impeccable English. "No decision that gets
made gets made in English," the pol responded.

Even if Anshu had picked up the language, the German establishment would still have looked down on him. The local media
insisted on pointing out, in just about every story, that he was
Indian. Sometimes the flagrant labeling was racist, in line with
The Economist's "Indian 'bond junkie' " sobriquet. Anshu turned
the other cheek, but his colleagues recognized that these preju-
dices would make it harder for him to effectively manage the
bank. Fitschen apologetically explained to one colleague that
Germans didn't look fondly upon outsiders in the banking sector.
That had been true back before the rise of the Nazis, when Jews
dominated—and then were erased from—the country's banking
scene, and it was true now, even if nobody wanted to admit it.

Nor was Jain fully prepared for the grueling daily task of managing a vast enterprise, of anticipating economic and political
shifts before they took place, of being able to make tough decisions as the co-CEO of an entire company, not just the leader of
one division. The most acute problem was that Deutsche's finances were in terrible shape. It was completely dependent on
borrowed money, a big warning sign to investors and regulators
who had watched during the crisis as seemingly secure funding
went poof in a heartbeat. The clearest reflection of this was
Deutsche's capital ratio—a measure of how much of a company's
balance sheet is supported by equity instead of much-riskier borrowed money—which at barely 6 percent was roughly half the
industry average at the time. The bank had hundreds of billions
of dollars in high-risk, hard-to-sell assets that were generating
big losses with no end in sight. To make matters worse, the dynamics of the entire banking industry at the moment Jain and
Fitschen took over were being turned on their heads. Regulators

in the United States and elsewhere, internalizing the lessons of the financial crisis, were suddenly making it much less profitable for banks to do business using borrowed funds and to gamble with their own (or depositors') money. This posed a grave threat to an institution like Deutsche, whose fortunes hinged on gobs of borrowed cash and whose profits derived largely from proprietary trading. Indeed, the bank was already seeing its finances slide into the red. Deutsche's business model was going to need to change radically.

Anshu, who had spent almost his entire career in sales and trading, wasn't ready for the seismic shift. His first priority had been to install his people in positions of power across the bank. As soon as it had become clear that he would become CEO, Ackermann's disciples, including Bänziger, had been informed that they should have their offices empty by the day of the annual meeting. Those spacious accommodations would now be occupied by executives who had been by Jain's side since the Merrill Lynch days. It was an understandable urge, to be surrounded by loyalists, but it meant that some executives were suddenly responsible for areas far removed from their skill sets.

Henry Ritchotte was named chief operating officer, with responsibility for, among other things, the bank's tangled web of technology systems—something in which he had no particular expertise. Michele Faissola was put in charge of the bank's asset- and wealth-management services worldwide, a job for which he had no discernible qualifications. And for Bänziger's chief risk officer job, Anshu selected Bill Broeksmit. Broeksmit initially worried that the job would be overwhelming, but Jain assured him that he'd be great, and Bill grudgingly agreed. It was a leap up from his current job: head of portfolio risk optimization in the investment bank. As chief risk officer, he would be responsible for the entire risk-management operation across the entire company, not just the investment bank. He would also join the bank's fabled vorstand, now known simply as the management board.

After Broeksmit's promotion became public, Deutsche decided it might be a good idea to run it by BaFin, which had the power under German law to veto such senior appointments. Broeksmit was dispatched to Bonn, where BaFin was located, to be interviewed by senior regulators. This was not the order in which things were supposed to happen; traditionally, banks gave BaFin a heads-up before finalizing big promotions. That way, if the regulator had qualms, they could be addressed, and if they were unresolvable, the appointment could be quietly abandoned before it became public.[9]

Anshu figured BaFin would rubber-stamp the appointment. Neither he nor Bill realized that behind the scenes, Hugo Bänziger, furious about being passed over for the CEO job and insulted by the brusqueness with which he'd been shown the door as the new team took over, was out for blood. He had spent months whispering in the ears of top BaFin officials, warning them that Jain was out of his depth, that he was surrounding himself with inexperienced cronies, that Broeksmit didn't have the skills to manage a large, complex, global risk-management operation. The surprising thing was that Bill and Hugo had been friends. Back in 2006, for example, Bill and Alla had attended Hugo's fiftieth birthday party at a luxury estate in the English countryside, dancing late into the night. But the long friendship was subordinate in Bänziger's mind to the paramount priority of damaging Jain. And what better way to do that than by dealing him a public defeat and simultaneously depriving him of Broeksmit's expertise?

Bänziger's sabotage campaign worked. BaFin, long in Deutsche's pocket, was beginning to realize that if it had any hope of fending off foreign authorities, it needed to start policing the bank and showing the public some results. After grilling Broeksmit in Bonn, BaFin came back with a stunning answer: He was unacceptable as chief risk officer. And so his promotion was rescinded.

It was the first time Bill had felt the sting of public humiliation. The promotion had garnered considerable attention in the business media. The congratulatory emails and phone calls had been pouring in all month. Now he had to explain, over and over and over, that the job had been revoked. He called his mother and got her voice mail. "Easy come, easy go," he told her, trying to sound nonchalant. When his brother Peter listened to the message, he could tell Bill was in pain. "There is no concealing the hurt," he emailed Bill. Broeksmit told John Breit, the old Merrill risk manager, that he knew he should be relieved given all the inevitable headaches and heartburn of such a high-pressure gig, "but once I started thinking about the job, I liked it." Anshu could tell he was devastated.

Worse was to come.

CHAPTER 18

DUMPING GROUND

Toward the end of 2012, the wretched selection/rejection pattern repeated itself. Anshu proposed giving Bill the job of running Deutsche's so-called noncore division—a part of the bank belatedly set up to get rid of its mountains of money-losing assets, including its misvalued derivatives. The job wasn't glamorous, but it was vital to the bank's prospects. Once again, BaFin said no.

Passed over for yet another high-profile gig, Broeksmit was relegated to the board of an obscure U.S. legal entity—Deutsche Bank Trust Company Americas, or DBTCA. This was the corporate husk of the old Bankers Trust business, and it had long been a dumping ground for unsavory businesses. The tax-avoiding trades with Renaissance Technologies were housed there. So were the loans to Donald Trump. Executives in London and Frankfurt weren't paying much attention to what happened inside this squirrelly unit. In fact, nobody was: DBTCA had barely a hundred employees, compared to the tens of thousands in other divisions, and it didn't have its own chief financial officer or risk department. But it had become a crucial holding company, through which almost all of its American businesses channeled their transactions.

For the past decade, the bank's U.S. operations had been run by Seth Waugh, whom some underlings derided as a lightweight. Waugh certainly hadn't kept a sufficiently close eye on what was happening in his division, preferring to spend his time hobnobbing on the golf course and promoting Deutsche's brand instead of toiling on important but mundane managerial tasks.

In 2012, with Jain and Fitschen poised to take the reins, Waugh decided to step down. He told acquaintances that Jürgen was a nice enough fellow but that Anshu wasn't trustworthy. Waugh's successor as CEO of the American business was the veteran investment banker Jack Brand, and he and Waugh recruited Broeksmit to the DBTCA board as part of an effort to improve the talent pool. Brand didn't know Broeksmit well, but he was aware of his reputation: a sharp mind, an honest man, a nice guy. Bill accepted the gig, telling Jack that it would give him an excuse to return to New York more frequently to visit his daughters.

Broeksmit and Brand were stunned by what they found inside DBTCA. Some problems were idiosyncratic, like the investment banker who was caught receiving kickbacks from a car-service company in exchange for extra business from Deutsche. Others were existential. State and federal regulators were crawling all over the place and had been for a decade—yet Deutsche hadn't seemed to do anything to address their concerns, as if the bank was determined to see how long it could get away with its bad practices before someone actually came down hard on them. Its relationship with the Federal Reserve, in particular, was awful.

Regulators feared DBTCA didn't have any systems in place to ensure that employees followed the law. They fretted that

DBTCA didn't have the wherewithal to figure out its own finances, much less to ensure their soundness. Its technology dated back to the Bankers Trust era. Many DBTCA employees relied on an ancient version of Lotus Notes. Others were manually entering the details of bespoke transactions into Excel spreadsheets; nothing was automated. When you pulled the bank's financial data from one computer program, it would spit out different numbers than if you pulled them from another system. The technology was such a mess, DBTCA's financial reporting so jumbled, that nobody really understood the underlying numbers. Officials from the compliance department sometimes resorted to asking executives to perform manual spot checks on their voluminous trading data to see if they were adhering to the law.

This all represented a very big problem, and not just for DBTCA. Because it was Deutsche's main vehicle for operating in the United States, the entity had the potential to get the entire bank in serious trouble. The worst-case scenario—which struck some executives as well within the realm of possibility—was that if the feds grew sufficiently angry, Deutsche might get kicked out of the world's biggest economy.

Broeksmit's mandate—in addition to continuing his regular risk-optimization job in London—was to help clean up this unholy mess.

Around the time he took on the DBTCA role, Bill reconnected with Edson's son Scott Mitchell. They had been out of touch for years, their relationship torched by the Broeksmits' support for Estelle, which the Mitchell clan viewed as an unforgivable act of disloyalty. But more than a decade had passed, and Scott realized that life was more complicated than he had understood as a teenager. It was time to move on.

In the spring of 2012, Scott was in London and visited Anshu. The framed photo of Edson was now perched on the top of a bookshelf, just above Jain's cricket paraphernalia. At the end of the meeting, as Scott got up to leave, Anshu suggested that perhaps it was time to rekindle the old Mitchell-Broeksmit friendship; he offered to have his assistant set up a meeting. Scott agreed, and Anshu's office booked a lunch for Scott and Bill at a Michelin-starred Indian restaurant in London.

When the date arrived, Scott flaked out. He was overcome with anxiety about seeing Uncle Bill, a man he had been trained to practically worship, and worried about his reaction when he learned that Scott had never amounted to much professionally. Scott knew that in certain situations—partly because of his physical appearance and partly because Edson's magnetism still had its pull—people saw his father in him; he could see the look in their eyes, the yearning in their voices, and it made him miserable.

A couple of months later, Scott and Bill tried again. This time it was Broeksmit's assistant who prodded the two men. After they both kept trying to reschedule, Bill's daughter Alessa took control and reserved a table at an expensive Japanese restaurant, 15 East, in New York's Union Square. Alessa planned to come to the dinner, and since Bill would have a wing-woman with him, Scott decided to bring one, too; he enlisted his younger sister Ellen, who lived in New Jersey. Scott flew in for the reunion.

It had been twelve years since Scott and Bill had last seen each other. Scott had indeed grown into a spitting image of his father, albeit a few inches shorter and with slightly redder hair. Bill rose to greet him when he spotted Scott walking to their table. "He's Edson, holy shit!" Alessa blurted. Trying to tame his nerves, Scott had downed several shots at the hotel before coming; now he was drunk and sweating. As the group sat at a polished wood table, it took a while for the two shy men to open up. But Bill selected some nice wine, and the more they drank, the more the tension eased. Scott fondly impersonated Anshu telling him that he had not lived up to expectations: "You are smarter than hell and talented," he said in a faux Indian lilt. "How do we get you up to your metrics?" Broeksmit loved it. Soon he and Scott were bantering about banking and politics. Bill lit up, as if a long-severed electrical connection had been soldered back together. As the dinner ended, Alessa pulled Scott aside. "This is him," she whispered, nodding in Bill's direction. "I haven't seen my father like this since Edson."

Late that summer, Bill and Alla invited Scott up to their place in Maine. They spent the day drinking and reminiscing, the old family bond now restored. Broeksmit joked about how he had dodged a bullet by not getting the chief risk officer gig. He said he was contemplating a third and final retirement. He asked about estate planning. He kept saying how much he still missed Edson.

Scott was a keen student of the banking industry, especially when it came to the institution that his father had helped build. He asked Bill what would have happened with Deutsche if Edson hadn't died. Would it be in better or in worse shape today? Bill paused for a moment, tugging at his eyebrow the way he did when he was deep in thought. "We would've made less money during the boom," he eventually answered. "But we would've lost less money during the bust."

CHAPTER 19

5,777 REQUESTS
FOR INFORMATION

n February 2013, after annual bonuses were handed out, Bill
asked Anshu if they could sit down for a meeting. He informed
the CEO—his on-again, off-again colleague of more than
twenty years—that he was ready to retire, for real this time.
He was tired and deflated. He told Anshu that he felt that he
wasn't pulling his weight inside the bank.

This was the last thing Anshu needed right now. His and Jürgen Fitschen's first months in the job had been turbulent at best.
Deutsche was bleeding money, with several divisions ringing up
losses of hundreds of millions of dollars. In December, more than
five hundred government agents in *polizei* vans and helicopters
had swarmed the bank's twin skyscrapers, occupying the lobby
and scouring the premises for evidence that the bank had committed tax evasion through its fraudulent emissions-permit
scheme—the ploy that Rod Stone had broken up a few years earlier. (The Germans had changed the law to block the scam, but
they were only now rounding up the perps.) With Stone's help,
German police had untangled a complex multinational tax fraud.

On the day of the December raid, the police, led by Frankfurt's top prosecutor, took five bank employees into custody; more than two dozen Deutsche officials would be investigated, including Fitschen, who had attested to the accuracy of the bank's fraudulent 2009 tax statements.[1] Barely a week later, another police raid on the headquarters further established that Deutsche had a big target on its back.

By the time Broeksmit declared that he was ready to throw in the towel, Jain was badly rattled. He pleaded with Bill, one of his most trusted, longest-serving lieutenants, to stay on for at least several more months and to remain a board member of DBTCA in perpetuity. Broeksmit relented. That represented a minor victory for Anshu. But things were about to get much worse.

The top concerns were financial. Ackermann had left on a high note, hailed by many German leaders as the greatest banker of his generation. (Shortly after he left Deutsche, the Institute of International Finance, which had amassed peerless power under his leadership, threw him a farewell bash at an ancient castle outside Copenhagen, complete with booming cannons and waitstaff in medieval garb.) Not many people realized that Deutsche was in tatters. That was because a bank's true health isn't measured by its profits in any given quarter. Instead, the numbers that really matter are complicated-sounding figures that gauge the company's reliance on borrowed funds (the leverage ratio) as opposed to money kicked in by shareholders in exchange for equity (as measured by its tier 1 capital ratio), and its stockpile of potentially dangerous but hard-to-sell financial instruments (its tier 3 assets). For Deutsche, those crucial health metrics were all in the danger zone, either way too low or way too high. There was no painless way to address these problems. Issuing new shares or asking existing investors to pony up more money would be agonizing for shareholders whose investments already had been clobbered. Disposing of more than $150 billion of unwanted money-losing assets was unquestionably the right thing to do, but their diminished values meant Deutsche would have to absorb heavy losses—likely well into the billions of dollars—when it sold them. Instead of ripping the Band-Aid off, Jain moved gingerly, prolonging the cleanup.

Meanwhile, a different class of crises was developing. Government authorities were finally catching on to Deutsche's tendency to prioritize profits over ethics. The problems began in Tuscany. A Deutsche investment-banking employee had not liked what he'd seen with the Monte dei Paschi transactions—part of a pattern, he thought, of the bank behaving in a reckless, belligerent manner all over the world. After leaving the bank, he leaked reams of paperwork about the Italian transactions to journalists and regulators. When Bloomberg News broke the story about Deutsche allegedly helping to hide losses inside the world's oldest bank, Paschi entered a fatal tailspin. Investors sprinted to sell its shares, and Italian authorities opened criminal and civil investigations, including into Deutsche's role in selling what looked like deceptive derivatives. The scary thing for Anshu was that Deutsche, after the initial success of the Paschi transaction, had been peddling similar transactions to banks in countries including Brazil and Greece.

Just as Broeksmit broke the news to Jain that he was retiring from full-time work at the bank (he left open the possibility of serving in a greatly reduced part-time role), Italian police investigating the transactions raided the Siena home of David Rossi, the communications director at Paschi. A fit, stylish man, Rossi had been more than a bank spokesman; he was a senior executive, crafting strategy and, it would turn out, providing personal financial services to some of the bank's clients. Two weeks after the police raid, on a rainy evening in March 2013, Rossi tumbled from the window of his fourth-floor office in Paschi's headquarters. For at least an hour, he lay in a courtyard, twitching occasionally, before his body finally stilled. The death—at the time, local authorities had ruled it a suicide—of a senior executive at a bank in the government's cross hairs made headlines worldwide, and it kicked the investigations of Paschi and Deutsche into a higher gear.

That summer, Deutsche produced a confidential internal report about its recent interactions with government authorities in countries all over the world.[2] In the first eight months of 2013, the bank had fielded 5,777 requests for information from regulators—an average of about one every hour, vastly more than the bank had received the prior year. "The remainder of 2013 indicates no signs of diminishing regulatory scrutiny," the memo predicted.

Everything that could go wrong seemed to be doing so. In August, the Chicago Mercantile Exchange alone identified forty-six instances where Deutsche had violated technical rules regarding the trading of derivatives. The Commodity Futures Trading Commission, another regulator of derivatives, "delivered strong messages and stressed urgency in remediating repeat findings and the need for prompt action," according to the bank's memo. The Federal Reserve, which was responsible for policing DBTCA, was especially grumpy. The Fed "has significantly changed its tone, delivering strong messages regarding the urgency in completing outstanding remediation issues," the memo said, referring to the long list of items that the bank was supposed to be fixing. One of the central bank's biggest concerns was the integrity of the financial data that DBTCA provided to the Fed and that the Fed then made public. Some of that data appeared to be wrong, and now the Fed was in the awkward position of having publicly disseminated faulty numbers.

It kept coming. There was Bob Roach's intensifying tax-avoidance investigation in the Senate. Then there were the allegations, now under investigation by Germany's central bank as well as the U.S. Securities and Exchange Commission, that Deutsche had deliberately hidden large losses during the financial crisis by inflating the value of derivatives by billions of dollars. (This was what Eric Ben-Artzi had reported to the SEC.) Regulators started interviewing former Deutsche employees, some of whom said there was one person they really needed to talk to, someone who understood derivatives and was more honest than anyone else in the bank's executive suites: Bill Broeksmit.[3]

The U.S. Justice Department, too, was coming after Deutsche on multiple fronts. Federal prosecutors sued MortgageIT, seeking $1 billion in damages, for "years of reckless lending" and dishonesty—a situation that should not have been a surprise, even based on Deutsche's scant due diligence prior to the acquisition. The Justice Department also was digging into the mortgage-backed securities Deutsche had sold all over the world.

And finally, there was Libor. In the United States and overseas, prosecutors had found stacks of evidence—traders and brokers had plotted many of their crimes in writing. Deutsche brought in outside auditors to take a closer look, and they found that Christian Bittar and his crew had engaged in an extensive campaign to manipulate the interest rate. Within weeks of the bank receiving requests for documents from American authorities, Bittar was transferred to Singapore—quite a coincidence, as regulators would later note. (He pleaded guilty to fraud in 2018 and was sentenced to more than five years in prison.[4])

One Friday afternoon, Deutsche's chief operating officer, Henry Ritchotte, asked the bank's legal department to deliver to him a few boxloads of the Libor evidence: transcripts of internal chat sessions and phone recordings, trading records, emails.

Ritchotte asked Broeksmit to swing by his office, and the two men sat around that evening, and then for much of the weekend, going through the damning materials. Ritchotte, who spoke fluent French, translated Bittar's communications for Broeksmit. By Monday morning, they could tell that Deutsche was in serious trouble.

The Russian business that Deutsche had leaped into with its 2006 acquisition of United Financial had grown into a sprawling enterprise. Its Moscow office, housed in an eight-story glass building near the Moskva River, had hundreds of employees and was raking in nearly $200 million a year in revenue.[5] Sure, some of the activities still made Deutsche executives queasy—did they really want to be in bed with oligarchs?—but such misgivings were salved by profits.

Then came the 2008 financial crisis. Revenues in Russia were chopped in half. To get things revved up, Deutsche used corrupt means to win business with the Kremlin. In one instance, the bank hired the daughter of Russia's deputy finance minister—an arrangement that was blessed by top executives in Moscow and London. The job quickly paid off, with the minister awarding Deutsche a lucrative role on a multibillion-dollar Russian bond offering. The next year, the bank gave a series of temporary jobs to the son of a senior executive at a state-owned company in Russia. The son performed poorly—Deutsche's HR department noted that he wasn't showing up at work and had cheated on an exam—but the bank won work with the father's company.[6]

The biggest play was the elevation of Andrey Kostin Jr., who had moved from Deutsche's London offices to its Moscow branch. Goateed and with piercing black eyes, Kostin Jr. was promoted in 2009 to a senior executive role, helping expand Deutsche's sales and trading of Russian stocks and bonds. Having an employee surnamed Kostin provided immeasurable benefits in Putin's Russia, and business poured in to Deutsche from deals it did with VTB Bank, still run by his father and still linked to the Kremlin's intelligence apparatus. "We found the nature and concentration of their business with VTB quite galling," the head of Goldman Sachs's Moscow office at the time told the journalist Luke Harding. "Nobody else could touch VTB."[7]

At the beginning of 2011, Kostin Jr. was once again promoted—this time to essentially run Deutsche's entire Moscow operation. He reported to the bank's country head, Igor Lojevsky, who was Charlie Ryan's successor in the job. Lojevsky was a flashy dresser whose aggressive, risk-loving management style—and the fact that a number of his relatives scored jobs at the bank—alarmed some of his colleagues.

By this time, Deutsche was once again laundering money for Russian clients. The anti-laundering order that the Fed and New York regulators had imposed back in 2005 had been lifted in 2008, and Deutsche swiftly reverted to form. Participants had uncreatively dubbed the latest arrangement the Laundromat, and Russian criminals—some with ties to the Kremlin—used it to wash their looted money out of Russia and into the European financial system. Deutsche was a crucial cog in the Laundromat, processing cross-border transactions for banks that were too small to have offices outside their home countries. (Deutsche was legally required to vet the sources of the money it was helping local lenders move, but that rarely happened.) Deutsche helped these smaller banks wire the freshly cleansed money around the world on behalf of the Russians, pocketing a tiny slice of each transaction. By 2014, tens of billions of dollars would cycle through the Laundromat, and Deutsche's Moscow corps was booking desperately needed profits.[8]

Things were looking good until a sunny Saturday in July 2011.

Kostin Jr. was riding an all-terrain vehicle through a forest out-side the Russian city of Yaroslavl. The four-wheeler flipped into a ditch and collided with a tree. Kostin Jr. was killed. Just like that, Deutsche's inside edge in Russia was blunted if not obliterated.

How would Deutsche recover? Around that time, a group of Moscow employees, led by a handsome young American named Tim Wiswell,[9] cooked up a new scheme to reinvigorate things. Wiswell had gotten his start at United Financial, slowly climb-ing through the ranks. In 2008, Deutsche promoted the twenty-nine-year-old—nicknamed Wiz, he was an avid sailor and skier—to be its head of Russian equities.[10] Now his squad devised a plan to help Russians secretly whisk their money out of the country.[11] A Russian customer would give his money to a Russian brokerage firm. The brokerage would then buy shares of a blue-chip stock from Deutsche's Moscow office, paying in rubles. Then the same brokerage—using a legal entity incorporated in an opaque jurisdiction like Cyprus—would sell the same quantity of shares back to Deutsche's London arm, which would pay the Russian brokerage in dollars. The stock trades canceled each other out, but now the money was in dollars rather than rubles. And those dollars were then transferred to a bank account in a Western democracy in the original Russian customer's name. Be-cause the two trades were reverse images of each other, the illicit transactions were known as *mirror trades*.[12]

Colleagues understood that Wiz had the blessings of his supe-riors, who on occasion pushed him to charge higher fees for this unique offering. As word spread about this valuable money-laundering service, Deutsche's Moscow offices became a go-to destination for shadowy Russians. Over the next several years, thousands of the mirror trades, representing more than $10 bil-lion, would flow from Moscow to London, then through DBTCA in New York, where the money was converted into dollars, then back to Cyprus or other parts of Europe.¹³ Among the customers were Putin's relatives and close friends.¹⁴ Profits poured in. Wiz and his crew partied hard, sometimes on the bank's dime, with heli-skiing and plane-jumping excursions, not to mention vodka-drenched nights at Moscow's high-end bars and strip clubs. "We lived like rock stars," one of Wiz's colleagues would write.¹⁵

At a well-run bank, any number of warnings would have sounded to alert compliance officials that something suspicious was going on. There was the fact that the back-to-back transactions were precisely the same size, albeit in different currencies. There was the fact that many of the customers the bank was serving had records of legal trouble, and in some cases those troubles were so public that even the tightly controlled Russian media had written about them. (Anyone who bothered to do a simple Google search would have seen the articles.) And there was the fact that the volume of business the bank was doing in Russia—a country notorious for organized crime and state-sanctioned thievery—was suddenly rocketing higher.

But Deutsche was not a well-run bank. Its computer systems in Moscow and London and New York didn't communicate with each other, which in this case had the convenient effect of disguising the similarities in size and timing of many of the mirror trades. In Moscow, a lone lawyer without any experience in compliance simultaneously served as Deutsche's local head of compliance, head of legal, and chief anti-money-laundering officer.¹⁶ The bank's due-diligence procedures there consisted of little more than asking customers to fill in a brief form stating where they got the money they were seeking to use.¹⁷ And unlike most of its peers, the bank—perhaps because of its long involvement with Russia and its 2006 acquisition of United Financial—hadn't assigned the country a high-risk rating that would automatically subject transactions originating there to greater internal vetting.¹⁸

Indeed, Deutsche had been conditioned under Ackermann to adore Russia and to do whatever it took to survive there. This worked out well for Ackermann. A month after he stepped down from Deutsche, he traveled to Saint Petersburg for an economic forum. Putin invited him to a private meeting. The Russian president had a proposition: Would he be interested in working for the Kremlin? Putin said the job on offer involved helping to run the country's enormous and not-always-squeaky-clean sovereign-wealth fund.[19] Ackermann said he was open to considering the gig. The job ultimately fell through, but it signaled just how intimate Deutsche had become with the Kremlin under Ackermann's leadership.

Directly off a busy parkway in Jacksonville, Florida, just down the street from the FBI's field office, a three-story white office building with blue-tinted windows blended into the suburban sprawl. Brightly colored muscle cars, many with license plates indicating their owners' military service, were parked outside. In case visitors didn't spot the NO TRESPASSING sign along the driveway, security guards cruised the premises in white golf carts as seagulls circled overhead. Every day, hundreds of workers marched past the palm trees and manicured lawns and into one of Deutsche's least glamorous, but arguably most important, offices.

The bank had assembled an army of not-very-well-paid employees and contractors to sift through thousands of transactions a day that the bank was doing for clients all over the world. The job of the workers was to sniff out potential money laundering or other financial crimes. Teams churned through dozens of case files a day, cross-checking client names against a series of databases to see if any obvious legal or reputational problems jumped out. Many did. "We had a ton of stuff that we knew was Rus-

sian," one employee recalls. "They'd be incorporated in one country and banking in another, but their address would be Russian.
It was crazy." The bank was moving many millions of dollars a
day for these Russians, often via untraceable shell companies.
There was no definitive way to tell if the LLCs and the like belonged to innocuous rich people or corrupt government officials
or oligarchs. It didn't help that many of Deutsche's Jacksonville
employees and contractors were young, often a year or two out of
local colleges, and that they received scant training. Many employees didn't understand how they were supposed to tell a risky
client from a merely secretive one.

There were a couple of ways to handle these situations. One
was to blacklist just about every murky client and to file a "suspicious activity report" with the Financial Crimes Enforcement
Network, or FinCEN. That had the benefit of partly covering the
bank's backside, but it didn't stop the transactions from going
through. Inside the Jacksonville offices' cubicle farms, some
teams filed dozens of the reports every day. Then a month or two
later, another transaction would land on an employee's desk involving the same Russian-linked shell companies, and the employees would again file a suspicious-activity report, and again
nothing would happen. It was disheartening and confusing—
why didn't Deutsche just stop doing business with these shady
clients? (The answer, employees recognized, was that handling
the transactions was profitable.)

That was one approach. Other teams inside the Jacksonville
complex adopted a different, simpler tactic: just wave everything
through. This had the advantage of making it easier to meet the
weekly and monthly quotas for clearing transactions through
Deutsche's pipes. "The culture was to just close [complete] the
transaction," another former employee explains.

All of this meant there were few restraints on ambitious,

envelope-pushing traders like Wiswell. On a couple of occasions in 2012 and 2013, someone in London inquired about why all these strange Russian trades were appearing on the bank's ledgers. Vague assurances came back from Moscow—by now under the leadership of a Russian economist whose previous employer had also been implicated in money laundering—but they didn't shed any light on the identities of the customers or the purposes of the transactions. Nobody asked follow-up questions.[20]

CHAPTER 20

STRESS

n a lakeside Swiss village in August 2013, a few days before
Bill's retirement became official, Pierre Wauthier killed himself. His wife found him hanging inside a converted hotel in
which he lived with her and their two children. Wauthier,
fifty-three years old, was the chief financial officer of Zurich Insurance Group. His typed suicide note blamed the company's
chairman for putting him under unbearable pressure to boost
profits. The chairman was Joe Ackermann.[1]

After Putin's job offer fell through, Ackermann had arrived at
Zurich Insurance to lead the company's board of directors. It
didn't take long for him and Wauthier to begin feuding over
Zurich's finances. Ackermann, of course, was not a man who
liked to be disappointed. And the company's numbers—especially
its all-important return on equity, the same metric that Ackermann had obsessed over at Deutsche—were sagging. Wauthier
had been on the receiving end of Ackermann's tirades.

A few days after Wauthier committed suicide, Ackermann resigned from the insurance company's board. "I have reasons to
believe that the family is of the opinion that I should take my
share of responsibility, as unfounded as any allegations might

be," he explained.* Broeksmit and some of his friends knew Wauthier from when he had worked at JPMorgan. Emailing with each other, they discussed the tragedy. "Ackermann does [not] look too good in this," Flavio Bartmann wrote to the group.

Broeksmit's last day of work was August 31. "There was really no logical next step for me at DB after board appointment fell thru, which is fine," he explained to Val in an email, referring to the ill-fated chief risk officer job. "I lasted a lot longer than I thought I would." Two months later, Jain hosted a small lunch in Broeksmit's honor in a dining suite in the bank's London head-quarters. About a dozen people attended. As the bankers ate a light three-course meal—salad, lamb, and fruit—Jain gave a little speech, toasting Broeksmit for his hard work.

Bill turned fifty-eight that fall. He and Alla intended to stay in London for at least another year. They made plans to tour South Africa and Iran the following spring. He tried to learn French, enrolled in a writing class, and prepared to get his British driver's license. He experimented in the kitchen, engineering recipes the way he used to engineer derivatives. And he found himself drinking more and more, because it was something to do.

At Thanksgiving, Bill and Alla flew to New York. Broeksmit had lunch with a former Deutsche colleague, Saman Majd, who was now a professor at Yale. Broeksmit complained that he missed his job, the markets, the adrenaline, the intellectual challenge. "How do you manage it?" he asked Majd about retirement. Majd said he had discovered fulfillment in academia. He suggested that Bill find something new to engage his mind.

---

* Three years later, Wauthier's old boss at Zurich Insurance also committed suicide.

Broeksmit, though, remained immersed in his DBTCA work, unable to step away. Once a month, he flew to New York to participate in board meetings; he could have phoned in, but that struck Bill as irresponsible.

There were so many problems. It struck Broeksmit that while nobody in Europe was paying attention to what this subsidiary was doing, DBTCA also didn't have much of its own senior staff. Broeksmit pushed for DBTCA to hire a chief financial officer—not a crazy idea for a company with tens of billions of dollars of assets coursing through it—and for an internal investigation into why on earth DBTCA had been making complex, poorly documented loans to other Deutsche entities around the world. "I know this won't be a popular suggestion but perhaps we need a more radical break from the past than so far proposed," he emailed Jack Brand. In fact, Brand was trying to recruit more staff, but it was hard to find high-quality people who were palatable to his German bosses. At one point, he was hoping to hire a former FBI agent or prosecutor to be in charge of preventing financial crime. He presented a few promising candidates. The response came back from Frankfurt that none were acceptable because they didn't speak German. The job ultimately went to a German speaker who lasted six months before being pushed out.[2] And the CFO position that Broeksmit had lobbied for never got filled.

Brand had moved quickly to build relationships with officials at the Federal Reserve, seeking to quell their concerns but also to protect himself should things go south. He explained to the Fed over and over that his superiors in London and Frankfurt didn't seem to be taking seriously the urgent need to expand the ranks of compliance, legal, finance, and tech staffers. Sometimes he invited the Fed to come to internal meetings when he knew a senior executive was visiting from Frankfurt. (The presence of powerful regulators at a closed-door meeting tended to serve as a helpful wake-up call for the German guests.) Brand figured the Fed would exert pressure on Deutsche, and that would help him accomplish things that were in the bank's long-term interests, even if the bank didn't realize it.

In September 2013, the Fed reported the results of an intensive on-site examination of DBTCA. The bank's systems were the "worst of our peers," a DBTCA official emailed board members, recounting the dressing down they had just received from the Fed. "Every key area has issues," the bank had "missed big time" when trying to address its deficiencies, and the problems the Fed had identified "are just scratching the surface." The central bank soon downgraded a crucial rating that governed how much money DBTCA could borrow from the central bank. It was a bad sign.

Broeksmit feared that more problems lurked ahead. "I am still tangled up in DB legacy matters," he emailed his long-ago Merrill colleague John Breit. The Fed conducted periodic stress tests on the companies it regulated, and Broeksmit thought that DBTCA wasn't taking the exams seriously. He repeatedly told his colleagues in the bank's newly created "Center of Excellence"— established to overcome a history of governance that was less than excellent—that the simulations they were running were far too mild, that it looked like the bank was cherry-picking favorable data while ignoring figures that would raise uncomfortable questions. "Bottom line: I think we should be more conservative," he wrote. Some of Bill's colleagues sensed his mounting discomfort. "It really bothered him that everything he'd helped build"— namely, the bank's Wall Street business—"became the root cause of so many problems," a fellow DBTCA board member would explain. Broeksmit felt he was being forced into defending an institution that he no longer believed in.

One afternoon in December, Bill arranged to see his old Deutsche partner Martin Loat. Bill showed up at Gail's coffee shop in Chelsea, sweating in his gym clothes. The two men sat in the crowded café and reminisced about old times. Loat had been out of the banking industry for a decade now, ever since he quit in frustration with Ackermann, and he told Broeksmit that he had pared down his life. He lived in a smallish house by the River Thames—or at least it was small compared to the Belgravia mansion he'd previously occupied. He spent his time jogging, skiing, and going to pub quizzes (trivia nights) with his mates. "All the simple things," Loat explained. He tried to get Broeksmit enthusiastic about this new phase of his life, but his former co-worker was still dwelling on Deutsche. He asked Martin about that time, many years earlier, when Bill had advised him to cancel the derivatives deal with the confused client and then had relayed to him Reverend Jack's lesson: Do right by others, be honest with them and treat them ethically, and things will work out in the end. Loat got the clear impression that Broeksmit was now wrestling with the same sort of problem at Deutsche— sketchy derivatives, big losses, an ethical morass. He asked Bill what was going on, but he demurred. Loat could tell that his friend was deeply troubled, but he didn't push. After a few quiet moments, Bill changed the topic, and Martin let the conversation move on.

Before Christmas, Bill and Alla flew from London to Virgin Gorda in the Caribbean. After a few days at the Little Dix Bay resort with their daughters—during which Bill phoned in to a DBTCA board meeting to discuss the bank's escalating problems with the Fed—they joined Bill's close friend and Wall Street veteran Michael Morandi on his forty-seven-foot sailboat. They swam, snorkeled, drank cocktails, smoked, ran out of cigarettes, searched the boat's ashtrays for half-smoked butts, and drank some more. When it was time to go, Bill and Alla sailed to the airport across choppy waters. Broeksmit, ruinously hung over, got sick. "Took several hours of being on land to regain my equilibrium," he later emailed a friend.

When they returned to London, a DHL package was waiting for Bill at the Evelyn Gardens apartment. Inside was a thick stack of Deutsche documents, largely about how to pacify the Fed, sent to Bill in advance of an all-day DBTCA board meeting scheduled for the last week of January in New York. Bill and Alla both planned to make the trip. Beyond the DBTCA gathering, Broeksmit had some other business to attend to in New York. He told Alla that he was scheduled to sit down with federal officials— he didn't specify which ones, and she didn't ask. Broeksmit also had arranged to meet with his personal lawyers to sign an updated will.

In Italy, the collapse of Monte dei Paschi shook confidence in the rest of the country's banking sector, and the government prepared to bail out other banks. Deutsche had recently reached a private settlement with the people responsible for winding down what was left of Paschi—essentially Deutsche's way of apologizing for helping torpedo the world's oldest bank. But even with that civil matter resolved, criminal investigations into the bank and its employees were under way. Michele Faissola would be among those charged with aiding the Italian bank as it deceived investors and regulators about its finances.

BaFin prepared to open an investigation into whether Deutsche helped Paschi conceal losses. The inquiry, led by an outside law firm, was scheduled to begin on Monday, January 27, 2014.[3]

On Friday, January 24, Anshu was in the Swiss ski village of Davos. The annual meeting of the World Economic Forum—where the world's most important and self-important people gather each year to admire each other under the guise of making the world a better place—was in full swing. Among its longtime skeptics was Broeksmit. "That's where the world's great issues are really solved, with the aid of alcohol and unburdened of opposing viewpoints," he had snarked in an email to his friends several months earlier.

Jain, though, was in his element. Like other captains of industry and finance, he packed scores of meetings into each day, with enough time left over to hold forth on weighty matters in front of captive audiences and TV cameras. At one point, he and other bank CEOs met with Mark Carney, the governor of the Bank of England, who privately chastised them for continuously getting in trouble with the authorities. Jain made some small waves by urging Carney and his fellow regulators to back off.[4]

That same day, Anshu and his wife, Geetika, were at an event when they spotted Ackermann across the room. He had been their nemesis, the one thing standing between Jain and the throne he deserved. Now Ackermann was waving at them. Anshu and Geetika walked over and greeted him. They told him he looked great—had he lost weight?—and invited him to stop by a party Deutsche was throwing that evening.

The festivities took place at the Belvédère Hotel, a once-grand lodge that had snipers stationed on the roof to protect dignitaries during the World Economic Forum. The venue for the bank's party was a windowless room that normally housed a swimming pool. The lights were low, music was pulsing, and waiters milled through the crowd with trays of refreshments. This night, the pool had been covered up with temporary flooring, and partygoers had no idea that an inch or two of carpeted plywood was all that stood between them and several feet of chlorinated water. The pool might have been invisible, but it created a muggy atmosphere, Deutsche's festive facade failing to conceal the murk below. Bald men's heads shined with sweat.

Jain and Jürgen Fitschen worked the room, greeting the mostly German clients. Their goal was more than just making their customers feel loved. They also were trying to make a statement about their ability to work together; rumors had been circulating in the German media that Jain was trying to oust Fitschen and be the sole man atop Deutsche. Anshu, who had struggled so mightily to win over the German establishment, had help this evening: Geetika was cosmopolitan, charismatic, and attractive. Good at chitchat, wowing strangers with tales of her adventures as a travel writer, she humanized her husband.

To the Jains' surprise, Ackermann made an appearance at the party. Maybe it was the fact that he'd been chastened by the Zurich Insurance disaster, but he seemed to have mellowed. The two rivals spoke wistfully about their years together at the bank, breezing past their recent acrimony.

The party ran into the early hours of Saturday morning. The alcohol kept flowing, and Anshu and Jürgen draped their arms around each other's shoulders in a public display of camaraderie. In this small Alpine town, far away from the daily drumbeat of awful news, it seemed like a fine moment for Deutsche Bank—its leaders united (and perhaps drunk), its clients happy, its future bright.

A few hundred miles to the northwest, Bill and Alla went out to dinner in London. Afterward, lying in bed together, they had a quiet talk. "How could we be more happy than we are right now?" Bill asked rhetorically. "We're so lucky." Then, for the final time, he fell asleep.

PART II

CHAPTER 21

VALENTIN

Thirty-eight years earlier, in the Ukrainian capital of Kiev, a boy named Valentin was born to Alla and Alexander Cherednichenko. They were a young couple, Alla only eighteen. She dreamed of becoming a painter, but she was Jewish, and Ukraine in the 1970s was an inhospitable place for both artists and Jews. State-sanctioned persecution of anyone with an intellectual bent was rampant. Memories of the Holocaust tormented Alla's parents, who feared that one day the Nazis—or others like them—would stomp through the streets of Kiev. After graduating from the Moscow College of Agriculture in 1977, Alla obtained exit visas for herself, Alexander, her younger sister, her mother, and the toddler Valentin.

Their first stop was Vienna, where they stayed for a couple of months. Alla was twenty, and it was her first time outside the Soviet Union. Next they went to Rome, where they awaited visas to the United States. When their immigration papers came, the family set out for Chicago in 1979. The city was home to a growing population of Soviet Jewish refugees—roughly 2,000 arrived there between 1973 and 1978.[1] "It can be called a mass exodus," the head of the Jewish Community Centers of Chicago told a local newspaper, a few months before the Cherednichenko family arrived.[2]

Valentin picked up two languages: Russian from his parents, English from the television. The marriage frayed, and by 1982, Alla and Alexander had split up. Valentin—known in America as Val—went to live with his father. One hot day in May 1982, the Cook County Juvenile Court took custody of Val. "The minor is neglected in that the minor's parent does not provide the care necessary for the minor's well-being," a court filing stated, citing "the mental and/or physical disability of the parent."[3] Court officers tried and failed to track down Alla[4] and Val was dispatched to a foster family in the suburbs outside Chicago.

On occasion, Val was driven to a social worker's office, where Alexander and Alla—who by then had learned of her son's whereabouts—could come to see him. His mother visited every couple of weeks. His father stopped by once in a while to play board games. But the intervals between his visits grew longer and longer until Val realized that he hadn't seen his father in months and probably never would again.

Val spent the next three years drifting through the Cook County foster-care system. His mother met Bill Broeksmit, married him, and moved to New Jersey. More than a year later, around Thanksgiving 1985, an Illinois judge granted Alla custody of her son, by now nine years old. Bill legally adopted Val. "You're now a Broeksmit," Alla explained to the boy.

Three years later, Bill and Alla had Alessa. Three years after that, Katarina was born.

Val was a troubled, angry boy. He disrupted class and disrespected authority figures. Bill tried to bond, sometimes bringing him to the Merrill trading floor. To a twelve-year-old boy, the place was overwhelming: a frenzied hive of shouting, jostling guys working multiple phone lines, a digital ticker tape snaking around the cavernous room. Broeksmit introduced colleagues to his son. "Oh, I can see the resemblance," one trader remarked. Bill and Val looked at each other and chuckled. "It's an inside joke," Broeksmit assured the confused employee. But Bill's face lit up around his daughters, and friends and colleagues noticed a comparative lack of warmth toward Val. "Your dad's not your real dad!" became a common taunt that friends hurled at Val when they were squabbling.

When Val was thirteen, he was sent to board at the Dublin School in New Hampshire. He felt he was once more being ejected from his family, and he acted out. Before long, he was expelled for smoking cigarettes and being caught with weed in his room.

Val often asked why he'd been put in foster care, but he never received a satisfactory response. His grandmother—Alla's mom—told him that his birth father was a drunk and a druggie and that's why he had vanished.

Neither Bill nor Alla knew quite what to do with their wayward son, whose only passion and source of solace was music. After his expulsion from the Dublin School, they eventually sent Val to another, tougher boarding school, Idaho's Rocky Mountain Academy, where he would spend his junior and senior years of high school. RMA was an experimental, cult-like operation, in vogue for rich parents struggling with hard-to-tame offspring. The school put its charges to work chopping wood and performing other manual labor, often in unpleasant conditions. Those who didn't bend were subjected to sleep deprivation and freezing nights in tepees.[5]

One of Val's classmates was a sixteen-year-old Texan named Jonathan Avila. He was a dork, and tormenting him became a popular pastime for Val and his peers. One day in 1994, Avila used a belt to hang himself from a pipe in a dorm room. A student giving a tour to parents discovered his dangling body.[6] Val never got over the feeling that he had played a part in pushing the boy over the edge. Over the years, he would wonder to himself about Avila. How must he have felt as he looped that belt around his neck? How desperate, how hopeless must he have been?

When Val went to Albright College in Pennsylvania, his misbehavior intensified. He was the one egging everyone on to find some coke at three o'clock in the morning. He went out of his way to thumb his nose at whoever was in charge, teaching his friends the maxim he lived by: that it is better to ask for forgiveness than permission. Once he coaxed some of his buddies to join him in a middle-of-the-night heist. They sneaked into the college's unlocked music room and swiped a bunch of electronics, including a dozen microphones and some recording equipment. The supplies would be useful for Val, who was the leader of a band he called the Good Time Charlies. He explained to his friends that it was the college's fault for not properly securing the equipment. "I thought it was pretty badass," remembers a conspirator, Matt Goldsborough. They never got caught.

After graduating from Albright in 1999, Val moved to New

York and took film and TV production classes. His parents bankrolled his education, but his relationship with them was a source of gnawing discomfort, and Val remained on the outskirts of the Broeksmit family. (Many of Bill's colleagues knew he had two daughters but didn't realize he had a son.) Bill, with his gift for seeing things through other people's eyes, at least tried to understand Val's rebelliousness. Val told friends that he felt like he had been a burden to his mother ever since she fled Ukraine with a toddler in tow.

Val bounced between odd jobs. He did some web programming. His obsession remained music. The Good Time Charlies became Bikini Robot Army. (The name had something to do with humans' attempts to assign meaning and individuality to stuff that's meaningless and common—like dressing a robot in a bikini.) The band was basically Val and those he was jamming with at that moment. He was a talented musician and songwriter, tapping his deep well of painful memories for inspiration. The result was mournful, angry, beautiful guitar or piano ballads like "Hey Momma," which he wrote in 2002, around the time that Joe Ackermann became Deutsche's CEO.

Maybe you think it's better to be the fool?
I've tried acting cool.
I've tried acting cruel.

Aren't creatures like you supposed to rattle before you strike?
I'm too tired to fight,
I'm too tired tonight.

Hey momma
Don't you love your only son?
Hey momma?
Come and see your lovely son. . . .

Aren't you ever gonna come by and see?
What's happening with me,
What happened to me.

Val possessed a manic charisma, and he charmed his way into recording studios and meetings with music-industry professionals. His catalogue of songs expanded. He got gigs. "It's less lonely with an audience," he would say.

In 2008, before performing at Irving Plaza in Manhattan, he met a cute British woman selling merchandise out front. Her name was Jenny. They started dating and, on a whim, moved to London, renting a two-bedroom flat in Kentish Town, a hipster enclave in the northern part of the city. Val was back in the same town as his parents—Bill had just rejoined Deutsche. He saw them monthly, and they paid his rent and distributed about $30,000 a year to him in spending money. Bill never seemed thrilled with the setup. "You're nuts. Earn some money," he snapped when Val requested that his monthly stipend increase by $1,800. Well into his thirties, Val had rarely held a steady job, although he earned money with irregular performances. He did a lot of drugs. Tall and thin, he sported an unkempt beard, and while his shoulder-length hair was mangy on the sides, the top of his head was as bald as a coot's. "He looked like a right tramp," one British friend recalls.

One night in 2011, Val went to a party at a friend's house. A redheaded Welsh woman named Beth spotted him holding court across the room. There was something magnetic about him. She walked over, and they started talking, and Beth was captivated. Soon Jenny was out of the picture, and Beth moved into Val's Kentish Town apartment.

"Want to go see some tennis?" Bill asked Val in June 2013. "Just you and me. No girls." They took a train to Wimbledon. They roamed from grass court to grass court, doing as much people-watching as tennis-spectating. They posed for a photo together outside the entrance to the All England Lawn Tennis & Croquet Club, a study in contrasts: Bill, in a blue button-down shirt tucked into his khakis, his graying hair neatly trimmed, a slight smile parting his lips; Val, a few inches taller, in brown-tinted sunglasses and a faded San Francisco Giants hat, wearing a half-buttoned denim shirt that exposed his chest, his bearded face projecting too-cool-for-school detachment. The two men stood side by side, not touching each other.

Six months later, on December 15, Val and Beth met his parents for an early holiday dinner, as Bill and Alla would soon be going on vacation for a couple of weeks. At the end of the meal, as a gospel choir sang in the restaurant, Bill hugged Val and handed him a holiday card with a short note: "Enjoy the holidays

here and we'll see you in January." The front of the card featured
a picture of Daisy, drawn by Alla. The entire card was blue and
white, except for the red of the dog's leash.

CHAPTER 22

LIFE EXTINCT

On the morning of January 26, 2014, Bill got himself out of bed and pulled on jeans and a button-down shirt. Rain was falling, and the water dripped down his flat's windowpanes, warping his view of the world outside. He and Alla had a Sunday routine of going to a local café, but Bill said he wasn't in the mood. Around 11:45 A.M., Alla stalked out of the apartment, miffed that she was going alone. The heavy outer door of their brick building clicked, the latch locking, as she stepped into the drizzle.

Alla and Bill were scheduled to meet Val at a restaurant in the nearby Saatchi Gallery for brunch in a little more than an hour. Bill placed seven handwritten letters in Daisy's bed. The off-white envelopes stood out on the colorful dog cushion. He took Daisy's red leash. He attached one end to the handle on the apartment's tall French doors. He arced the leash over the top of one door. Bill cinched the other end around his neck, made sure it was secure, and lunged forward.

Around 12:25, Alla returned from the café. She climbed the two flights of stairs and opened the door to flat 4. They had a few minutes before they had to set out to meet Val. She walked into the apartment. Bill was hanging from the leash, unconscious. She dialed 999.* The dispatcher told her help was on its way.

Alla raced into the kitchen and grabbed a knife to cut Bill down and sliced the leash. Alla tried CPR, but nothing happened.

Paramedics from the London Ambulance Service arrived at 12:31, three minutes after they'd received radio calls from their dispatcher. Alla was crouched over Bill, still trying CPR.

An EMT removed the leash from Bill's neck, checking his breathing and his pulse. There was no sign of either. Another paramedic clamped on a neck brace, inserted a tube into Bill's throat to open his obstructed airway, and started pumping in oxygen. They hooked up an IV and poured adrenaline into Bill's bloodstream. Someone radioed for a helicopter ambulance.

It was too late. At one o'clock, the emergency responders pronounced Bill "life extinct." Alla stammered that he had been depressed and was taking heart medication. Ten minutes later, as the paramedics packed their equipment, Val arrived from the Taschen bookstore.

* Britain's version of 911.

CHAPTER 23

EVERYTHING IS UPSIDE DOWN

O n a coffee table in the apartment's family room was a copy of Bill's recently revised will—which was supposed to be signed in the presence of his lawyers in New York in a couple of days—and an inch-thick stack of paperwork, the Deutsche Bank documents that had recently been delivered by DHL. Val thumbed through the papers. The acronym DBTCA kept popping up. He had no idea what it stood for.

Someone found the letters in Daisy's bed: one each for Alla, Alessa, Katarina, Val, Mom, Anshu, and Michael Morandi, their names written on the envelopes in black ink. Val opened his. Inside was a sheet of white printer paper.

Dear Val,

I am so sorry I was such a cold father. You are a warm-hearted, witty young man and a loving brother to your sisters and a loving son.

All of my friends enjoy your company and you have always had lovely girlfriends. You are a credit to the name I gave you and then disgraced.

Dad

Val stuffed the letter back into its envelope. The words didn't sink in.

The paramedics told Val that the police would be arriving soon. Instinctively distrustful of the cops, Val snapped some pictures of the awful scene with his iPhone. He asked his mother who to call for help; did the family have a lawyer? "Call Michele," Alla managed. Val fished his father's cell phone out of his pants pocket, looked up Michele Faissola, and dialed. "This is Val, William's son," he said, trying to sound calm. "We need your help. My dad is dead." Faissola, who lived nearby, rushed over.

The police arrived and inspected the suicide notes. "Val, is this your father's handwriting?" an officer asked, beckoning to him to look at one of the notes. Reading the four-sentence note Bill had left for him had pushed Val to the brink; there was no way he was about to inflict additional readings on himself. "I can't look at them," he protested. The cop told him he had to, and he placed one of the letters in Val's hands. Val glanced, burst into tears, and confirmed that the handwriting was his father's. Then the officer handed him the next note. Val turned away. "Just push on," the cop urged. "You don't have to read every sentence." He peeked at each note and confirmed his father had written them. He didn't read the words. The only thing Val processed was that the letter to his mother, written on checkered graphing paper, ran page after page after page. The notes to his sisters were on fancy greeting cards. And the short note to Anshu Jain was on the same plain printer paper that Val's was written on.

Beth had spent the weekend in Wales for her mother's birthday. She was on a bus back to London, quietly fuming about her unreliable boyfriend, who hadn't responded to her many text messages that afternoon. Finally a text arrived: "My dad is dead." Beth figured Val must have gotten word that his long-lost birth father had passed away. She called Val and heard that no, it was Bill who was dead. It didn't make sense—he had seemed so happy the last time she'd seen him, gossiping about pop music at the dinner while the gospel choir sang in the background. Beth wept for the rest of the ride.

Back in London, she went to their flat, packed an overnight bag, and took a taxi to Evelyn Gardens. Val was waiting for her in the building's arched white entryway. Shell-shocked, he didn't utter a word. Beth embraced him. By then the police were gone, and the coroner had removed Bill's body. A sad, stunned silence blanketed the apartment. Faissola's wife, Maria, came over to take care of Alla. The Broeksmits occupied two adjoining flats in the building, one serving as the living area and the other, across the hall, functioning as Bill's office suite. Faissola and Val went into the office. "Is this your dad's computer?" Faissola asked. "Can I check some things?" Val watched over Faissola's shoulder as he rummaged through the Apple desktop.*

That evening, Val and Beth went into the office flat to sleep on a foldout couch. Val's brain was churning, flitting from one half-crazed thought to another. Why had his father hung himself with Daisy's leash and placed the suicide notes in her dog bed? Was it a clue? Was it supposed to symbolize something? Was it just because he loved his dog? His mind flashed back to watching a TV prison drama with his father years earlier. An inmate hung himself from a door handle, and Val now remembered discussing whether it was really possible to do that; the answer, they concluded after a brief physics discourse, was yes, it was actually pretty easy; you could suffocate while kneeling. Val shuddered.

Alone with Beth in Bill's office, Val rifled through his father's

---

* This is Val's recollection, corroborated by another person who said they witnessed it. Faissola vehemently denies touching Bill's computer.

computer. The machine, which Bill had used to log into Deutsche's secure computer network, was stashed with two decades of Bill's personal and work files. His Yahoo and Gmail accounts were signed in, and Val started looking for secrets that might explain his father's unfathomable act. Did he have another family? Was he deep in debt? As he perused the emails, Val saw that Bill had been forwarding huge quantities—hundreds, it looked like—of Deutsche Bank emails to his personal accounts. And since his retirement a few months earlier, he had been using his Yahoo account to receive and send messages about his ongoing work on DBTCA's oversight board. Even as Val wandered through the computer, one final Deutsche email arrived at 8:42 P.M. There was a DBTCA board meeting scheduled for the following week, and the bank's corporate secretary wanted to inform Bill that there had been some delays in delivering materials beforehand. The paperwork would be waiting for him at his Park Avenue apartment in New York, the message said.

None of this meant anything to Val. He swallowed a handful of morphine and Xanax pills and tried to sleep.

Michael Morandi flew in overnight to deal with everything. He helped Anshu draft an email informing Deutsche's entire staff about Bill's death. The message went out under Jain and Jürgen Fitschen's names. "It is our sad duty to inform you that our former colleague, Bill Broeksmit, 58, died on Sunday at his home in London," they wrote. They described Broeksmit as having been "instrumental as a founder of our investment bank. . . . He was considered by many of his peers to be among the finest minds in the fields of risk and capital management."

The bank dispatched a beefy security man to the Broeksmit flat. Reporters, photographers, and cameramen had set up outside—it was the latest banker suicide, more evidence of the rot inside London's financial sector and within one of the world's largest and most troubled banks, and it was especially lurid because Bill had been one of Anshu's closest confidants. And someone needed to stand guard.

Deutsche was notorious for its aggressive efforts to control the media. Some of the bank's spokespeople and executives had earned reputations for lying. The penchant for secrecy was so intense that when the bank handed out documents to board members, each piece of paper was embedded with a hidden code—perhaps a slightly different dollar amount in one paragraph or a different date at the top of the document—so that the bank could trace the leak if the materials ended up in the media's hands. Now Deutsche deployed these tactics in an attempt to sway the coverage of Bill's suicide. The first priority was to try to tamp down media interest. The bank sent a public relations person to counsel the family on how to handle the flood of inbound media inquiries. The simple advice: say nothing. Deutsche's spin doctors argued to journalists that his death had nothing at all to do with his time at the bank—a claim they couldn't possibly make with any credibility so soon after his death.

Notwithstanding those efforts, details about the suicide soon started trickling out. The German media learned that one of Bill's suicide notes was to Anshu. Rumors swirled that the note was similar in tone to the one Pierre Wauthier had left blaming Joe Ackermann at Zurich Insurance. When reporters called the bank's PR people to see if any of this was true, they grudgingly confirmed that Anshu had received a letter—but they insisted that it was innocuous. "It was a friendly note," one of them said, claiming to have seen it firsthand.[1]

Family members, friends, and former colleagues paraded through Bill and Alla's flat, bringing copious quantities of food and booze. "Everything's upside down and sideways right now,"

Val emailed his ex-girlfriend, Jenny. He wanted to walk around the block a dozen times and clear his head, to chain-smoke some cigarettes, to get away from all these friends and relatives whom he didn't really know but who nonetheless claimed to share his sadness and anger and confusion. But Alla forbade Val from leaving—he looked like a homeless man, and the pack of journalists outside the flat was certain to pounce on her loose-cannon son if he emerged from the building. Val grew so desperate that he cooked up an excuse that he figured would appeal to his mother: He wanted to get a haircut and clean himself up. The ruse backfired. Alla's hairdresser was summoned to the flat. Val sat at his father's desk and got pampered.

That afternoon, the bank's security man downstairs admitted into the apartment a skinny tech guy that Deutsche had sent over. His assignment was to copy the contents of Bill's computer onto portable hard drives. Val logged him on and watched him work. After Faissola, this was the second person from Deutsche to show interest in Bill's computer. Val wondered if there was something on there that the bank was worried about. (Unbeknownst to Val, Michael Morandi had invited the bank to send someone over to preserve the computer's contents.) Val thought it would be prudent to make sure he and his family maintained their access to his father's electronic files. On the computer, he found a list of passwords for all of Bill's email, financial, and other digital accounts. He jotted them down on a piece of paper.

The media soon moved on, and it became safe for Val to venture outside. Back in his own apartment, he lay in bed, exhausted but unable to sleep. Whenever he shut his eyes, he saw his father on the floor, covered by a white bedsheet, a tube jutting out of his mouth, the neck brace angling his head. He wondered if he'd ever be able to wash that image away. He gave up on sleep and opted for music. He turned on Sinéad O'Connor's "The Last Day of Our Acquaintance"—the same ballad that Bill had put on repeat after Edson's death. Now Val replicated the ritual, listening to the gloomy song over and over.

Anshu brought the note that Broeksmit had left him into Deutsche's offices. He showed it to the bank's deputy general counsel, Simon Dodds. Dodds read the short letter. He asked Jain what Bill had been referring to. "Damned if I know," Anshu said.

Dodds took the note and locked it in a safe.

Alla flew to New York, and Val followed a couple of days later, on the same plane as his father's coffin; someone needed to escort Bill on his final flight. At Heathrow, a border guard checked Val's passport and discovered that his visa had long since expired; he was in Britain illegally. The guard handed him a form stating that he was not welcome back—a bad start to a wretched journey. The Virgin Atlantic plane touched down at JFK shortly before ten P.M., and a hearse drove onto the tarmac to collect the coffin.

The memorial service was held on February 8. Hundreds of guests, bundled against the freezing wind, hurried into the red-brick Presbyterian church on Park Avenue. As they entered, each person was handed a laminated card with a picture of a smiling, suit-wearing Bill on one side, and on the other a famous Ralph Waldo Emerson poem about the meaning of a successful life. The church's long rows of wooden pews filled, and mourners crowded into the balconies.

Bill's brother Bob stood in the pulpit. He recounted the stories about Bill's subcontracting of his newspaper route and his insistence on picking up the tab for a relative's medical care. He talked about how Bill had hated to lose on the tennis court and how he had been "a force of nature in the kitchen." At Bob's behest, Val recited a few lines from scripture: "For we know that if the earthly tent we live in is destroyed, we have a building from God, a house not made with hands, eternal in heaven." Michael Morandi, in his eulogy, gestured to the full house and noted how Bill always had been uncomfortable in the spotlight. "If he's looking down on this assembly, he'd wonder what all the fuss is about," Morandi concluded.

Then it was Alla's turn. Through tears, she recited W. H. Auden's funereal poem "Stop All the Clocks."

Afterward, scores of people returned to the family's apartment to eat, drink, and tell stories. Poster-sized photos of Bill—on a lawn chair, reading the *Financial Times*, with Daisy crouched at his feet—were placed around the apartment. Jain, Faissola, and other Deutsche executives crowded in. One of the guests was Estelle, still heartbroken thirteen years after Edson's death. She approached Alla, and the two women hugged. Now they had both lost their men.

"They are together now," Alla whispered.

CHAPTER 24

NO REASON FOR CONCERN

A round the time of Broeksmit's death, a small lender in Cyprus, Hellenic Bank, got suspicious. Someone from Russia had set up accounts with Hellenic, and obscene sums of money were pouring in.[1]

That strange things were happening in Cyprus was not a shock. The island was a popular place for people with shady backgrounds to do their banking. Cyprus was part of both the European Union and the euro currency area, where government regulations were robust, so in theory, at least, Cyprus's financial system was safer than in many other parts of the world. Yet the country also tended to do the absolute minimum when it came to blocking illicit transactions. By design, that made it a go-to destination for Russians and others searching for somewhere to hide ill-gotten cash. Aside from its sunny weather, the laxity of its financial system and its integration into Europe were perhaps Cyprus's biggest selling points.

It took a lot to make a Cypriot banker queasy, but nearly $700 million had flooded into these particular Russian bank accounts in a short period of time, and that did the trick. Officials at Hellenic looked into where the money was coming from—a basic first step when conducting due diligence on such gigantic money flows—and saw that the source was Deutsche Bank. This should have been a reassuring sign. For all its problems, Deutsche was a mainstream, heavily regulated European financial institution—not the kind of dodgy outfit likely to be involved in brazen money laundering.

But there was a protocol for Hellenic to follow in such situations, and it called for the filing of a "request for assistance" with Deutsche in order to get more information on the unusual wire transfers. That request was submitted to Deutsche's London office, where the transactions had originated, in January 2014. It asked Deutsche to explain its relationship with the Russian customer and the purpose of the transfers, as well as whether Deutsche had "any reason to believe that the transactions . . . are in any way of a suspicious nature." Deutsche probably could have put the matter to rest with a quick response, but instead it ignored the query. The next month, Hellenic sent a reminder. That, too, received no answer. A third inquiry followed in March. This time, the request was routed to a different part of Deutsche, and someone there directed it to another office, and that office in turn forwarded it on to Tim Wiswell in Moscow.

Wiz knew all about these transactions. The Russian customer was participating in mirror trades with Deutsche to extract rubles from Russia and convert them into dollars, using Deutsche's U.S. operations—DBTCA—as a Laundromat. Then the dollars were being zapped over to Cyprus, where the Russian beneficiary could do with the money as he pleased—except for the fact that Hellenic had now grown suspicious.[2] Wiz needed to quell the concerns; otherwise Deutsche and its client would have to find another, less scrupulous destination for the freshly laundered funds. Wiz assured Hellenic that Deutsche had thoroughly vetted the customer and saw "no reason for concern here."[3]

Hellenic, however, was not satisfied. Apparently realizing that the money was being routed through the United States, which had a reputation for imposing crippling penalties on institutions that violated American law, it sent a final inquiry. This one went to a DBTCA employee in New York who was in charge of protecting against financial crime inside the bank. As Broeksmit had warned months earlier, DBTCA was so short-staffed that it didn't have its own chief financial officer or compliance team. And sure enough, the internal cop never responded or looked into the matter. He would later explain to regulators that he had been too busy and "had to deal with many things and had to prioritize."[4]

It wouldn't be until October 2014—after prodding from the Kremlin, which was trying to halt an exodus of cash from the country[5]—that Deutsche's headquarters would realize that there was a massive Russian money-laundering scheme operating out of its Moscow outpost, with a helping hand, perhaps unwitting, from the bank's London and New York offices.[6] A year after Hellenic Bank had first flagged the suspicious transactions, Deutsche alerted regulators in multiple countries to what it had uncovered. Government investigations were launched in the United States and Britain, and they eventually would find that Wiz's wife had offshore bank accounts with what looked like millions of dollars she had received from Russians, at least some of which had originated with the bank's mirror-trading clients and paid to her via DBTCA.[7] (Wiz also sometimes received bags of cash.[8]) Broeksmit's concerns about DBTCA's laxity were proving prescient.

For the better part of a year, Anshu had been publicly insisting that Deutsche had more than enough capital to protect it in the event of another financial crash. Few investors or regulators believed him, partly because the bank's shock absorbers were thinner than those of its peers and partly because the bank was still loaded with trillions of dollars of derivatives, which could go from valuable to valueless in a heartbeat. The drip-drip-drip of bad news and the constantly sinking stock price had made Deutsche's clients increasingly nervous, too. Banks rely on the faith of customers, investors, regulators, and other banks— otherwise everyone will pull their money out and the institution will quickly capsize—so this was a perilous situation.

While Jain projected confidence in public, he and his lieutenants acknowledged privately that they had a problem on their hands. Numbers didn't lie, and the bank's stock price was in the gutter; the market clearly lacked confidence in the bank's future. Anshu had a preferred solution to this mess: He wanted to get rid of Deutsche's retail-banking business in Germany. The country was notorious for having far too many banks with far too many branches (Deutsche itself had well over a thousand, thanks in part to Ackermann's acquisition of Postbank), and the competition drove profits into the ground. This was great for consumers, but not so great for bankers. Jain told Paul Achleitner, the chairman of the supervisory board, that they should jettison the business and return to Deutsche's old model. After all, in its original incarnation, the bank hadn't bothered with small-time retail customers, focusing instead on German exporters and multinational companies. "It's not in our DNA," Henry Ritchotte, still the bank's chief operating officer, explained to board members, hoping to win them over to this radical idea. But the plan was stillborn. There was no way Achleitner or the rest of Deutsche's board—stocked with labor representatives who were obligated to act on behalf of the bank's rank-and-file German employees—were going to bless a proposal that would result in many of those employees losing their jobs. Anshu's inner circle would later lament that they hadn't just announced their idea to the public unilaterally; that would have made it much harder for Achleitner and his boardroom colleagues to stand in their way.

Jain felt like everyone at Deutsche knew that he'd been thwarted. He thought a substantial majority of the bank's 100,000-plus employees hated him—whether because of his brown skin and inability to speak German, or because his preferred corporate strategy would have cost many of them their jobs. Geetika was sick of watching her husband being publicly pummeled and spending his evenings lamenting his failings; she urged him to quit. In March 2014, Anshu spent the long flight back to Europe from a Singapore business trip weighing his options. By the time the plane touched down in Frankfurt, he had made up his mind. He took Achleitner out to dinner and told the chairman that he had underestimated how hard this job would be and how little support he could count on from the bank's supervisory board and employees. Jain doubted the bank's current strategy would succeed. He thought he should resign.

Achleitner wasn't thrilled with Jain's performance thus far, but he knew that his abrupt departure could spark a devastating crisis of confidence. The chairman had long sensed in Anshu a deep well of insecurity, and so he pledged his support and begged him to stay. Jain, calmed by these reassurances, agreed to remain as co-CEO.

Bucked up with new confidence, Jain realized the time had come for the bank to start taking its medicine. In May 2014, he announced that Deutsche would issue eight billion euros (about $11 billion) worth of new shares. The infusion gave Deutsche a little breathing room, and Jain decided to use some of the outside money to accelerate growth in the United States and elsewhere. Some of Deutsche's board members questioned this decision, arguing to Jain and Achleitner that the money should be used to insulate the bank from future storms. The two men waved off such conservatism. Jain's plan was for Deutsche to be the only "universal bank" headquartered in Europe—a distinction that he believed would win it lots of business from European clients as well as overseas companies trying to do business on the continent. And so, while other crisis-scarred banks retreated, Deutsche cruised in the opposite direction. It was another big mistake.

All the while, government investigations into the bank were accelerating, and the cases threatened to become more than public embarrassments. Regulators and prosecutors, sick of being ridiculed as toothless (years of pip-squeak penalties having had no discernible effect on banks' conduct), were beginning to impose larger and larger fines on badly behaved banks. Fines of $10 billion or more were no longer out of the question. A penalty of that size was enough to wipe out nearly all of the capital that Deutsche had just raised.

The soon-to-be-launched investigations into Wiz's Russian money laundering were just one item on a growing list of threats. (Deutsche still hadn't discovered the separate Laundromat operation that predated the mirror-trading scheme.) In New York, regulators were finishing up a damning investigation into how the bank deliberately violated international sanctions by doing business with entities in Iran, Syria, Burma, Libya, and Sudan. (In 2015, the New York Department of Financial Services would fine Deutsche $258 million, require it to fire employees, and install an independent monitor inside the bank to try to prevent it from committing more crimes.[9])

In the Libor case, prosecutors and regulators in at least three countries had concluded that Deutsche was one of the worst offenders, with responsibility for the scandal up and down the corporate ladder. Penalties would surely stretch into the billions.

And in Washington, Bob Roach's Senate committee had just finished its tax-avoidance investigation, and the result was a scathing report spelling out how Deutsche had enabled giant hedge funds like Renaissance Technologies to avoid billions of dollars in federal taxes. Shortly before the report was published, the Broeksmit family got an unsettling heads-up from the bank: Bill might be mentioned in an unfavorable light. The moment the report was posted online, Val searched the document, and sure enough, his father was named eight times in the ninety-six-page report. The cameos were brief but important. Back in 2008, as Deutsche's lucrative work with Renaissance had intensified, Jain had dispatched Broeksmit to make sure everything was kosher. Bill had spent weeks trying to understand the byzantine structure that Deutsche's traders had erected for the hedge fund. He had eventually concluded that aside from some mild objections about the structures consuming too much of the bank's financial resources, there was nothing fundamentally wrong with the way the trades were being handled. But in a phone call with a colleague, Satish Ramakrishna, Broeksmit had been candid about the fact that the transactions were designed "for tax reasons." The bank recorded all calls over its phone systems, and this one was eventually discovered in the files that the Senate subpoenaed from Deutsche. This was a problem. The bank's defense was that the Renaissance trades had legitimate business purposes and weren't designed purely to avoid taxes.[10] A couple of senior executives had prepared extensive Senate testimony that was devoted largely to exhibiting those supposed non-tax rationales. But here was Broeksmit openly declaring what everyone knew but no one else had been honest or naive enough to say aloud.

Months before his death, Broeksmit had learned that Senate investigators were homing in on this recorded conversation. One late summer afternoon in 2013, attorneys from the law firm Paul, Weiss, Rifkind, Wharton & Garrison had been in London to interview him about the Renaissance trades. The goal of the meeting was to figure out what Bill knew and to get his take on the documents and recordings that the Senate investigators had obtained. The men sat at a wooden table so polished that Broeksmit could see his reflection in it. The lawyers told him that there was a chance he would have to go to Washington to be interviewed on Capitol Hill, perhaps under oath. Broeksmit was polite and forthcoming, but he struck the legal team as beaten down and world-weary. After the meeting, as the attorneys were in a Heathrow lounge awaiting their flight back to New York, Bill phoned one of them. He peppered the lawyer with questions about what he needed to do next. The way Broeksmit talked, he seemed to be bracing for a world of shit to land on him at any moment.

The Senate's report was unveiled with fanfare in July 2014, paired with congressional hearings—just as the co-head of Renaissance, Robert Mercer, was beginning to bankroll a series of right-wing initiatives, such as Breitbart News, aimed at upending the Western political order. Senator Carl Levin, the chairman of the investigations committee, convened the first public hearing at 9:30 one July morning in the Hart Senate Office Building. Levin and Roach had plotted lines of questioning with the witnesses. One of them was Deutsche's Satish Ramakrishna. Nearly four hours into the hearing, Ramakrishna claimed not to know much about the trades' tax-avoiding purpose. "Did you ever have a conversation with a man named Broeksmit?" Levin demanded. Ramakrishna acknowledged the phone call had taken place but insisted that Bill was merely observing that taxes were one of many reasons for the trades. Levin noted that just a minute earlier, Ramakrishna had maintained his ignorance about the tax rationale. Ramakrishna now acknowledged what the recorded phone call made plain—and what Deutsche had been so determined to deny. "He did say tax benefit was one of the benefits, yes," Ramakrishna conceded. "He knew as well as I did."[11]

It was the first public hint that Broeksmit might have been snared in a dangerous situation.

As all of this was unfolding, Deutsche executives were rushing to contain the damage. One day in May 2014, Colin Fan walked into a makeshift TV studio to record a video for the entire staff of the investment bank. Born in Beijing, raised in Canada, and educated at Harvard, Fan was a towering man with spiky black hair and such a young, chubby face that people regularly mistook him for being in his twenties. In fact, he was forty-one years old and, riding Anshu's coattails, had ascended to the top of Deutsche's investment-banking division. It was Fan's legions of envelope-pushing traders and salesmen who were responsible for many of the bank's current legal troubles. In case after case, his traders had been so cocky or clueless that they had committed their misconduct in writing, blabbing over email and in electronic chat rooms about exactly what they were doing, and why. If these guys had been just a little more careful, the bank might have avoided heaps of very expensive legal problems.

That was the point Fan decided to convey to his thousands of employees. "This is an important message," he began. "You need to pay close attention." He was wearing a purple tie and a black suit, and his hands were clasped behind his back as he stared into the camera. "You may not realize it, but right now, because of regulatory scrutiny, all your communications may be reviewed." The camera zoomed in for a tighter shot of Fan's face and shoulders. "Some of you are falling waaaaaay short of our established standards. Let's be clear: Our reputation is everything. Being boastful, indiscreet, and vulgar is not okay. It will have serious consequences for your career." He took a breath and continued in a calm, almost chirpy tone. "And I have lost patience on this issue. Communications that run even a small chance of being seen as unprofessional stop right now."

It might have been Fan's deadpan delivery, as if he were barely managing to suppress a smirk. Maybe it was his implicit admission that misconduct was rampant inside the investment bank. Or perhaps it was his focus on addressing communications about bad behavior, rather than the bad behavior itself. Whatever the case, when the video leaked online, it went viral.

As recriminations flew over who was to blame for all the trouble Deutsche found itself in, there were two distinct camps. In the bank's London and New York offices, the bogeymen were overzealous regulators and out-of-touch German executives and board members, the old Forces of Darkness whom Edson had railed against. Employees in Frankfurt had a different perspective. A malignant and fast-spreading Anglo-American investment-banking virus had infected the bank twenty years ago, and the disease had ravaged this once-healthy institution.

There was at least one other big problem looming for Deutsche. It was one that nobody knew about yet and that, even if someone had, would not have been easy to defuse or even control. The problem had a name: Val.

CHAPTER 25

THE FIRST LEAK

The front page of *The Wall Street Journal* on July 23, 2014, featured five articles: one each about Israel, Obamacare, Russia, cocktail-scented household cleaning supplies, and a certain German bank. "Fed Raps Deutsche Bank for Shoddy Reporting" was the headline in the newspaper's lower right corner. The *Journal* had obtained a letter sent to the bank months earlier by Daniel Muccia, a senior vice president at the Federal Reserve in New York, one of the people responsible for regulating Deutsche on a day-to-day basis. In the letter, excerpts of which the *Journal* posted online, Muccia blasted Deutsche for the problems in its U.S. arm, DBTCA. He accused the bank of producing financial reports that "are of low quality, inaccurate and unreliable. The size and breadth of errors strongly suggest that the firm's entire U.S. regulatory reporting structure requires wide-ranging remedial action." Muccia went on to warn that the shortcomings constitute a "systemic breakdown [and] expose the firm to significant operational risk and misstated regulatory reports."

In the parched lexicon of central bankers and regulators, understatements reign. Muccia's letter qualified as a fiery condemnation. It gave voice to more than a decade of mounting frustration inside the Fed about Deutsche's inability or unwillingness to fix its long-standing problems. The letter noted that examiners from the Fed had been complaining about this to Deutsche since 2002, yet the problems hadn't been addressed. If anything, they seemed to have worsened.

As a DBTCA board member, Broeksmit had witnessed first-hand the Fed's rising anger. In fact, this very letter had landed in his Yahoo email account about a month before he died. It was not a coincidence that it was now appearing on the cover of *The Wall Street Journal*.

A few days after his father's memorial service, Val had come to terms with the fact that his life was a mess. For years, he had been abusing painkillers, part of an unsuccessful strategy to suppress his inner misery. Getting opioids in America without a prescription was proving to be much harder than it had been in England. After Beth returned to London, Val sat down with his family to discuss his rehab options. Alla didn't exactly leap at the opportunity to foot the bill for a resort-quality withdrawal and recovery experience. She urged Val to hunker down for a few days at the cushy University Club, where he'd been staying on her dime, and try to snap his addictions. Val knew that such an unsupervised approach wouldn't work, and he eventually persuaded his mother to send him to rehab.

He started out in a facility in Palm Beach, Florida, but after a couple of weeks he got kicked out because he was unleashing his anger on patients and staff. Val by now had concluded that maybe rehab wasn't such a good idea after all, but his family arranged for him to be transferred to another outfit, Alta Mira, in the Sausalito foothills outside San Francisco. For $50,000 a month, residents lounged on the back patio, enjoying the soft Pacific breeze and a view of the Golden Gate Bridge, and dined on food prepared by gourmet chefs. Val felt like a prisoner.

That spring, Alla and Beth flew to San Francisco to participate in "family week" at Alta Mira. On walks with Beth around Sausalito, Val seethed with anger—especially toward his mother, who he felt had used her husband's death as an excuse to abandon her son once and for all, albeit in a luxe rehab joint. Val verbally attacked her, shredding some of the remaining threads tethering him to his family. Beth, too, said goodbye to Val and flew back to London, their relationship essentially over.

Early in the summer of 2014, Alla and her daughters scattered Bill's ashes. Val was devastated not to be invited. He wondered if his mother was icing him out because she was trying to hide something. It didn't occur to him that his behavior may have been the reason.

Val slowly burned off some of his anger and began opening up in group therapy sessions. He made friends with people who saw a sensitive, tortured soul. "He was a wounded little boy," says Sidney Davis. "He wanted to be loved by his mother." One day a new guest arrived: a middle-aged woman with blond hair, a guitar, and a dog. Val spotted her, alone and crying, on a concrete staircase that led up a hillside, and he sat down next to her. They spent two hours chain-smoking and talking. Her name was Margaret, and her marriage had just imploded. She was considering suicide. Val told her how his father had recently killed himself, and they grieved together about each other's misfortunes. She later told Val her real name: Pegi Young. She was an accomplished musician and the founder of the famed Bridge School in California, but she was best known as the soon-to-be-ex-wife of the rock star Neil Young. "Are you fucking kidding me?" Val asked. Listening to Pegi's description of her broken marriage, he knew he could never enjoy Neil Young's music again.

Pegi eventually left Alta Mira, and Val followed in July 2014. Warming to the role of surrogate mother, she helped him relocate to a "sober living" house in Strawberry Manor, a waterfront enclave north of San Francisco. Val spent his time stewing—about Beth, Bill, and Jonathan Avila, whose method of suicide was now linked in Val's mind with his father.

Val's roommate at the Strawberry Manor house was a twenty-two-year-old named Spencer. One afternoon he, Val, and another resident were sitting around chatting. Spencer excused himself and went to the bathroom. When he didn't return after a while, Val and his housemate went looking for him. They knocked on the bathroom door. Spencer didn't answer. They tried to open the door, but something had wedged it shut. Val kicked it in. Spencer was passed out on the floor, his face blue, overdosing. Someone called 911. Waiting for the paramedics to arrive, Val cradled Spencer's unconscious head, trying to keep him from choking on his vomit and wondering if this was going to be the second time this year he'd been in a room with a dead man. Fortunately, the paramedics managed to resuscitate him.

A drug overdose was simple. Val knew firsthand how easy it was to push things too far. What he couldn't understand—what continued to drive him crazy—is what had led his father to die. Despite the coldness Bill had acknowledged in his farewell note to Val, he had defended his son when others did not. His suicide had destabilized the family in a way that left Val, already the black sheep, on the road to being erased. He needed to know *why.*

There may have been a case for holding Deutsche Bank accountable and seeking financial compensation after Bill's years of tireless work. There were plenty of recent examples in the finance industry of wrongful-death lawsuits: In April 2014, a former senior executive at a big Dutch bank had murdered his wife and daughter before killing himself.[1] The prior year had brought Pierre Wauthier's suicide in Switzerland, as well as David Rossi's fall out of his Monte dei Paschi window. And there was a recent case in which an employee successfully sued Deutsche for workplace bullying, which might help make the case that the bank had not done enough to protect Bill. In the end, no lawsuit would be filed.

Before leaving London, Val had written down all of his father's computer passwords. Now he signed into his dad's Yahoo and Gmail accounts, wandering, more or less aimlessly, through thousands of messages. He hadn't given up hope that he would encounter evidence of a secret lover or crushing debts or some other awful secret that, while painful to confront, would reveal why his father felt he had no choice but to die. After a couple of days, though, Val concluded that even if such a clean explanation existed—and he was beginning to doubt it—it wouldn't be easy to find.

There were three main types of messages in Bill's email accounts. The first was personal stuff: years of detailed records of Bill's arranging dinners or vacations or trips to the Russian and Turkish Baths, bantering about finance or politics with friends and colleagues, and dealing with an enormous volume of logistics and financial management for his wife, children, and extended family. These were interesting to Val in a voyeuristic way, but they weren't enlightening.

The second category of emails was spam. Bill had been constantly bombarded with the usual offers of porn, magical weight-loss pills, surgical enlargements, and Republican National Committee fundraisers.

The final variety was stuff related to Deutsche, and this was the area to which Val started to devote most of his waking hours. Through process of elimination, he had begun to suspect that whatever had led his father to kill himself might have had something to do with his job. There must be something in those emails, Val figured; why else would Deutsche officials have poked around in Bill's computer right after his death? And the fact that one of his farewell notes was to Anshu, one of the world's most powerful bankers, added to Val's conviction that Deutsche had been on his mind when he decided to die. Val had glanced at Jain's letter when the police forced him to identify his father's handwriting, but he hadn't read the words.

Some of the Deutsche emails made sense to Val. It quickly became clear, for example, that Anshu had turned to Bill again and again to extinguish problems that were burning the bank. It was also obvious that Bill at times felt overwhelmed, concluding that banks of Deutsche's size were simply too big to manage. ("Hard to know how banks keep track of the hundreds of billions flowing through their pipes every day," Broeksmit wrote in one email to a friend.) And Val knew his father well enough to detect when he was angry, as he clearly was when he was scolding his DBTCA colleagues for their lackadaisical approach to the Fed's stress tests. But the overwhelming majority of the messages were incomprehensible, jammed with jargon, acronyms, and big numbers. Val needed guidance about what to search for and someone to translate what he found.

Five months earlier, I had contacted Val. I was part of a group in *The Wall Street Journal*'s London bureau that had set out to learn everything we could about the circumstances of Broeksmit's suicide. Gossip about his having been involved in government investigations and angry at Jain was making the rounds in the city's

banking circles. (Further piquing our curiosity was the grisly recent pattern of bankers killing themselves. Two days after Bill's
death, a JPMorgan worker in London jumped from the top of the
bank's Canary Wharf skyscraper.) Val maintained an active social
media presence, and I quickly found his email address. In early
February, nine days after Bill's death, I sent him a note asking to
speak with him for a potential story about his father. He responded
the next day: "What is it you want to know?" I told him that we
had heard that Broeksmit had expressed regrets about his time at
Deutsche and that I'd be happy to go into more detail over the
phone. Val asked me to leave his mother and sisters alone, and perhaps he would speak to me when things settled down. "Everyone
is very sad and grieving right now," he wrote.

After a couple of weeks of my pestering, Val grudgingly got on
the phone. It was the middle of the night in London and evening
in Florida, where Val had recently arrived to enroll in rehab. I
paced in my darkened apartment, my wife and infant son sleeping, as Val berated me for digging into his father's life. He was
rambling, and his speech was slurred; he didn't sound sober. He
insisted, falsely, that his family already knew the true reasons
Bill had killed himself and assured me that those reasons had
nothing to do with Deutsche. His message was that there was no
story here. The conversation ended with Val's agreeing to remain
available to answer questions and my promising to keep him ap-
prised about what we planned to write.

We kept in sporadic touch. He seemed to enjoy teasing me
with provocative messages, only to disappear without explaining
what he meant. "I think I know what happened," he emailed me
in March 2014, saying he would call me as soon as he could. He
didn't call, but a few days later, apropos of nothing, he emailed
me a low-resolution iPhone photo of a building on fire in downtown San Francisco, black smoke billowing across the cloudless

dusk sky. "Thought you reporters needed a pic," he wrote cryptically. (The photo, we figured out from data embedded in the file,
was taken on Alta Mira's back patio.) Over the next four months,
I periodically emailed and texted him, asking if he was ready to
talk. He rarely replied.

And then, on a Tuesday evening in mid-July, about two weeks
after Pegi Young had deposited him at the Strawberry Manor
house, Val sent me an email: "Are you still looking into deutsche?"
He explained that he had gained access to his father's work
emails. He said it looked like there was some interesting stuff,
but he didn't know what he was doing and there were thousands
of messages to sift through. Could I provide some keywords and
names to narrow his search?

My colleague Jenny Strasburg and I drew up a list of words,
phrases, and acronyms like "subpoena" and "DOJ" (Department
of Justice). Within a couple of hours, Val started sending me
items that his searches had turned up. There were exchanges between Bill and Anshu, memos about upcoming board meetings,
and emails with befuddling snippets like "persistent non-
arbitrageable price differential with a long-term drift with mean
zero." Some of this was interesting—journalists rarely get unvarnished peeks at the private communications of top corporate
executives—but nothing jumped out as newsworthy.

That changed at 1:33 in the morning of July 18. Val sent me an
item that he said included at least three of our search terms:
"BaFin," "subpoena," and "FRBNY." "Don't know what it
means," Val cautioned. I started skimming and realized it was
the very unhappy letter to Deutsche from the Fed's Daniel
Muccia. Given Deutsche's vast size, the Fed's discomfort had big
implications for investors, fellow banks, and just about anyone
who had a stake in the global financial system. Trying not to
show my excitement, I asked Val if he would be okay with my

writing a story about this document. I braced for a protracted negotiating session, but Val surprised me. "If you'd [like] to write a story and leave my dad out of it, that's cool," he answered. "Please don't tell anyone where you're getting this info."

Four days later, we published the story. "An examination by the Federal Reserve Bank of New York found that Deutsche Bank AG's giant U.S. operations suffer from a litany of serious problems, including shoddy financial reporting, inadequate auditing and oversight, and weak technology systems, according to documents reviewed by The Wall Street Journal," the first sentence read. Deutsche's already beaten-down stock tumbled 3 percent. Val read the article and contemplated the effect of his actions. He liked the feeling of having knocked more than $1 billion off Deutsche's market value—of having made a difference.

CHAPTER 26

THE NORTH KOREANS

On a cool, cloudy morning in October 2014, in a white-brick townhouse in the Bay Ridge neighborhood of Brooklyn, Calogero Gambino hung himself from a banister on his second-floor balcony.

Gambino, whom everyone knew as Charlie, was forty-one, the father of two young children. A lawyer, he had spent the past eleven years working in Deutsche Bank's New York offices. His title was associate general counsel, which meant he was one of the bank's top attorneys working on the multitude of investigations and other legal problems dogging the company. Gambino was popular with his colleagues. Some of them knew he suffered from depression and worried that he'd been pushing himself too hard; among other things, Gambino had been enmeshed in the Libor case, a topic he had discussed with Bill on at least a couple of occasions. Now, less than nine months after Broeksmit hung himself in London, Gambino had done so in New York. Despite Deutsche's staunch efforts to deny it—tearful public relations employees insisted that there was no way Gambino killed himself because of work issues, and they continued to assert that Broeksmit's suicide, too, was not connected to the bank—there was no avoiding the appearance of a deadly pattern.[1]

That's certainly how it looked to Val. As the high wore off from having planted a story on the front page of *The Wall Street Journal*, Gambino's death was the equivalent of another hit, giving Val the energy to push forward in his personal investigation into the reasons for his father's death. Solving that puzzle—or even being able to determine its outer boundaries—became Val's addiction. "Think of suicide as the most rational act a human can make," Val explained to me at one point. "Then work backwards from that. . . . Sure, it's an emotional act, which is why many get lost and explain it away as 'crazy' or 'unknowable.' But if you look at the reasoning, it makes sense. Unfortunately my father didn't leave a reason. But he left clues."

Those clues, though, were like hieroglyphics to Val. He found help on his iPhone, which came pre-installed with an app called iTunes U, which offered free university classes. Val downloaded an introductory finance course, taught by a Yale professor named John Geanakoplos. "Why study finance?" Geanakoplos asked in the first session. "It's to understand the financial system, which is really part of the economic system. . . . The language that you learn is the language that's spoken on Wall Street." Val binged on the classes. Before long, he could explain what a derivative was, at least in fuzzy terms. He grasped the concept of leverage. Finance was filled with jargon and acronyms, but they often served to obscure more than illuminate. Val called the curly-haired professor's classes his "finance decoder ring."

A few weeks after Gambino died, a shadowy group of hackers, calling themselves the Guardians of Peace, penetrated the computer systems of Sony Pictures, the giant movie studio. It was the work of North Korea, whose government was irate about Sony's planned release of a Seth Rogen comedy that depicted the assassination of Kim Jong Un. Sony raced to pull its entire global computer system offline, but it was too late. The hackers already had made off with a devastating cache of materials: hundreds of gigabytes of internal files, emails, and unreleased movies.

When Sony employees switched on their computers after the hack, they were greeted with a jarring image: A demonic red skeleton appeared under the heading "Hacked by #GOP." "We've obtained all your internal data," the warning from the Guardians of Peace read. "If you don't obey us, we'll release data shown below to the world." At the bottom of the image were links to a few different hacker websites.

The hack became public a few days before Thanksgiving 2014. Val—having dabbled in TV work and mingled over the years with film people—watched with fascination. "Amazing," he tweeted on November 24. "They shut down a massive studio with a keyboard and a bag of crisps!" He read a story about the hack that included a photo of the image and links that had flashed on Sony employees' screens. Out of curiosity, he typed one of the links into his browser. A bare-bones website came up, containing little more than a link to another page. Val clicked and then followed instructions to download a zip file (a compressed package of other files). Normally, this would be a reliable recipe for getting your computer infected with a virus, but Val lucked out. The files were filled with computer code, and at the bottom of one, Val found three words he understood: "For more information," it said, and then listed a few email addresses.

Val had spent the past forty-eight hours wondering: If Sony's computer systems were so porous, did other global corporations have similar vulnerabilities? Could this be a way to figure out what had been going on inside Deutsche? It was early evening, and Val was alone in the Strawberry Manor house. He typed a

message to one of the Guardians of Peace addresses: "I'm interesting [*sic*] in joining your GOP, but I'm afraid my computer
skills are sophomoric at best. If I can help in any other facility
please let me know."

Val doubted the hackers would reply, but a day or two later, an
email arrived with a primer on how to access Sony's stolen documents, which the hackers were preparing to release in the near
future. Val had been added to the hackers' email list—a feat that
had eluded many journalists who were covering the electronic
attack. On December 11, Val received another email from the
Guardians of Peace, this one with links to several anonymous
websites. Sony's internal materials were there for the taking. Val
started downloading the enormous files. While he was waiting
for the process to complete, he emailed the hackers: "Hey, you
guys ever thought about going after Deutsche Bank? Their [*sic*]
tons of evidence on their servers of worldwide fraud, some of it
even contributed to the very sad and tragic suicides of two of
their employees." Val knew the FBI was pursuing the Guardians
of Peace, and now he was encouraging them, in writing, to go
after another global company. He was relieved that the hackers
never responded.

Val meandered through the Sony files. In email after email,
executives trash-talked movie stars and discussed their studio's
budgets and upcoming films. Val took to Twitter, where his
Bikini Robot Army account had several thousand followers. He
posted screenshots of internal Sony documents and emails: deliberations over who—Martin Scorsese or Francis Ford Coppola—
might direct a planned remake of *Cleopatra*; Brad Pitt freaking
out about the edit of the World War II film *Fury*; a confidential
three-year schedule of Sony's planned movie releases. His tweets
reached larger and larger audiences as people shared them across
the social network.

Val was hardly the only one disseminating Sony's salacious materials, but his prolific postings set him apart. A week later, Sony's outside lawyer, the hyperaggressive David Boies, sent Twitter's general counsel a letter warning of legal action if it didn't shut down the @bikinirobotarmy account. Twitter forwarded the letter to Val, who received a similar missive from Sony's vice president for content protection. Sony warned it would "hold you responsible for any damage or loss" stemming from the materials he had published.

Val now had a choice. He could delete his fifty or so posts that contained Sony's materials. He could keep them up but stop tweeting new stuff. Or he could just thumb his nose at Sony and its fancy lawyers and keep posting materials. Val chose option 3—and then shared with me the lawyers' letters he had received. A few days before Christmas, the *Journal* published a story about Sony and David Boies threatening this random musician.

The article made Val a little famous. (The legal threats fizzled.) "What about freedom of speech? What about First Amendment rights?" an anchor on the Fox Business Network asked during an "exclusive" phone interview with Val. She invited him to describe Boies's letter, and Val, pacing in the backyard of the Strawberry Manor house, gave a creative rendition: "He said, 'Stop tweeting or we're going to come over and kill your hard drive and bury it underground and beat it with baseball bats.'" As Fox rolled footage of Val's Twitter feed, another anchor chimed in: "It seems like somebody's trying to make you the fall guy, doesn't it, Val?"

"A little bit, yeah!" he agreed.[2]

The lesson here for Val was powerful: The public had ravenous appetites for documents that exposed the inner workings of giant corporations. Spreading such materials seemed virtuous. And Val had plenty of stuff to spread.

Weeks earlier, Val had received an out-of-the-blue email from a reporter at Reuters, the business newswire, named Charles Levinson. "I'm writing because a source of mine told me that you might be looking for a reporter to talk to," Levinson explained cryptically. "I believe it possible that, if senior Deutsche officials believed your father might be able to tell investigators something that could be used against them or the bank, they might be willing to find ways to exert pressure to prevent that from happening," Levinson wrote. "I suppose it's possible that they found some means of exerting pressure, some threat, that could have driven someone to despair."

This was catnip to Val's conspiracy-inclined mind, and he said he'd be willing to meet Levinson, who promptly booked a flight to California. They met at the Mountain Home Inn, a rustic hotel on the slope of Mount Tamalpais. It was a chilly November afternoon, and they sat alone on the hotel's patio. Levinson drained a few beers, while Val chain-smoked Marlboro Reds. He told Levinson his father's life story. Levinson said that he would like to write about Bill and his role at Deutsche. To do that, he explained, he would need to explore a little in Bill's emails.

Val was game. About a month later, Levinson returned to San Francisco. It didn't take him long to find something juicy in Bill's accounts. There were lots of email chains from about a year earlier in which Broeksmit had browbeaten his DBTCA colleagues for their haphazard approach to the Federal Reserve's stress tests. It was a clear example of how Deutsche seemed to be trying to pull the wool over regulators' eyes, so much so that a prominent and well-regarded (and soon-to-be-dead) executive had expressed grave concerns.

Levinson's story ran in March 2015, under the headline

"Former Risk Chief Warned Deutsche Bank on Stress Tests, Emails Show."[3] The article quoted Bill's writing to his colleagues that they needed to "stress harder," that their financial forecasts were "way too optimistic," and that the losses they were anticipating in an economic storm were "way too small compared to history." With *The Wall Street Journal*, with the Sony hack, and now with Levinson, Val had possessed something valuable. At long last, he was not only seen as an adult—he was a player.

CHAPTER 27

NO CONFIDENCE

n May 2015, Christian Sewing walked onto a floodlit stage with the rest of Deutsche's top executives and board members. Tall and baby-faced, wearing stylish horn-rimmed glasses, he stood out among the row of mostly older men assembled at the front of Frankfurt's vast Festhalle.

Sewing had joined Deutsche straight out of high school. Growing up in the German region of Westphalia, he'd been a star tennis player. His father insisted that he get some work experience before going to university, and in 1989 Sewing scored a coveted two-year apprenticeship in a local branch of Deutsche.[1] Even though Sewing spent much of his time opening mail, there was something invigorating about working for this proud German institution. When the apprenticeship ended, Sewing stuck around, forgoing traditional higher education.

After six years in Germany, the bank cycled Sewing through Singapore and Toronto, and he started learning about the derivatives and investment-banking businesses that were becoming a crucial part of the company's genetic makeup. Following further stints in London and Tokyo, he returned to Frankfurt after the Bankers Trust acquisition. He was alarmed at what he saw: a bank whose businesses were becoming lopsided, an institution that was losing its heritage in the pursuit of Wall Street. He voiced his concerns to Hugo Bänziger. "Let's not make the mistake that we leave our roots," he warned. Bänziger didn't care what Sewing thought, and at the end of 2004, the thirty-four-year-old resigned in frustration.

Sewing spent the next couple of years at a smaller German bank. Initially he was relieved to be away from Deutsche, but that soon turned to boredom. Every time he opened a newspaper, he scanned the headlines looking for stories about Deutsche. "You are cheating, because your heart is not with the bank you work for," Sewing's wife told him. He knew she was right, and in April 2007, months before the onset of the financial crisis, he returned to Deutsche.

Now, eight years later, Sewing was a senior executive at arguably Europe's most important company, bestowed for the first time with the honor of being onstage at the annual meeting. It was a warm, sunny day, and a dozen blue Deutsche flags flapped in the breeze outside the Festhalle. Investors filled up the floor seats, moved into the risers at the back, and then crowded into the balconies. As the meeting started, Anshu Jain, wearing a black suit and a textured blue tie, stood at a lectern emblazoned with the bank's logo. His image was projected onto a giant screen, along with slides showing the bank's recent financial metrics.

This was Jain's third annual meeting as co-CEO. In 2013 and 2014, he had spent weeks memorizing his speeches in German, stammering through words that he didn't understand, trying to impress his German regulators, customers, investors, colleagues. This time, he started off the same way. "Welcome on behalf of the board," he began in German. "This is a very important day. Today we discuss, critically and constructively, where your bank stands. Every word is important on this day. That is why," he continued, "I allow myself to continue in my mother tongue." Journalists in the audience glanced at one another. Anshu started up again, now speaking in English, to groans from the audience. The bank muted Jain's microphone and piped a German voice-over into the hall. Up on the dais, Sewing looked out at the audience and could see that Anshu's English was going over about as well as the bank's lead-weighted stock price. It was just as Sewing had warned the bank's PR staff a few days earlier when they gave him a heads-up about Jain's plan: The public would see it not as Jain's lack of mastery of German; they would perceive it as his not caring about Germany.

Shareholders were angry—and with good reason. In the three years with Jain and Fitschen in charge, the company's stock had sunk slightly; over the same period, the shares of Deutsche's rivals had rocketed higher, in some cases doubling or tripling. Under the duo, the bank's return on equity—the figure that Ackermann had demanded soar to 25 percent—hadn't breached 3 percent. That was in no small part because Deutsche had recently been shelling out billions to resolve its long list of government investigations and other legal matters. And the problems showed no signs of letting up; by the bank's tally, it still faced roughly 7,000 outstanding lawsuits and regulatory actions around the world.[2]

Deutsche had refused to cut its losses and fundamentally alter its business model. Without exception, its European rivals that had harbored Wall Street ambitions had shelved those plans, a concession to a new era of tougher regulations and less tolerance for investment-banking adventures. Deutsche was alone in sticking to its guns—a reflection in part of the reality that for all its problems, the investment bank remained the company's biggest profit producer. It also reflected Anshu's biases. There was no way this creature of Wall Street would be the one to rethink the investment bank's primacy within the overall organization. Nor was it even clear that jettisoning the investment bank would solve the underlying crisis of confidence; after all, most of Deutsche's other businesses continued to flail.

Deutsche's problems had been on vivid display in recent months, as had Jain's inability to deal with them. Things had gotten off on the wrong foot in January, when he was back in the Swiss Alps for the World Economic Forum. In closed-door meetings with government officials including the U.S. Treasury secretary and the governor of the Bank of England, Jain lashed out, blaming overbearing regulators for causing recent market turbulence. His insolence—he was either ignoring or had forgotten the reasons for regulators' newly hands-on approach to overseeing giant banks—drew sharp rebukes, especially because the bank was in serious trouble with regulators all over the world.[3] That spring, Deutsche was penalized $55 million by the SEC for hiding up to $3.3 billion in losses on derivatives during the financial crisis—a judgment that was based in part on what Eric Ben-Artzi and other bank employees had complained about years earlier. Deutsche also disclosed for the first time that it was under investigation for the Russian mirror-trading money laundering.

Then, in late April, Deutsche had shelled out an astronomical $2.5 billion to U.S. and British authorities to settle the Libor investigation. (That was on top of $1 billion it had previously paid to European antitrust authorities for colluding to manipulate another important benchmark interest rate.) It was by far the largest penalty any bank had paid to resolve such a case. One reason was the enormous scale of the bank's misconduct, which went far beyond Christian Bittar's scheme; it seemed that more or less the entire bank had been involved or complicit. Another was that the bank dragged its feet on handing over evidence to the government—and that even after the bank had been or-

dered to preserve relevant materials, Deutsche had destroyed 482
tapes of recorded phone calls. A normally restrained British regulator went on the record with reporters to blast the bank for
"repeatedly misleading us."[4] Miraculously, Alan Cloete, the executive responsible for the division where the misconduct occurred, remained in a senior leadership role at the bank.*

Shortly after the $2.5 billion penalty was announced, Jain
held a conference call for hundreds of the bank's senior managers. The call was to discuss Deutsche's latest financial results, but
given the harsh tone of the Libor judgments, participants expected him to at least acknowledge how badly the bank had
screwed up. Some members of the supervisory board dialed in to
hear how Jain would handle the delicate situation. Anshu's solution was to ignore it: He gushed about the bank's few areas of
strength and didn't mention the Libor case or Deutsche's inescap-
able pattern of misconduct. The board members were appalled.[5]
This did not seem like a man up to the leadership challenge at
hand.

Around this time, one exasperated board member confronted
Anshu and the also-still-employed Colin Fan and scolded them
for not accepting responsibility for the huge lapses that had taken
place on their watch. Jain was indignant. He insisted that the
board member didn't understand how things worked at Deutsche;
different members of the management board—the old vorstand—
had distinct responsibilities for compliance and accounting and
legal. So the failings weren't his or Fan's fault. "That's how German governance works," he lectured.

"Bullshit!" the board member shot back. "You're the CEO of
the entire company."

---

* Cloete told me that he "was cleared in every investigation on the Libor
matter."

The next month—a couple of weeks before Deutsche's annual meeting—a top regulator at BaFin, given the unpleasant responsibility of supervising Deutsche, finally lost her cool. Frauke Menke, fifty-five years old, was a small woman with short blond hair and pale blue eyes. She had joined Germany's financial regulator after receiving a law degree in 1995, initially specializing in money-laundering cases. She slowly ascended through the ranks of the agency that became BaFin. By 2012, she was in charge of overseeing Germany's largest financial institutions. The cocksure men atop these leading banks had routinely made the mistake of underestimating this quiet woman. It was Menke who, three years earlier, had derailed Broeksmit's promotion to be chief risk officer. Predictably, the German media obsessed over the notion that a woman was putting the kibosh on the careers of powerful men. One magazine, *Cicero*, called her "Das Phantom," citing her mysterious clout, rare public appearances, and "pageboy" haircut.[6]

For the past couple of years, Menke had been monitoring the agency's investigation into Deutsche's role in the Libor scandal and had been trying to assess the management team's capacity to act responsibly. She had watched with mounting alarm as the bank repeatedly stiff-armed regulators, as Jain surrounded himself with what looked like yes-men, as it became clear that the rampant misconduct was not an accident but the inevitable consequence of the culture, incentives, and neglect emanating from the top of Deutsche.

On May 11, Menke sent a letter to the bank. The ostensible purpose was to convey the results of an outside review into the Libor case. But Menke's real goal seemed to be to draw blood. The thirty-seven-page letter—written in German and promptly translated into English for broader distribution among the bank's stunned executives and legal counselors—skewered Anshu and his team for creating a toxic culture, for allowing horrible behavior, for encouraging conflicts of interest, and for deceiving regulators. "If the measures required for proper management had been taken here in a timely manner or if the matter had at least subsequently been dealt with differently on the whole," she wrote, "this could not only have saved immense costs for the bank, but the trustworthiness of the bank would not have been harmed in such a manner either."

One by one, Menke went through the bank's senior executives and explained how each had at best fallen down on his job. In one piercing attack, she described how the general counsel, Dick Walker, had seemed to take a minimalist approach to dealing with regulatory inquiries. "It appears to me that this is a manifestation of part of the culture that is possibly still characteristic to your bank, i.e. to prefer hiding, covering up, or entirely negating problems instead of addressing them openly and actively in order to prevent similar issues in the future."

As for Jain, Menke rattled off a long list of lapses, including how he had fought to secure the huge cash payouts to Christian Bittar. "I consider the failures with which Mr. Jain is charged to be serious," she summed up. "They display improper management and organization of the business." Given the letter's tone—it made the 2013 missive from Daniel Muccia at the New York Fed seem mild—the point was clear: The company's most important regulator was calling for a transfusion of new blood.

Everywhere one looked, new crises seemed to be erupting, posing dire threats to Anshu's grasp on power. In Germany, powerful labor unions were in a state of open revolt over the bank's plans to eliminate thousands of jobs. A letter circulated among employees demanding Jain's ouster, and some senior executives passed it around among themselves, agreeing with its proposed remedy. In Berlin, protesters—including more than a few right-wing extremists angry about an Indian running a German institution—marched with signs denouncing Anshu as a rat. Someone threw rocks with his name on them through the plate-glass window of a Deutsche branch.

Even among the people who should have been his biggest boosters, Jain was wearing out his welcome. When he held a town hall meeting in London for investment bankers, he told them he understood their frustrations about the bank's flagging stock price and general malaise. Intended to improve morale, the pep talk irritated executives, who felt Jain was emoting without strategizing.[7]

With Anshu's muted face appearing on the Festhalle's jumbotron on May 21, investors cast their votes for the bank's board members. Such polls are usually a rubber stamp of a company's incumbent leadership; executives and directors generally receive support in excess of 90 percent. But when the results came in at the end of Deutsche's meeting, barely 60 percent had endorsed Jain and Fitschen—an extraordinary no-confidence vote in Deutsche's CEOs. During the meeting's question-and-answer session, two shareholders walked to microphones and called, literally, for Anshu's head.

After the meeting, Jain and the bank's senior executives met in private. Anshu was visibly upset. He asked colleagues to look up online how many times in German corporate history a CEO had received such paltry support. "I don't want to stand in the way of the development of the bank, and if necessary, I will step aside," he offered.[8] No one took him up on that, but the supervisory board soon met to discuss the rebellion. It was clear to them that investors weren't the only ones who had lost confidence. Employees and the board members themselves had, too. Even some major customers had been complaining that the uncertainty around the bank's stability was leading them to consider taking their money elsewhere.[9] That was a scary prospect: If customers started pulling their funds, it could quickly escalate into a run on the bank. It was time, the board decided, for Anshu to go.

Jain saw it coming. About a week after the annual meeting, he told Fitschen that his inability to speak German or to blend into German society was becoming a hindrance to the bank, and his colleague didn't do much to dissuade him. Jain phoned Achleitner and told him he would prefer to resign than to wait for the bank's board to ask him to leave. Unlike a year earlier, this time Achleitner didn't try to talk Jain out of it. In fact, the chairman had already scouted out some German-speaking replacements.[10]

A few days later, on a Sunday afternoon in Frankfurt, Achleitner summoned the supervisory board to an emergency meeting. Their normal practice was to gather in a boardroom high up in Tower A of the bank's headquarters, but Achleitner was worried that reporters might notice the procession of armored limousines, so they instead convened at the nearby Jumeirah hotel. In a conference room whose floor-to-ceiling windows looked out upon an eighteenth-century palace, Achleitner told the directors why they were there: Jain had decided to leave, and Fitschen would step down the following spring. The board voted to accept their resignations. The chairman then explained that the only available replacement was one of their own: John Cryan, a longtime British financier who had served for a few years on Deutsche's supervisory board. Without much debate, the directors anointed Cryan as the incoming CEO.

That afternoon, the news leaked, and Jain's phone buzzed with hundreds of commiserating emails and text messages. "It's a relief. You had no chance," Rajeev Misra sympathized, noting that Anshu had been doomed from the start by his lack of German heritage. By the end of the week, Anshu would receive more than

2,000 such messages from colleagues and clients, many mourning what they figured was the end of the German bank's investment-banking era—an era that had begun, exactly twenty years earlier, when Edson Mitchell had quit Merrill and arrived at Deutsche.

Jain emphasized to anyone who would listen that his departure was voluntary, that this was simply the right time to make way for new leadership. He tried to cheer himself up by having his personal assistant assemble all the condolence messages into a keepsake book. The night that his resignation was announced, he flew back to London and had a quiet evening at home with Geetika. She, for one, was relieved it was over.

John Cryan, a former chief financial officer at the Swiss bank UBS, had a freckled bald head and a creased hangdog face; colleagues had nicknamed him Mr. Grumpy. He was well regarded by investors, known for a methodical approach and a candid demeanor. ("He is the anti-Anshu," a former colleague observed.[11]) Investors celebrated Cryan's ascent. Deutsche's shares soared 8 percent the day after the change was announced. Hoping to act during a honeymoon period, Cryan announced that he was shutting down Deutsche's investment-banking operations in Russia, which had been in the news because of its latest money-laundering troubles. He would also soon move to cleanse the bank of the remnants of Anshu's Army: Michele Faissola, atop the wealth management business; Henry Ritchotte, the chief operating officer; and Colin Fan, in charge of the investment-banking division—all would be out or demoted.[12]

Such housekeeping, though, was months in the future. On the morning of June 9, less than forty-eight hours after Cryan had been chosen as the incoming CEO, ten police cars, their sirens wailing, pulled up outside Deutsche's headquarters. Thirty armed officers rushed inside, looking for information related to one of the many ongoing investigations into the bank. If there was any question about whether Anshu's departure would easily resolve Deutsche's smorgasbord of problems, the raid provided an emphatic answer: no.

CHAPTER 28

TRUMP ENDEAVOR 12 LLC

The week after Anshu's June 2015 ouster, Donald Trump rode a golden escalator down to the ground floor of the Manhattan skyscraper in which he lived and worked. Trump Tower's marbled lobby was festooned with American flags and "Make America Great Again" paraphernalia. In front of a pack of TV cameras, cheering fans, and his extended family, Trump declared his candidacy to be the forty-fifth president of the United States. Then, for good measure and gobs of free publicity, he denounced the "rapists" that he claimed were flooding across America's southern border.

This sort of provocative bombast would come to define Trump's candidacy and then his presidency. But even before his dig at supposed Mexican rapists, he had made racism a crucial part of his public shtick. More than any major American politician in decades, Trump had recognized that there was nothing stopping him from mining the potent seams of race and ethnicity for his political advantage. That is why he had spent years spreading the lie that Barack Obama wasn't born in the United States and therefore was an illegitimate president. It didn't matter that the assertion was false. The point was to grab attention and to inflame passions, and Trump—the star of his own popular reality-TV show—had an undeniable knack for doing exactly that.

Trump's business record was a centerpiece of his campaign. To maintain the mirage of success, he needed to do splashy deals. How would he pay for that? In addition to his rich history of defaults, his increasingly polarizing politics were a problem, too. The banking industry is rightly maligned for prioritizing profits over principles, but in the years after the financial crisis, many leading banks started evaluating reputational risks as an important factor in weighing whether to green-light transactions. The prospect of ugly headlines or political blowback made banks like Citigroup, JPMorgan, and even Goldman Sachs at least slightly less likely to finance oligarchs or tobacco and gun companies or Malaysian billionaire playboys or genocidal governments. The idea was that the character of your clients should be treated as an important reflection of your values as an institution. (And that bad publicity was bad for profits.) Not many banks seemed eager to project Trumpian values.

Deutsche, via Rosemary Vrablic, already had financed Trump's acquisition of the Doral golf resort in Florida and had provided the $48 million loan tied to his Chicago tower. Two years later, in early 2014, the Buffalo Bills football team came up for sale after its longtime owner died. An auction for the NFL franchise got under way, and Trump called Vrablic and told her he was thinking about bidding. A successful offer would have to be in the vicinity of $1 billion, and Trump wasn't about to pony up his own money, so would Deutsche be willing to front him some cash? At the very least, would the bank be able to vouch to the NFL that Trump (who in the 1980s was part of the failed United States Football League) had the financial wherewithal to pull off such a transaction? Deutsche's answer came back: yes.

It was no secret within Deutsche that Vrablic had been enlarging the bank's relationship with Trump. Every big loan the private bank extended—including the Trump transactions—was entered into a spreadsheet that was presented every three months to senior executives. Emails went out to DBTCA's board members notifying them whenever a loan was granted to Trump's companies. A few weeks after Jain became CEO in 2012, he had come to New York, and executives in the wealth management division briefed him on their ten biggest clients; Trump was near the top of that list. Not long after that, at an annual gathering in Barcelona of Deutsche's fifty or so top executives, the wealth-management team presented a video in which clients lavished the division with praise. One of those clients was Ivanka Trump, who thanked Deutsche for being so easy to do business with—and singled out her family's relationship manager for being such a pro. (Years later, when these loans became politically radioactive, a succession of senior executives would pretend they had no clue that Trump was getting all this money from their bank.)

In the end, Trump's bid for the Bills was rejected in favor of a $1.4 billion offer from another businessman. Since Trump wasn't buying the team, there was no need for the loan from Deutsche. But another lending opportunity would pop up within months.

In 1899, a grand new building opened in Washington, D.C. A few blocks down Pennsylvania Avenue from the White House, the castle-like structure was out of place among the rows of boxy government buildings. Its 315-foot clock tower afforded panoramic views of the entire capital; aside from the Washington Monument, it was the city's tallest edifice. For fifteen years, the proud granite building served as the headquarters of the U.S. Postal Service. But eventually it lost its main tenant, and over the ensuing decades an alphabet soup of other federal agencies cycled through the Old Post Office building, and it gradually fell into disrepair. Preservationists secured its status as a National Historic Landmark in the 1970s, saving it from demolition, but cobwebs and boarded-up windows pocked the place well into the 2000s.

This seemed like a colossal waste of a beautiful property in a prime location. In 2011, the U.S. General Services Administration, which manages the federal government's real estate, invited private developers to submit bids for how they might use the Old Post Office building, and what they'd be willing to pay for the privilege. Ten detailed offers arrived, including one from the Trump Organization, which proposed transforming the building into a luxury hotel. Trump envisioned more than 260 rooms, a ballroom, a spa, restaurants, shops, and continued public access to the building's tower.[1] In February 2012, just as Trump negotiated for the Doral and Chicago loans from Deutsche, the GSA named him the winner of its bidding process.[2]

Trump and his business partner, a California private equity firm called Colony Capital, run by billionaire Tom Barrack, agreed to invest $200 million in renovating and cleaning up the building. In exchange, they got a sixty-year lease, which required them to pay the government at least $3 million a year. Rival bidders scoffed that the financial assumptions underpinning the Trump International Hotel proposal were fantastical—to break even, the hotel would have to charge an exorbitant $700 a night for rooms, a price point that experienced hoteliers declared unrealistic in the Washington market. Who in D.C. would want to stay in a gaudy, Trump-branded hotel, anyway?[3] Such skepticism didn't faze Trump or the government. "In the Trump Organization, we have found a partner who understands both the privileges and responsibilities of our historic assets—and who understands that historic preservation is good business," a top GSA official declared at the 2013 unveiling of Trump's plans.

The plan was for Colony Capital, with its deep well of funds from private investors, to kick in almost all of the money for this massive project. But Colony soon backed out. That left Trump on the hook for the $200 million that he had promised would be spent redeveloping the building. Quickly lining up that kind of money was not easy, especially for a man with a well-established pattern of defaulting on loans. "Every bank wants to do the deal," Trump claimed.[4] "We don't even need financing. We could do it in cash."

That last part might or might not have been true (the first part was clearly not), but at best it would have made the project infinitely riskier for Trump. So once again, in the summer of 2014, he and Ivanka sat down with Vrablic. The banker and her superiors were willing to dole out more money—at the exact time that their star client was delving further into demagoguery. His latest issue was Ebola. The disease was spreading in parts of western Africa. Trump demanded, over and over again, that the federal government immediately halt all inbound flights "from Ebola-infected countries." His concerns seemed less grounded in public health than in trying to stir up racial animus. But he was an important client, and at least on the surface, Trump's behavior didn't change the financial attractiveness of lending him money. In case Deutsche was on the fence, Vrablic had persuaded Trump to sweeten the deal by informally agreeing to stash tens of millions of dollars more in Deutsche accounts, an arrangement that generated substantial fees for the bank. Vrablic noted the tacit quid pro quo in her write-up of the loan as she sought sign-off from her superiors.

Helping seal the deal's outcome was the fact that Vrablic's

higher-ups perceived her and Anshu as having a strong bond. Tagging along to meet Vrablic's best clients, the CEO appeared to get a rush out of meeting celebrities—"he seemed star-struck," says an executive who went with them—and Deutsche colleagues noticed how the CEO went out of his way to praise her in front of clients. She was the only one in the private bank who enjoyed such reverential treatment. One foggy day, Jain accompanied Vrablic to Trump Tower for lunch with her prized client. Trump's executive assistant, Rhona Graff, greeted her like an old friend, and it was instantly clear to Jain that Vrablic was a regular there. Inside Trump's cluttered office, Vrablic was warm and casual not only with Trump but also with Ivanka when she popped in. Before the meeting, Jain had received a small dossier describing Trump's background and the bank's relationship with him, and over lunch they had a brief chat about Trump's finances. Anshu commented that he was surprised by Donald's relatively low levels of debt. Jain left the meeting feeling impressed with Vrablic, who returned to her office and told colleagues that the CEO had sounded upbeat about lending to Trump.

Deutsche—via DBTCA—soon agreed to lend $170 million to Trump Old Post Office LLC, a newly incorporated company in Delaware. The loan didn't have to be fully paid back for a decade, but Trump was personally on the hook for most of the money; if he defaulted, Deutsche could come after his personal assets.[5]

A couple of years later, on the presidential campaign trail, Trump would cite his new Washington hotel as proof of the financial and management acumen he would bring to the White House. And there was some truth to his savvy at wringing every last cent out of his patrons at Deutsche Bank—though that was not necessarily the type of talent Trump was trying to boast about. Like the Doral loan, whose low interest rate had stunned Rich Byrne, the Old Post Office transaction was surprisingly inexpensive for a borrower whose credit history was scarred by repeated defaults. "I'm borrowing money at numbers like 2 percent," Trump exclaimed to the journalist William Cohan.[6] "It's crazy! I've never seen anything like it." Inside Deutsche, after the initial furor over the resuscitation of the Trump relationship, the Post Office loan didn't receive so much scrutiny. Like the prior loans, it was written up in a report that was sent to members of the DBTCA oversight board. Directors had the authority to summon executives to explain why on earth they were shoveling so much money in Trump's direction, especially when no other bank dared touch him. But nobody asked questions.

Deutsche's work by now extended well beyond loans to Donald Trump and his company. In 2009, Trump's son Don Jr. had started a company, Titan Atlas Manufacturing, that he bragged would revolutionize the prefab-home industry. By 2011, the business was unraveling. Don Jr. turned to Vrablic for help, and Deutsche coughed up a nearly $4 million mortgage, repayable in three years. That preserved for a short while the fantasy of Don Jr. as a not-unsuccessful businessman. Days before the loan's due date, the elder Trump used a specially created LLC—DB Pace Acquisitions—to buy the loan from Deutsche Bank (hence the *DB*). This was yet another favor to Trump—normal bank customers couldn't just walk in and purchase a family member's problematic loan. When Don Jr. predictably defaulted, DB Pace foreclosed on the warehouse, thus keeping it in the hands of the Trump family and out of reach of Titan Atlas's other creditors.[7]

The Kushners started receiving personal loans from Vrablic's department, too. This had been impossible for years because Charles Kushner, Jared's father, had been convicted of tax evasion and witness tampering. Even at a lender as uninterested in its clients' reputation as Deutsche was, the family patriarch's incarceration had made the entire family essentially off-limits. But Vrablic and Ivanka had grown tight—they weren't quite friends, but they saw a lot of each other at social events—and she'd known Jared Kushner since before her arrival at Deutsche. Vrablic started bringing Deutsche executives along to meet him, impressing them with their easy, familiar rapport.

Jared returned the favor. He owned *The New York Observer*, an influential weekly tabloid, and soon it was apparently being used as a lever with Deutsche. One top investment-banking executive who had lobbied against lending to Trump was pretty sure that a series of negative stories about him in the *Observer* had been planted by a longtime Deutsche rival who happened to be close to the Kushner and Trump families.

The *Observer* had created a couple of offshoot magazines to write about the real estate business, and in late 2012, Kushner approached Carl Gaines, the editor of the *Mortgage Observer*, with an idea. "Why don't you write a profile of this Rosemary Vrablic woman at Deutsche Bank?" he asked. Gaines poked around a little and realized that Vrablic was Kushner's personal banker. He told Kushner he wasn't sure this would make a very compelling story. "Just go meet with her," Kushner said. "You'll figure something out." So Gaines arranged an interview at Deutsche's Park Avenue offices, and he and Vrablic spent a couple of hours talking about how she'd gotten into banking. Gaines dutifully wrote a gauzy profile that ran in February 2013. "Got a chunk of change lying around?" the article began. "With a book of business north of $5.5 billion, Rosemary Vrablic, a managing director in the asset and wealth management division at Deutsche Bank, can help."[8] (It was one of the only on-the-record media interviews that the elusive Vrablic ever granted.) In an accompanying portrait, she perched on a ledge inside Deutsche's midtown offices, skyscrapers in the background and the winter sun illuminating her face and her magenta jacket.

After the profile ran, Vrablic sometimes attended *Observer* events that Kushner hosted. Gaines saw the whole affair as an overt, almost clumsy, effort by his boss to suck up to a banker who had the potential to help his family company—an impression that gained credence as Kushner continued cozying up to Vrablic in public. The following October, they attended an annual fundraising dinner together at the Frick Collection's mansion turned art museum. Photos from the night captured Kushner, in a bow tie and suspenders, and Vrablic, wearing a partly translucent black gown, posing together. At one point Kushner slung his arm around Vrablic, and the banker and her client smiled warmly.

A year later, in 2015, Vrablic's group at Deutsche extended a $15 million personal credit line to Jared and his mother, Seryl Kushner. It was the largest lending facility they had, and they quickly borrowed $10 million at a very favorable interest rate.[9]

On the evening of August 6, 2015, ten Republicans gathered in Cleveland's Quicken Loans Arena for the party's first presidential debate. Two months into his candidacy, Trump had amassed a remarkable double-digit lead in early polls. Almost everyone dismissed it as a fluke, but there was no denying that Trump, at least for now, was leading the pack. Fox News was the sponsor of the two-hour debate, and one of the moderators was Megyn Kelly. Her first question was for Trump: "You've called women you don't like fat pigs, dogs, slobs, and disgusting animals," Kelly punched. "Does that sound to you like the temperament of a man we should elect as president?"

Trump barely blinked. "I think the big problem this country has is being politically correct." He shrugged.

By most accounts, Trump emerged from the debate largely unscathed—quite a feat given his front-runner status, his lack of experience, and the considerable number of skeletons crammed inside his walk-in closets. But that night, as his private Boeing 757 whisked him back to New York, Trump became furious with what he regarded as the unfair treatment he had received at the hands of the Fox moderators, Kelly in particular. "Wow, @megynkelly really bombed tonight," he tweeted at 3:40 in the morning. The following evening, still fuming, Trump called in to a CNN show hosted by Don Lemon for a thirty-minute interview. He continued to assault Kelly. "You could see there was blood coming out of her eyes, blood coming out of her wherever," Trump spat.

In the hours between his plane touching down at LaGuardia Airport and his conducting what would become a notoriously misogynistic CNN interview, Trump had attended to some personal business in New York. One of the loans Deutsche had made in 2012 to finance his purchase and renovation of the Doral resort—by now rechristened the Trump National Doral—was coming due. Trump was pumping huge sums of his own money into his presidential campaign, and rustling up the cash to repay Deutsche for the maturing loan was not ideal right now. Trump asked Vrablic if he could refinance it with a new loan. Deutsche agreed. On August 7, an entity called Trump Endeavor 12 LLC took out a new $19 million loan from Deutsche. The bank had agreed to slice the interest rate to an even lower rate than on the original loan. That day, in the middle of a frenzied White House campaign, Trump found the time to personally sign the loan documents.[10]

CHAPTER 29

THE DAMAGE I HAVE DONE

n the shade of a palm tree, Val sat on the concrete steps leading to the rear entrance of the Belamar Hotel. He was burning through Marlboros, and his Mac laptop was whirring so vigorously that it was hot to the touch. The Belamar was located on a busy Los Angeles avenue, with a strip mall on one side and a gas station on the other. But it was less than a mile away from the beach, and the ocean breeze made the noise and pollution of the round-the-clock traffic a little easier to bear. Unlike some of the other places where Val had recently been crashing, at least the Belamar had Wi-Fi, which was crucial to his task as he stared at his computer screen on this evening in June 2015.

Six months earlier, he had left the Strawberry Manor house. Pegi Young had driven him in a Lexus SUV down to Los Angeles, where he moved into another substance-free facility, Indigo Ranch. Val had confided to her about his role leaking documents to *The Wall Street Journal* and Reuters, and she cheered him on. "Go for those fuckers, Val," she said. "Let's get Deutsche!" Indigo Ranch—in a Tudor mansion on a Malibu hillside—required Val to see a therapist, and the staff recommended an addiction specialist named Larry Meltzer. He was a mustachioed ex-hippie, and therapy sessions were held in a loft in his palatial hilltop compound. Meltzer wasn't one of those old-fashioned shrinks who would coax you along with Socratic questions. He was happy to inject himself into the lives of his clients, as he called them. "I am a solution-focused therapist," he liked to say.

In their first session, Val took in the loft's spectacular views, stretching from the mountains to the ocean. He told Meltzer that he was on a quest to understand why his father had killed himself, but that the mission was being thwarted by his inability to communicate with his mother, who possessed crucial information to unravel the mystery—not least, Bill's suicide notes.

Access to those notes seemed like an impossibility, given the amount of anger and distrust between mother and son that had built up over the years. Most recently, Val had wrongly accused Alla of cutting him out of Bill's will and demanded that she fork over money. She stopped returning his phone calls.

"I need someone to intermediate for me," Val explained to Meltzer.

"That's what I do," replied Meltzer. "That's my job."

The first time that Meltzer got on the phone with Alla, his top priority was to convince her to increase Val's monthly allowance so that he could afford a decent place to stay. (After a fight with a staff member, Val had been kicked out of Indigo Ranch. He had shacked up in a dirty Rodeway Inn, where he stumbled back into his opioid habit.) Meltzer eventually wore her down, and since she was no longer footing the bill for rehab, she agreed to bump Val's monthly allowance up to $2,500 from $300. That allowed him to upgrade to the Belamar.

Meltzer told me that he encouraged Val to continue his investigation into what had been going on inside Bill's head—and inside Deutsche—at the time of his death. Perhaps some answers, or at least exhausting the possibility of finding any, would bring him some peace. The key to all of this, Val figured, was lodged in his mother's email account. She kept everything in there—phone numbers, credit cards, online passwords—and he bet the suicide notes were there, too. She had probably needed to share them with her lawyers or police or family members.

One of the lessons he'd learned from his Sony adventure was that computer security tended to be weak; there likely was a way for him to sneak into his mother's Gmail. He tried guessing her password. No luck. So he went to Google and typed a question: "How do you hack a Gmail account?" The search engine came back with millions of hits—including step-by-step tutorials. First, Val downloaded a piece of software called a packet sniffer. The data that flow across the Internet—emails, pictures, credit-card transactions—are made up of lots of byte-sized packets; this software positioned Val to intercept and decipher some of those packets. For it to work, though, Val had to trick other people's computers into allowing his sniffing software to see the data they were transmitting. The best way to do that was to disguise his computer as a trusted Wi-Fi network. That was step two. The online tutorials instructed Val on how to create a spoof Wi-Fi signal. For a trial run, he set up a fake hot spot with the same name as the Belamar's network for hotel guests. No smoking was allowed inside the hotel, so Val propped open a fire exit with a room-service menu, took a seat on the concrete steps, and watched, mesmerized, as hotel guests blindly logged onto the Internet through his computer. The software allowed him to see their emails, online passwords, and credit-card information. It was a little scary how easy this was.

Val was now confident that if he got near his mother's apartment in New York, he would be able to replicate the trick and nab her Gmail password so that he could freely snoop around. Meltzer negotiated with Alla to provide $20,000 for Val to buy a car, arguing to her that it would increase the odds of Val's becoming self-sufficient. Val snorted some heroin, went to a nearby used-car lot, and plunked down all twenty grand on a silver Audi Q5, fully loaded.

His eastward expedition began on Father's Day. It was warm and hazy as Val pulled onto the freeway, his windows rolled down so he could smoke while crawling through the L.A. traffic. His first stop was Las Vegas, where he hoped to shore up his finances by playing poker. Within a few hours, he had lost $1,500. His unlucky streak continued when he spilled the remainder of his heroin in his hotel room, the powder disappearing into the Hard Rock Hotel's shag carpeting.

Before going to New York, Val arranged to have a reunion in Philadelphia with some of his college bandmates, including Matt Goldsborough. He set out from Nevada and, fueled by Ritalin, drove thirty hours straight, fantasizing about what he might find in his mother's emails and how it might help him decode his father's death. Sleep-deprived, stressed, and hopped up on stimulants, by the time he neared the Pennsylvania border Val was hallucinating. At a gas station, he realized that other motorists were plotting to murder him in order to stop him from solving his father's riddle. He needed to call the police, but he was pretty sure his iPhone was wiretapped. The only way to get the authorities' attention was to ram his car into the gas pumps and cause an explosion. It was three A.M. when he called Goldsborough to lay out his plan. Goldsborough was on an overnight Greyhound to Pittsburgh, where he was supposed to rendezvous with Val. "Do you believe that I'm your friend and I love you?" Goldsborough whispered, trying not to wake his fellow passengers. Yes, Val allowed. "Then you have to trust me. You have to not do that. Just get back on the road and get to Pittsburgh." After several minutes of urgent directives and more than a few dirty looks from groggy passengers, Goldsborough was surprised when Val obeyed. In Pittsburgh, they went to a friend's house. Someone made Val a cup of tea and sent him to bed.

A couple of weeks later, after spending time with his old band-mates and restocking his supply of heroin, Val drove to New York. He arrived at his mother's Upper East Side apartment building in the early evening. It was the first time he'd been there since his father's memorial service a year and a half ear-lier. Val marched through the arched granite entryway into the building's tree-lined courtyard. A doorman admitted him into the elevator to ride, unannounced, up to the fifteenth floor. He knocked on the door of unit 15D. Alla looked through the peep-hole, saw it was her son, and refused to open the door. Val hol-lered to let him in. Alla shouted that this wasn't a good time. Val plopped down on the hallway floor with his MacBook and laid his trap, creating a spoof Wi-Fi network to trick his mother's phone and computer into transmitting data through Val's lap-top. It took half an hour to intercept a bunch of packets from Alla's computer.

He drove to the Lower East Side. The temperature that day had hit 95, and the night was sticky with heat, humidity, and the stench of rotting garbage. Packs of young people roamed the streets. These used to be Val's stomping grounds; just down the road was a venue where Bikini Robot Army had performed years earlier. Val sat in his Audi, the air conditioning cranked up, and opened his laptop. The packet-sniffing program had re-trieved an impressive lode of data, and Val quickly found what looked like his mother's email password. He went to Gmail, en-tered her credentials, and held his breath. The page loaded; he was in.

In the inbox, he found his mother's log-in credentials for the University Club and booked himself a suite. Penniless, at least he now had shelter—around the corner from Deutsche's midtown offices, where Mike Offit and Justin Kennedy had once worked. The University Club allowed him to charge food to Alla's account, and though it didn't sell cigarettes, it did offer a variety of Cuban-style cigars. Val tried not to choke while inhaling their acrid smoke. His suite reeked of old, faded money: an overstuffed armchair, plush green carpeting, and salmon-colored walls hung with oil paintings and lamps that emitted a weak yellow glow. Val started pawing through his mother's messages. He didn't feel guilty; he had convinced himself that his mother deserved this invasion of privacy, not to mention his unauthorized use of her University Club expense account. But the voyeuristic rush of looking through her personal correspondence soon yielded to hollowness. He saw signs of his mother and sisters traveling, gossiping, going out to dinner together, laying plans for the future. None of it included him. Hardly any of it even *mentioned* him. Val's mind crashed backward to his days in foster care. Did he even have a real family? Had either of his fathers loved him? What about his mother? The same physical pain that he'd felt as a child in foster care washed through his body. He shut his laptop and got high.

Within hours, Val was lured back. Sitting at his suite's scuffed wooden desk, he entered two words into the search field of his mother's Gmail: "notes Bill." A handful of items came up. One of them was an email with a scanned document attached. Val opened the PDF file. He instantly recognized his father's semi-cursive scrawl. Val carried his laptop to the bathroom, the only place in the suite where he could crack open a window. He sat on the toilet, balanced his computer on his knees, and lit a cigar.

The PDF contained scanned copies of all seven suicide notes. Val started reading Bill's letter to Alla. Written on graphing paper, with a grid of faint vertical and horizontal blue lines, it ran about ten pages. Until now, Val's main recollections of the letter had been that it was long. It was: page after page of Bill's fears, insecurity, self-loathing, and paranoia—how the Xanax had stopped working, how alcohol no longer cured his pain, how he felt terrible about his work for Deutsche.

Val tapped ash out the window, and it floated into the courtyard below. The cigar was spewing an alarming amount of smoke. He worried it would waft into the hallway. He turned on the hot water in the old-fashioned bathtub, hoping that might mask the smell. Soon the small bathroom's air was thick with smoke and steam. Val felt like gagging.

He read the other notes. Alessa's and Katarina's were on elegant greeting cards, while the one to Bill's mother was on lined notebook paper. Michael Morandi's note asked him to please take care of Bill's family. There was the short one to Val, calling him a credit to the Broeksmit name. At the back of the PDF was one last letter—to Anshu. (The original version remained entombed in a vault inside Deutsche.) It was written in black ink on a piece of white printer paper. An uneven crease was visible where the note had been stuffed into the envelope. The handwriting was slightly messier than in the other letters, and almost violent, as if Bill had been jamming his pen onto the page as he expelled the sour words.

Anshu,

You were so good to me and I have repaid you with carelessness. I betrayed your trust and hid my horrible

nature from you. I can't even begin to fathom the damage
I have done.

I am eternally sorry and condemned.

Bill

Val read the note again, and then a third time. It didn't make sense. How had his father been careless? What damage had he done to Deutsche? His "horrible nature"? In what way had he betrayed Anshu's trust? Val had long ago concluded, without a whole lot of evidence, that Bill's suicide must have been related to Deutsche. Sitting on the toilet, he finally had what looked like proof—even if it wasn't what he had expected. There now was no question that Bill felt remorse about his work for the bank and that it was on his mind when he decided to die. But what could have been *so* bad as to lead him to loop Daisy's leash around his neck? In the University Club's white-tiled bathroom, the swirling cigar smoke mixed with mist from the hot water in the tub. Val slumped on the toilet and wept.

CHAPTER 30

PERSON OF INTEREST

n the United Kingdom, all deaths that are considered "violent and unnatural" are subject to a thorough examination. Broeksmit's suicide fit that designation, and in early 2014, Fiona Wilcox, a senior coroner in the London council of Westminster, had been assigned the task of determining the causes and circumstances of his death. There was plenty of material for her to draw on, not least the bundle of suicide notes. Wilcox also learned that in 2013 Broeksmit had gone to his physician, Simon Moore, and complained that he was having trouble sleeping. Moore had given him some sleeping pills, prescribed Xanax, and referred him to a psychologist, William Mitchell. In February 2014, an aide in Wilcox's office had written to Moore and Mitchell, seeking any information they could provide about their patient's state of mind in the months before his death.

Moore responded with a summary of his interactions with Bill the prior summer—including a mysterious reference to his fear of government scrutiny. "He explained he was being investigated by US and European Courts and was extremely anxious," Moore wrote.[1]

The nature of that anxiety became clearer when Mitchell responded to the coroner's letter. "It was with considerable sadness that I heard about Mr Broeksmit's death," he wrote. He recounted what had happened during their one session: Bill had told the shrink about his career, his family, his problems, his anxieties. The key thing that was gnawing at him, Mitchell explained to the coroner, was work-related: "He was suffering from high levels of anxiety related to investigations into the Libor allegations by the US and EU authorities. He was catastrophising, imagining worst case outcomes including prosecution, loss of his wealth and reputation. He was sleeping badly and was constantly preoccupied by those concerns. . . . His self esteem and normal resilience had been greatly undermined as being named 'a person of interest' in the Libor case and in the EU investigation."

At the time of the inquest, the revelation that Broeksmit had feared being prosecuted in the Libor case would have upended Deutsche's narrative that his suicide was unrelated to work (and that the Libor investigation was no big deal for the bank). Wilcox had scheduled a public hearing for March 25 to discuss the findings of her inquest. A few days beforehand, she informed lawyers whom Deutsche had hired for the Broeksmit family that she planned to read aloud portions of the doctors' letters about Bill's anxiety about the government investigations. On the morning of the inquest, the lawyers found Wilcox at the Royal Courts of Justice, an ornate marbled courthouse in central London, and urged her not to mention any specifics from the doctors' letters, citing the family's desperation for privacy. Wilcox initially stood her ground. "She reminded me that by law she was under a duty to investigate all deaths fearlessly and without favor," one lawyer wrote in a memo. But as the complaining dragged on, Wilcox accepted a compromise: She would read the doctors' letters in court, but they could be edited beforehand.

Nearly everything about Broeksmit's specific anxieties was

expunged. The fact that he had told his psychologist that he had been named as a "person of interest" in the Libor investigation was gone. Where Mitchell had written that Bill feared being prosecuted and having his reputation destroyed, the words were crossed out and replaced with the statement that "He imagined various issues." The same trick was pulled with Moore's letter. It described how Bill the previous July was "worried about going to prison or going bankrupt even though he knew he was innocent. He kept on thinking back over all the thousands of emails he had sent over the years. He knew how lawyers can twist things round and was worried they would take extracts from emails." All of that was deleted and replaced with two anodyne sentences: "He told me he had been extremely anxious. He explained he was retiring in September." (Nobody seemed bothered about fabricating the doctors' words.)

Only one stray line hinted at the truth, noting that Bill had expressed concern about an unidentified investigation. The journalists at the inquest had no clue that most of the doctors' explanations had been redacted.

Extensive documents—lawyers' reports detailing how they censored the coroner; the original doctors' letters, with much of their findings crossed out with a pink highlighter and new wording penciled in; a flurry of emails about what the coroner was expected to say—had been emailed to Alla. Now Val found them. Once again, it looked like Deutsche had attempted to rewrite history, sanitizing an event that threatened to cast a pall over the institution and its leaders.

Back inside his father's files, Val stumbled upon a number of emails with a man named Mark Stein. Stein was a New York lawyer from a high-priced corporate law firm, Simpson Thacher. Deutsche had hired him to help Bill deal with the variety of U.S.

government investigations in which he was at least tangentially involved. Reading through the email chains, Val could tell that his father had been upset. Even after retiring, he had regularly checked in with Stein to see if there were any updates from the Justice Department or Deutsche about whether he was in trouble or what the next steps were. "Total silence on the investigation," Stein had assured him in late September. "So all good." Bill, however, hadn't seemed convinced.

The investigation Stein was referring to was Libor. And Stein knew why his client had been so worried. Five years before Broeksmit's suicide, Christian Bittar had been poised to pocket his whopping nine-figure bonus. At the same time that Deutsche's "Business Integrity Review Group" assigned a lone employee to flip through the communications of Bittar's group, Jain had asked Broeksmit to take a look as well. Bill's mandate had been to figure out if everything was aboveboard and if the profits generated by Bittar's team were legitimate.

Broeksmit had spent a couple of weeks poring over financial data and trading "tickets." He also spoke to some of the guys on Bittar's interest-rate swaps desk. Broeksmit's conclusion was that the traders had a plausible strategy to make money off of rates moving in very specific directions, by very specific amounts. He told Anshu that he had not found evidence of Bittar's doing anything improper; the profits appeared real. That was enough for the star trader to get paid—and as it turned out, for Bittar and his colleagues to keep their scheme alive and for Deutsche to keep making money.

It was a huge mistake. If Broeksmit had dug deeper, Deutsche might not have landed in the middle of an international criminal case. As the investigative temperature had started to rise, Broeksmit had been hauled in for interviews with the bank's accountants and lawyers and then had been questioned by German

regulators about his failure to notice or stop the Libor manipulation. Subsequently, his name—and the missed opportunity that
his review represented—was mentioned in a confidential report
produced by European antitrust regulators, who had busted a
long list of banks, including Deutsche, for attempting to rig interest rates.[2] Next up was the Justice Department, which was
considering criminal charges against traders and managers at
Deutsche and other banks. Bill was under the impression that he
was a "person of interest" in the American investigation, a suspicion that would turn out to be well founded.

In April 2015, eight days before the bank reached the $2.5 bil-
lion settlement with the U.S. and British governments, the Justice
Department had circulated a draft summarizing its main findings. It noted that "senior managers failed to detect the pervasive
fraud and collusion at the bank"—and then in the next sentence
cited Broeksmit's ill-fated review. Prosecutors wrote that it was
"almost inexplicable" that Broeksmit, identified as "Senior Man-
ager-5," had failed to turn up the misconduct.[3] (By the time
the final documents were made public on April 23, most of the
references to the involvement of senior executives—including
Broeksmit—had mysteriously vanished.)*

Bill, of course, didn't know that would happen. All he knew
was that the government had evidence of his lapses and that his
actions were under scrutiny as part of a long-running criminal
investigation. (The Justice Department also had turned up a
recording of a 2011 phone call in which a colleague had told
Broeksmit that the bank had ignored requests from the government to turn over materials related to Bittar's sky-high compensation.[4]) And he surely knew that FBI agents were summoning
other Deutsche executives in late 2013 and early 2014 to inter-

---

* The draft document was disclosed in an unrelated 2018 court filing.

views that would determine whether they faced criminal charges.[5] That was presumably why, in the months before he hung himself, Broeksmit had been repeatedly pinging Stein to see what was going on. A number of traders at Deutsche and other banks had already been arrested and criminally charged for their alleged roles trying to manipulate Libor. Would he be among the next? Unlikely—after all, he hadn't participated in any of the manipulative activity. But would his reputation be tarred, his bank accounts sapped by endless legal fees and civil penalties? That was a little easier to imagine.

Before long, Val found a report written by another lawyer, Victor Rocco. Portly and mustachioed, Rocco had once been a federal prosecutor, running the criminal division of the U.S. attorney's office in Brooklyn. In recent decades, he'd been in private practice, often defending companies and individuals who were in trouble with the government. Now, referred by a Broeksmit family member, he was representing Alla.

At lunchtime on an unseasonably warm day in January 2015, Rocco had arrived at Deutsche's skyscraper at 60 Wall Street. Two flags—one American, one Deutsche's—fluttered above the building's entrance. Nearly a year earlier, Anshu had commissioned an internal review to learn more about Bill's suicide; he hadn't felt like he had a choice after the jarring note that Bill had left him. Was Broeksmit harboring some financial secrets that drove him to desperation? Had the bank put him under too much pressure? Deutsche had hired a British law firm, Freshfields, to help go through its files and interview staff and others whom Broeksmit had interacted with as part of his job. Now, at the request of his family, the bank had agreed to share some of its findings.

Two executives were waiting for Rocco in a small conference room with modern German art hanging on the mahogany-paneled walls. One was Simon Dodds, the deputy general counsel to whom Jain had handed Broeksmit's suicide note. The other was Christian Sewing, the baby-faced, fast-rising Deutsche executive, who had been given the responsibility of overseeing the Broeksmit review. Reading from a highlighted memo, Sewing and Dodds walked Rocco through the report's main findings. They acknowledged that the Libor investigation might have caused Broeksmit some heartburn. They breezed through the rest of the issues that Bill had dealt with, shooting each down as a possible source of stress. For example, when it came to DBTCA, the bank acknowledged it was an unholy mess. But it wasn't Bill's mess—the report asserted that he was not responsible for DBTCA. That ignored the reality that as a board member Broeksmit unquestionably had responsibility, and he had spent months agonizing and squabbling over the health of the entity—and senior executives at the bank knew it. The review also looked at how Bill had been affected by BaFin's rejections of his promotions. Deutsche concluded that he had taken the disappointments in stride, bucked up by the steadfast support of his loyal colleagues. (Sewing and Dodds also insisted, contrary to Val's assertion, that the bank had never sent someone over to the Broeksmit flat in London to copy Bill's hard drive.) The bottom line: The review had turned up "nothing that shows a direct link between Broeksmit's death and his work at Deutsche Bank." The meeting lasted about ninety minutes.

Rocco didn't realize it, but there was one sign that Deutsche might have been economical with the truth and, at the very least, was hypersensitive about the report's contents. Some members of the bank's supervisory board had asked to see the report, or at least a detailed summary of its findings. They were denied access. Why? What was the bank hiding? "I was very suspicious," a board member would tell me.

Val soon discovered another poisonous issue that had touched his father: Monte dei Paschi. When Michele Faissola's division pioneered the controversial trades with the Italian bank, Broeksmit had been a member of the risk-management committee that reviewed them. In emails that Val found in his father's Yahoo account, Broeksmit had warned his colleagues that the transactions entailed significant "reputational risks" for Deutsche. He had cautioned that there was no telling what an angry government might do if it got wind of these creative structures, whose primary purpose seemed to be hiding losses, and he had urged his colleagues to run the transactions by Anshu. (There is no evidence that they did.) The risk group had approved the transaction, and the deal got done.[6] Soon Deutsche was replicating the Paschi structure for use with other banks. The transactions continued to make Broeksmit queasy. (They "may be a rounding error at this point, but [they are] growing quickly," he had emailed colleagues in 2009.) And yet, in a replay of the Orange County fiasco at Merrill Lynch in the early 1990s—when Broeksmit had presciently warned that the Californians were feasting on gluttonous quantities of derivatives—his cautions were ignored. Deutsche kept selling the derivatives.

By 2012, as the criminal and civil investigations into the destruction of the world's oldest bank were heating up, Deutsche's lawyers called Broeksmit in for interviews about his role. He was asked to explain how the trades worked and why he had been uncomfortable with them. Before long, government authorities were citing his earlier written warnings as indications that Deutsche should have known better. Should Bill have kept his troubling thoughts to himself rather than putting them in writing, setting his colleagues up for future trouble? Or should he have been louder and more insistent? If he had been, perhaps Faissola wouldn't be facing the likelihood of criminal charges. Deutsche's reputation in Italy—and, for that matter, across southern Europe—might not have been ruined. Monte dei Paschi might still be intact.

Val emailed Faissola and asked why he thought Bill had killed himself. Faissola deflected the question, urging Val not to read too much into reports of various investigations that Broeksmit might have been sucked into: "Unfortunately we live in a world where banks are perceived as evil and therefore senior people are unfairly attacked by the media, politicians and regulators." Val kept pressing, and eventually Faissola offered a more complete theory about what he believed had been going on inside Bill's brain. "I do not think the depression was caused by a specific work situation, but definitely work has contributed to it, and in the last few years the whole industry has entered a very difficult and dark time, we all got attacked and vilified," Faissola wrote. "I think he realized the end of his generation of managers was approaching and maybe he could not deal with it. Definitely the fact that in the last two years he did not have a clear job, due to BaFin opposition, did not help."

But even this theory seemed to skip what was becoming clear: that behind the sturdy facade, Bill had internalized Deutsche's many problems. His mental anguish wasn't all about Deutsche, of course—his life had been marked by what his friends and colleagues described as periodic bouts of darkness, not the kind that would lead them to expect suicide, but enough that they found it noteworthy, even before he killed himself. Yet Broeksmit's wide-ranging if ill-defined responsibilities at work had saddled him with enormous guilt when things went wrong, as they seemed to do at Deutsche with the rhythmic regularity of a metronome. As the pressure built, Bill had kept quiet about the torture he was enduring, about the fears he was harboring about his life and reputation being ruined. People had counted on him; he couldn't show weakness. Eventually it had become too much.

CHAPTER 31

SIENA

ooking up at Deutsche Bank's headquarters in Frankfurt, the parallel buildings seemed to bend toward each other as they soared skyward—an illusion that created the impression of two towers that nearly fused into one at the top. Val Broeksmit stood on the sidewalk, scowling at the hulking high-rises. From the ground, the structures—Credit and Debit—appeared ominous and almost black, their angled glass panels reflecting the night sky.

It was August 2016, and the bank was once again engulfed in a dangerous crisis. Investors had lost confidence in the assurances offered by its parade of chief executives, most recently John Cryan, that it had enough capital. They were sick of Deutsche's making less money than its rivals, partly due to billions of dollars in recent losses. The bank had become a giant casino for derivatives traders, and nobody trusted that its executives had come clean about the extent of losses lurking among the trillions of dollars of the instruments that remained parked on its balance sheet. Regulators had already faulted Deutsche for hiding more than $3 billion in such losses during the crisis. How many billions more were yet to be acknowledged? Equally frightening, there appeared to be no end in sight to the government investigations into Deutsche's years of misconduct. Even after dishing out billions of dollars to defuse a multitude of government probes, the bank remained under suspicion for manipulating currencies markets and violating sanctions and laundering money and deceiving customers and improperly peddling mortgage bonds— and that was just in the United States. The penalties for all this misconduct were certain to exceed $10 billion. Deutsche's market value at the time was less than $20 billion.

Indeed, to an increasing number of investors and regulators, the bank appeared not only short on capital but on the fast track to insolvency. Its stock price was circling the drain, reflecting, as CNBC put it, "mounting concerns about [Deutsche's] survival."[1] Deutsche was so big, and its holdings of derivatives were so vast, that if the bank buckled, the collateral damage was guaranteed to spread, viruslike, to hundreds of other institutions all over the world: Deutsche's customers, trading partners, and other banks. Two months earlier, the International Monetary Fund had given voice to such fears in a report that warned that Deutsche was "the most important net contributor to systemic risks in the global banking system."[2] Things were so bad that Cryan, the German government, and Christine Lagarde, the head of the IMF, all had to publicly deny rumors that the bank was in secret negotiations for a taxpayer bailout. (As a general rule, when a bank feels compelled to deny that it needs a bailout, it almost certainly needs a bailout.)

Val was vaguely aware of the existential dangers confronting his father's former employer. By his side was a pretty German art student named Julie, who had become Val's girlfriend and European traveling companion. She was fifteen years younger than Val and enamored of his seeming worldliness (and forgiving of his persistent drug use). Up in those dark towers, he told Julie, sat the guys who were responsible for his father's death—and for Deutsche's downward spiral. Craning her neck, feeling her boyfriend's hatred, Julie was filled with a sense of dread.

Val had flown to Paris in March 2016. He wanted answers, and he wanted an adventure, and he had the details of his mother's American Express card, which he'd fished out of her email, and he fantasized about the notoriety he would achieve if he managed to take down Deutsche Bank.

Before he'd even left Charles de Gaulle Airport, things had veered off course. He'd used Alla's Amex to buy a bunch of new Apple equipment and downloaded his father's files onto a laptop. After snorting a few lines of heroin in an airport bathroom, he briefly left his bags unattended, and much of his new computer equipment vanished. He called Larry Meltzer, and the therapist didn't do anything to calm his jittery client. It was possible, he cautioned, that Val was being followed, perhaps by someone from Deutsche who wanted to stop him from disseminating any more damaging information and had swiped his computer gear. Meltzer urged Val to be vigilant.

He rented a Nissan and drove to Amsterdam. One evening, someone smashed the car's window and stole his last laptop—the one with everything from his father's email accounts. That sealed it for Val: Deutsche had caught on to his plan and was determined to thwart him. Meltzer, too, thought a conspiracy might be afoot.

Val began running up enormous hotel bills on his mother's credit card. He didn't feel guilty. "This is the only way I can get at her," he told me. "This is the only jab I can take at her, the credit card." Alla's money manager eventually figured out what was happening and canceled the card. Cut off from his illicit subsidy, Val set up shop in a campground north of Amsterdam. He played occasional gigs there to earn his keep. That is where he met Julie, a twenty-four-year-old art student whose father had died in 2015 from a heart attack. "We shared the madness of death," she would say. They also shared lots of mushrooms.

When Val discovered another credit card in his mother's email, they escaped the campground and toured Europe, making a pit stop in Frankfurt on their way to Julie's hometown of Nuremberg. She was awed by Val's seemingly magical ability to charm strangers into handing over cash and guitars and hotel rooms in exchange for the credit-card digits he had committed to memory. (In another life, Val might have made a good derivatives salesman.)

That summer, Val contacted the lawyer for the widow of David Rossi, the Monte dei Paschi executive who had fallen out his office window in what had been ruled a suicide. Having discovered Bill's prophetic warnings about the Paschi transactions, Val now wondered if there were more clues in Italy about his mindset when he decided to die. (A *New York Post* editor, Michael Gray, had told Val that the Rossi family had surveillance footage showing him falling out of his window backwards—not a normal way to commit suicide—which triggered in Val a frenzy of conspiracy-theorizing about the circumstances of his father's death.*) Val explained to the widow's lawyer that his father was a dead banker, too, and that he would very much like to compare notes. "Maybe I can help, maybe we can help each other and perhaps also help other families of those who have suffered through all this misery," Val wrote.

The lawyer, Luca Goracci, said Val was welcome to come to Siena to talk. Val, his smashed Avis rental car replaced with a con-

---

* Val shared with Gray an iPhone photo he'd snapped of his father's body, and the *Post* published it. Val's family assumed that Val had sold it to the tabloid, which was not the case.

vertible, set out for the Tuscan hill town in August. He checked into a hotel with a view out his window into the palace headquarters of the 544-year-old Paschi. That evening, he walked to Goracci's small home office. An exposed lightbulb dangled from the ceiling, making Goracci reminiscent of a figure in a Caravaggio painting. Rossi's still-grieving widow, Antonella Tognazzi, was in the corner, clad all in black, and when she emerged from the shadows Val was so surprised that he let out a small yelp.

"What is it you want?" Tognazzi asked.

"I'm looking for connections," Val answered. He wanted to understand how Deutsche, his father, and people in his orbit like Michele Faissola were tangled up in the Monte dei Paschi mess. Was there something that linked the deaths of Broeksmit and Rossi?

By now, after two government bailouts, the Italian bank was a ward of the state. A number of Paschi executives had been convicted of fraud and sentenced to jail, and Deutsche and some employees—including Faissola—faced criminal charges for helping the Italian bank falsify its accounts.* Val, Tognazzi, and Goracci talked for an hour or so. Tognazzi was certain that her husband had been murdered, and she had some evidence to support her claim. One piece was the footage of Rossi falling backward out of the palace window. As he lay twitching on the ground, two shadowy men had walked up to him in the courtyard, observed his body, and returned to their car.[4] Tognazzi suspected that her husband's killing was related to Paschi's deep financial problems—the aftermath, in part, of its derivatives deals with Deutsche.

---

* While BaFin concluded in 2016 that no Deutsche employees intended to aid Paschi in misrepresenting its balance sheet, the Italian court convicted Faissola in November 2019 and sentenced him to four years, eight months in prison. He denied wrongdoing and is likely to appeal.

Val returned to the townhouse the next day. This time he was ushered into the family's living quarters, arranged around a small courtyard. An elaborate spread of meats and cheeses was laid out on the table. As they ate, Goracci painted a sordid picture of the corrupt relationship between Deutsche and Paschi. Paschi's connections to the local mob and corrupt politicians ran so deep and were such an open secret that anyone who had done minimal due diligence would have had trouble missing all the danger signs. Goracci reported that Rossi had been mixed up in some sinister-sounding stuff: Not least, he had been renting a car once a month and driving to Switzerland to deposit cash into secret bank accounts for clients who Goracci believed were connected to the local mafia. That, the lawyer concluded cryptically, probably had something to do with why Rossi had been murdered.

As Goracci dropped these bombshells, Val scribbled notes. He was intrigued by the unsolved mystery, which once again showed his father's former employer to be so obsessed with profits, so apathetic about its clients' reputations, that it had gotten mixed up in some deadly criminality. If Val was honest with himself, he also felt a pang of jealousy. Things would be easier to stomach if his father had been killed by someone other than himself.

On Val's way out, Goracci gave him a folder of documents he had gathered during his investigation. Outside, the ancient city glowed in the late-afternoon sunlight. Colorful flags hung from lampposts and balconies, enlivening the streets' faded hues. The decorations were on display for Siena's famous Palio horse race, two days away. Hordes of tourists had descended on the town to witness the summer ritual, and Siena seemed to be thriving. Beneath the surface, though, Paschi's demise had taken a big bite out of the region's economy. For centuries, the bank had been not just the go-to lender for projects large and small; its foundation—

endowed with a controlling interest in the bank's shares—also had been a generous benefactor of many of Siena's most important institutions. As the value of the bank's shares rose, the foundation had flourished, doling out more than 200 million euros a year. But then the bank's shares crumbled like the city's ancient walls, and the foundation's coffers were suddenly emptied. By the time of Val's visit, its yearly distribution had shriveled to 3 million euros.[5] Here was a vivid illustration of the real-world harm caused, at least in part, by Deutsche's recklessness. The world's oldest bank had been reduced to ruins, and Deutsche's fingerprints were all over the wreckage.

CHAPTER 32

ROSEMARY IS THE BOSS

The American presidential campaign was entering its homestretch, and the man in charge of Donald Trump's chaotic candidacy was happily anticipating the mayhem that would be unleashed if Deutsche continued to unravel. Steve Bannon, who had made a small fortune working at Goldman Sachs, was an unlikely populist, but he had watched with boiling fury as millions of people lost their homes and their savings during the financial crisis. His father was one of the victims, having seen his retirement fund wiped out. Triggered, Bannon recast himself as a fiery destroyer of the globalist order. Big institutions—governments, corporations, multinational alliances, national political parties, you name it—became his blood enemies. He called himself an "economic nationalist."[1]

In Deutsche, Bannon saw evil. It was, of course, one of the world's largest banks, and it had done more than its share to plunge America and the world into a savage recession, even as its traders and executives were bathed in riches. But more than that, Bannon was a fan of political disintegration in a literal sense. His bet was that if Deutsche went down—or even if it needed a government bailout, as looked increasingly likely—it would sow such mayhem that it would doom Germany's powerful chancellor, Angela Merkel. And with isolationist movements engulfing much of Europe—British voters had just opted to leave the European Union, for example—Merkel looked like one of the last things standing between Europe's political and financial union and the every-country-for-itself anarchy that Bannon craved. As Val sought vengeance and bank executives toiled to right their sinking ship, Bannon gossiped to American journalists that Deutsche was sinking and that it was taking Merkel, and the entire postwar European integration project, down with it.

What made Bannon's gleeful diatribes especially ridiculous was that the man he was trying to install in the Oval Office to enact his anti-globalist agenda was, at that moment, relying on Deutsche more than ever.

First of all, there was the money. At the behest of Jack Brand and Christian Sewing and others, Deutsche in March 2016 had overruled Rosemary Vrablic and shot down Trump's request to borrow money for his Scottish golf resort, Turnberry. In addition to the concerns about Trump's reputation, the bank's financial straits made it much harder to continue justifying tens of millions of dollars of loans at rock-bottom interest rates—which is what Trump had grown accustomed to. Trump by now owed the bank about $350 million, representing half of all of his outstanding debt. Deutsche was by far his biggest creditor, and Trump was the single biggest borrower from the private-banking division. To borrow that money, Trump had provided Deutsche with his personal financial guarantees. If he failed to pay the loans back, the bank could come after his personal assets, making his life—and his ability to project the public impression of massive wealth—exceedingly difficult.

There was also the loan to Don Jr. And there was the $15 million credit line to Jared Kushner and his mother, the biggest lending facility that Jared or either of his parents had access to.[2] That sum was soon dwarfed when, weeks before the election, Deutsche agreed to refinance a $370 million loan to the Kushner family real estate company that it had used to buy a 250,000-square-foot space in the former headquarters of *The New York Times*. Jared personally guaranteed the loan.[3]

In addition to all the money Deutsche had dispensed, the bank had become an occasional prop for the presidential candidate. One of the many critiques of Trump was his shaky record as a businessman. Exhibit A was the fact that his companies had repeatedly filed for bankruptcy. So lousy was Trump's record, critics observed, that he had been frozen out of the banking system. "He's written a lot of books about business—but they all seem to end at Chapter 11," Hillary Clinton sneered in a June 2016 speech in Columbus, Ohio. "Go figure. And over the years, he intentionally ran up huge amounts of debt on his companies and then he defaulted. He bankrupted his companies—not once, not twice, but four times."[4]

Sue Craig, a reporter at *The New York Times*, was preparing an article about Trump's excommunication from Wall Street. Her research and interviews were mostly done by the time in March that Trump picked up the phone and called her to dispute the fundamental premise of her story. "I can do business with the biggest banks in the world," he insisted. "I just don't need any money." That was not true, and Craig—who had an extensive network of Wall Street sources—persisted. Trump cited his relationship with Deutsche as proof that he was not entirely on the outs. "They are totally happy with me," he asserted. "Why don't you call the head of Deutsche Bank?" Craig knew that John Cryan was the bank's CEO, so she was taken aback by what came out of Trump's mouth next: "Her name is Rosemary Vrablic." He kept going. "They are very happy. I do business with them today. You have got to speak to the head of Deutsche Bank. Do you have Rosemary Vrablic's number? Why don't you call her? She is the boss."[5]

Was Trump confused or lying about Vrablic's role?* Either way, he was using his years-long ties to the German bank to knock down the notion that he was a pariah in the financial world.

After Edson Mitchell pushed him out of Deutsche, Mike Offit had puttered around on the outskirts of finance. He had done some consulting, but mostly he had retreated from Wall Street. His nerve damage made working at a bank unpleasant at best, and he didn't miss the politics of operating inside a huge institution. Anyway, he had plenty of money to live on, not least because his wife, Dara Mitchell, the Sotheby's art saleswoman, was raking in millions. Offit decided to follow in his father's footsteps and become a writer. He did some freelance pieces for finance publications and a stint as a columnist for a luxury lifestyle magazine. In 2014, he published a book, *Nothing Personal: A Novel of Wall Street*, about a pair of murders committed by and against employees of a fictional German investment bank. Characters and scenes were plucked from Offit's adventures in banking; he would tell people that one sleazy character was modeled on Steven Mnuchin, who had stiffed him at Goldman after he got sick. On the back cover were a few blurbs. "Michael Offit offers a colorful insight into how the big money is made—and/or taken—on Wall Street," one said. "*Nothing Personal* will hold your attention whether you are in finance or not. A riveting story." The blurb was from Donald Trump.

Two years later, in October 2016, the presidential campaign was

---

* After the interview, Ivanka Trump claimed to Craig that her father had only once described Vrablic as the bank's CEO and that he had simply misspoken. In fact, he had called her "the head of Deutsche Bank" at least three times during the brief interview.

winding down, and it was time for Offit to repay that favor. Trump was getting pilloried for his pattern of bankruptcies. Offit wasn't a big fan of Trump's politics, but he loathed Hillary, and he was willing to do just about anything to avoid her winning the White House. (Offit held his nose and tried to ignore the fact that Mnuchin was the finance chairman of Trump's campaign.) He pondered how Trump might be able to blunt the attacks about his personal finances. It didn't take him long to gin up a strategy. Who were the biggest financial villains out there? Hedge funds! And they were the villains Trump should blame for his checkered financial history. He'd had to declare bankruptcy because greedy hedge funds were so obsessed with wringing every last dollar out of poor Donald Trump that they had refused to let him renegotiate his crushing debts. This was not really true, but it sounded good, and the line of attack meshed with Trump's populist rhetoric on the campaign trail, where he'd accused hedge fund managers of getting away with "murder" through the tax code. "These are guys that shift paper around and they get lucky," he'd declared in a TV interview.[6]

Offit's wife had forbidden her husband from doing anything to assist Trump, who had grossed her out ever since Offit had worked with him at Deutsche. But the election was looking like a landslide, and Offit convinced her to let him email Trump with his political advice. On a Friday evening, Offit typed up a lengthy message, explaining that Trump's argument that he was simply using the bankruptcy law in an advantageous way wasn't resonating with voters. "I believe there is a much better answer, that may help defuse this issue, and am just arrogant enough to suggest it," Offit wrote. He got no response and wasn't even sure that Trump had read the email.

Tammy McFadden had worked in Deutsche's Jacksonville offices—a few buildings down from the FBI's field office—for eight years when, in the summer of 2016, some suspicious Jared Kushner transactions landed in her inspection queue. Deutsche's computer systems automatically scanned thousands of transactions every day, looking for any hints of impropriety, and then sent those flagged transactions to experts for review. McFadden, a veteran anti-money-laundering compliance officer attached to Deutsche's private-banking division, was one of those experts.

Over the years, McFadden had received a number of internal awards from the bank for her strong performance. But by 2015, she had begun making waves, standing up for what she thought was morally and ethically right. First, she protested that the private bank had created dozens of accounts for and was lending money to Jeffrey Epstein, a politically connected financier who had repeatedly been accused of sexually abusing girls and young women. (Epstein for many years had run his companies out of Henry Villard's old Madison Avenue mansion.) A few years after being convicted of soliciting prostitution from a minor, Epstein had been cut off from his previous bank, JPMorgan, at which point he decamped to Deutsche, as willing as ever to ignore clients' ugly backgrounds. Some of McFadden's colleagues had alerted superiors to suspicious overseas transactions in Epstein's accounts, fearing that he might have been moving money around as part of a sex-trafficking operation. Deutsche's higher-ups did nothing. McFadden, too, refused to sign off on Epstein's activity, but managers didn't want to hear it—he was a lucrative client. (He would remain a client until June 2019—weeks before he was criminally charged with sex trafficking of girls as young as fourteen.) "If they're willing to do business with Jeff, Lord help us all," McFadden would tell me.[7]

Next, in early 2016, McFadden had noticed that many customers of the private bank, including quite a few of Vrablic's super-rich clients, didn't have the proper documentation attached to their accounts. This was especially problematic for customers who were classified as "politically exposed persons"—a designation that is supposed to subject them to extra vetting because of the heightened risk that they could be involved in bribery or other public corruption. After initially noticing the problem in a couple of isolated accounts, McFadden did a broader review and found more than a hundred politically exposed clients who didn't have the requisite documentation showing things like where their money came from. Among those customers, she realized, were Donald Trump and his family members. When McFadden alerted her superiors, they told her not to worry about it. Mc-Fadden didn't let it go, lodging a complaint with the HR department and, in the process, angering her bosses.

Now, in the summer of 2016, with Trump having clinched the Republican nomination and Kushner serving as his adviser, Mc-Fadden was assigned the task of reviewing a number of transactions in the Kushner Companies' accounts that had triggered alerts in Deutsche's computer system. Right off the bat, she could see why the transactions had tripped up the software: Kushner's real estate company was moving money to a number of Russian individuals. That didn't mean there was anything improper—it certainly wasn't proof of money laundering—but it *was* unusual. McFadden did some research, looked into the recipients of the money and into the Kushner Companies' history of moving funds overseas, and concluded that the appropriate response was for Deutsche to file a "suspicious activity report" with FinCEN, the arm of the Treasury Department responsible for policing financial crimes. Banks file thousands of such reports every year, and this didn't strike McFadden as an especially close call. She typed up a report and sent it to her superiors.

Normally, a proposed suspicious activity report would be reviewed by another money-laundering expert, one who was outside the business unit where the transactions in question originated—in this case, the private-banking division. It was important to keep things separate; otherwise, employees with financial interests in seeing transactions go through unimpeded would be calling the shots, potentially compromising the effectiveness of Deutsche's already questionable anti-money-laundering safeguards. This time, though, word traveled back to McFadden that her report was being killed—by managers in the private bank.* McFadden was pretty sure this was an example of the private bank trying to preserve its lucrative relationship with the Kushners (and therefore the Trumps), at the cost of not adhering to anti-money-laundering laws.[8] She hadn't survived at banks for decades without knowing how to stand up for herself and her work—more than a decade earlier, she'd sued Bank of America for racially discriminating against her and other black employees—and now she started making more noise. That was not the way to get ahead at Deutsche, as guys like Eric Ben-Artzi could have told her. Bosses derided McFadden to colleagues as a crazy, difficult woman. Soon she was transferred to another division and then, in April 2018, fired.

McFadden had found something important. The Kushners—with their long-standing ties not just to Deutsche but also to Bank Leumi, which had its own problematic history of doing business with Russians—were moving money to Russians at the same time that Russia was interfering in the American presidential election, trying to tilt it in favor of Jared Kushner's father-in-law. (And Kushner's personal banker, Vrablic, had learned the nuts and bolts of banking at . . . Bank Leumi.) It was hard not to be a little suspicious.

---

* Deutsche Bank says that it acted properly and that a suspicious activity report wasn't warranted in this case. The Kushner Companies deny any involvement in money laundering.

What exactly were the purposes of the transactions that Mc-Fadden had spotted? What did they show about the interests of Kushner, Trump, or his presidential campaign in Russia? With McFadden gone, and her suspicious activity report deleted, the answers to those questions vanished inside Deutsche's computer systems.

CHAPTER 33

DO NOT UTTER THE
WORD "TRUMP"

On November 8, 2016, Donald Trump won the presidency. Almost no one—not him, his advisers, his opponent, the media, fellow Republicans—had anticipated his historic upset. The following morning was blustery and cold in Frankfurt, and Deutsche executives woke up to the nausea-inducing realization that they had a very big problem on their hands. For months, they had been fielding inquiries from journalists about how on earth their bank had ended up being the only conventional financial institution to lend money to the Republican nominee. The bank's official on-the-record response was that it couldn't possibly comment on matters pertaining to individual clients. Off the record, senior executives had a simpler answer: We don't really know. The bank's media-relations staff advised John Cryan and his lieutenants to just sit tight; they assumed, like everyone else, that such questions would go away after Clinton trounced Trump and he skulked out of the limelight once and for all.

Now shell-shocked executives and board members had to

reckon with a much different reality: The incoming president of the United States was deeply indebted to their institution. This was a public nightmare. Much of the world despised Trump, a man whom Deutsche had helped—not once, but over and over again—reach these unimaginable heights. With Trump in the White House, there would presumably be extensive digging into every deal he'd ever done, every partner he'd ever worked with, every loan he'd ever received—many of which involved Deutsche. And the facts that Trump's election was under a cloud because of Russia's efforts to sway the vote and that his leading lender had for years been engaged in money-laundering activity in Russia— well, it didn't take a genius to realize that real or imagined dots would soon be connected linking Deutsche to Russia to Donald Trump. This was especially true since the bank a decade earlier had connected Trump with wealthy Russians as he prepared to build his resorts in Hawaii and Mexico. (Adding fuel to the fire, Eric Trump had previously told a journalist that when it came to financing work on his family's golf courses, "we don't rely on American banks. We have all the funding we need out of Russia."[1] Deutsche had bankrolled the Doral; was that loan funded with Russian money?) This was the kind of story that had the potential to do more than generate reputation-tarnishing headlines; it could get bank executives dragged before congressional committees and grand juries.

A few days after Trump's victory, Deutsche's senior executives commissioned a review of the bank's relationships with the president-elect, his company, and the Kushners. Lawyers fanned out to question employees in Rosemary Vrablic's unit and in the investment bank, which had recently packaged some of the loans to Kushner's company into salable securities. The tone of these interviews was accusatory; employees started referring to them as depositions and interrogations. The result, a few weeks later, was a presentation that was handed out to a small group at the top of the bank. The confidential document, more than twenty pages long, included a family tree, going back to Trump's grandparents and extending down to Ivanka, Don Jr., Eric, and Jared Kushner. It went through each outstanding loan to the Trumps and Kushners and listed their accounts at Deutsche. And it traced the history, back to Offit and the loan to refurbish 40 Wall Street. Executives in Germany flipped through the document and shook their heads—here was another mess the Americans had sucked their bank into.

Deutsche's supervisory board also rushed to figure out what had just happened. The board assigned the task to its "integrity committee," which—after reviewing bank documents and interviewing employees—soon produced its own report. Its main focus was why, not long after the investment bank had imposed a no-Trump policy following the 2008 Chicago litigation, Deutsche's private-banking unit had begun practically throwing money at Trump. One factor, the integrity committee found, was that Vrablic's bosses had been star-struck; the allure of doing business with The Donald had overridden any self-preservation instincts. That was embarrassing for Deutsche, but what was more alarming to the board members was that the bank had produced a number of documents over the years that flagged the large volume of business they were doing with this one client. These were called exposure reports, and their purpose was to make sure that someone up the hierarchy was aware of the full extent of a relationship that, if it soured, had the potential to inflict serious financial or reputational damage on the bank. Yet as far as the supervisory board could determine from talking to executives, the reports had never been viewed by anyone at a senior level. The blame, the board concluded, rested in large part with Deutsche's antiquated technology and a compartmentalized management setup in which just about everyone could plausibly claim that policing a relationship with a big client wasn't their responsibility—a relic of the vorstand's narrow divisions of labor. The fact that one arm of Deutsche refused to do business with Trump and another arm considered him a marquee client was a perfect illustration of the bank's dysfunction. "It was obvious," one board member would lament after reviewing the Trump relationship, "that the bank was not properly managed."

Both reports noted that the recent Trump loans had been financed through DBTCA. Bill Broeksmit, of course, had been on the unit's board up until his death, complaining, without much effect, about the lack of rigorous financial controls that might have prevented precisely this sort of situation.

There was some truth to the reports' conclusions that the Trump relationship was the product of organizational disarray. But that masked a more sobering, problematic reality: Despite not seeing the official exposure reports, quite a few of the bank's highest-ranking executives, including Ackermann and Jain, had more or less known what was going on—and, in fact, both CEOs had seemed to bless aspects of the relationship. They'd known about Trump's reputation for demagogy and defaults, for racism and recklessness, but the allure of quick profits superseded those concerns. Now the bank was pinning the blame for the relationship on a roguish American outpost and trying to hide the entire institution's culpability.

In the weeks after the 2016 election, executives hustled to devise a plan. One immediate step was to reduce the bank's exposure to Russia. A decade earlier, Deutsche had extended a $1 billion credit line to VTB, the Kremlin bank with which Ackermann had forged such close ties. By 2016, about $600 million was outstanding. There was nothing wrong with two banks lending each other money; bank-to-bank transactions were the lifeblood of the financial system. But this was a large loan to a bank with links to Russian intelligence, and Deutsche executives were scared about what might happen if it became public. In the weeks after the election, bankers raced to get the loan off Deutsche's books, selling a large chunk of it to another Russian bank at a discounted price.[2]

The bigger problem, Deutsche executives concluded, was the fact that Trump had given his personal guarantees on hundreds of millions of dollars of outstanding loans. At the time, this had seemed like the safest course, partly shielding the bank if Trump defaulted. Now, though, it meant that the incoming American president was deep in hock to a foreign institution, one over which his administration wielded enormous power. One possibility was to just let Trump off the hook for his personal guarantees; the loan agreements could be amended to delete those provisions, and then it would be the Trump Organization, not Trump himself, that owed all the money. But when Deutsche's discussions about that idea leaked, the outcry was swift. The bank was facing multiple federal investigations, which would now be in the hands of the Trump administration, and giving the president-elect a big financial break smelled corrupt. "It looks terrible," one ethics expert remarked.[3]

The bank decided to revert to its typical plan in such crises: Keep quiet, downplay the severity of the problem, and hope everyone gets distracted and moves on. In Jacksonville, when top executives came to town to hold question-and-answer sessions in the corporate auditorium, employees were warned beforehand against asking questions about Trump. On Wall Street, an edict was issued to the bank's traders and salesmen: They were not to utter the word "Trump" in internal or external communications.

Edicts were rarely adhered to at Deutsche, and before long a number of traders and salesmen had included the forbidden word in emails to their clients as they mused about the effects of a Trump presidency on different parts of the markets. One Deutsche sales guy made the mistake of including a bit of snark about Trump in a note that was widely circulated on Wall Street. He was summoned to a dressing down with officials from the bank's compliance and legal teams. Perhaps, they said, he hadn't grasped the importance of not fanning the Trump flames. They explained why they cared. Deutsche higher-ups were very worried that the incoming president might stop paying back the money he owed, in which case Deutsche would be left with the ugly choice between seizing the president's personal assets or not enforcing the loan terms and, in effect, dispensing a very lucrative gift to the American president. The last thing the bank needed was its employees' jokes drawing unwanted attention to the Deutsche/Trump relationship.

For all the handwringing in the executive suites, the mood on the bank's Wall Street trading floors was jolly. Few employees were all that concerned about the harm that the Trump relationship might inflict on Deutsche; after all, not many of these traders, salesmen, and investment bankers expected to hang around forever. Instead, they dwelled on the positive: The Republican sweep in 2016 was likely to usher in a new era of tax cuts and deregulation. That was superb news for rich Americans, who would benefit directly from lower taxes and only slightly less directly from a stock-market rally caused by the unshackling of heavily regulated industries. While some Deutsche bankers on November 9 were tearful, others huddled in communal kitchens and in elevator bays, grinning and exchanging quiet congratulations about their good fortunes. Their moods only brightened in

the coming weeks as Trump picked one Wall Streeter after another for top jobs in his administration: Wilbur Ross, Steven
Mnuchin, Gary Cohn, Dina Powell—the list went on.

On Tuesday, January 20, Trump arrived at the Capitol to be
sworn in as the forty-fifth president. It was a mild, dreary day in
Washington, and the anticipated hordes of Trump adorers were
slow to materialize on the National Mall. At ground level, facing
the bunting-bedecked stage, was a fenced-off seating area for a
few hundred VIPs. This was where many of Trump's friends,
business associates, and former colleagues, as well as a smattering of foreign officials, would witness the unlikely spectacle of
him becoming the most powerful man in the world.

After taking the oath of office, Trump walked to the lectern
to deliver his fiery Inaugural address. He waved, acknowledg-
ing the cheering crowd. Off to his left in the VIP section sat a
slim, gray-haired woman in a stars-and-stripes scarf and a white
parka. As Trump spoke, it began to rain, and she pulled up her
faux-fur-lined hood. Sixty years earlier, Hermann Abs—the
war criminal who led Deutsche in the postwar era—had attended Eisenhower's second Inaugural as a guest of the president. Now another Deutsche executive received a similar honor:
Rosemary Vrablic.[4]

Val was in Prague, and things were not going well. Julie had
bailed, and he'd picked up an OxyContin habit, crushing eighty-
milligram pills and snorting the powder several times a day. He
shared Goracci's Monte dei Paschi documents with journalists,
leading to a small flurry of stories about the Tuscan bank's she-
nanigans with Deutsche. At one point, Val went to the U.S. Justice Department's website and filled out an email form: "I'm
writing in hopes of speaking to someone at the DOJ in reference
to the evidence I have showing major fraud at one of the world's

largest banks." A month later, he received a formulaic reply from the Justice Department. No one else got in touch.

One day in September 2016, Val stopped at a Vodafone store to get a new SIM card. He returned to his convertible, lit a cigarette, and was preparing to drive away when a hulking man yanked his door open. The man, with a bushy black beard and tight, acid-washed jeans, gestured angrily for Val to get out of the car. They started kicking each other. "Leave me the fuck alone, asshole!" Val yelled. "You piece of shit, fucker!" All he could think was that someone had been sent to kill him to stop him from disseminating information about Deutsche or Paschi. Soon the police arrived. It turned out the burly guy was an Italian repo man, not an assassin. Avis had dispatched him to recover its rental car because Val owed the company thousands of dollars. The police released both men, and the Italian drove off with the convertible. Val didn't see how his life could get any worse.

On November 8, he stayed up all night to watch the election results roll in. As the sun rose over Prague, the TV networks declared Trump the victor. *The whole world's gone mad,* Val thought to himself. Soon he started getting calls from reporters he'd talked to over the past two years. Did his father's files, still accessible by logging into Bill's Gmail and Yahoo accounts, have anything on Deutsche's relationship with Trump? Val's quick search turned up nothing.

Winter descended on the Czech capital. Snow dusted the old city's reddish rooftops. Alla once again canceled her credit card, wising up to her son's latest theft, and Val's funds were low. He migrated south, to Athens and then Rome. One day Catherine Belton, who identified herself as a reporter with the *Financial Times*, emailed Val. She told him that she'd heard about him from a fellow journalist, and she expressed interest in writing about him and his father—not the first reporter to pitch such a yarn. Val took the bait, and Belton flew to Rome on New Year's Eve. They spent the chilly night wandering the city. Val told his story, Belton interrupting to point out this ruin or that historic church. Val periodically excused himself to go to the bathroom to snort Oxy. He and Belton ended up at the Colosseum shortly before midnight. Fireworks exploded, illuminating the ancient stadium in yellows, reds, and greens.

The next day, Val offered Belton a glimpse inside his father's files. She left Rome, promising to be back in touch.

Val soon departed for Lisbon—a cheaper city than Rome. His money and Oxy were nearly exhausted. He called Belton. "I'm in trouble," he pleaded. "I don't know what to do." He needed money. The only asset he had was his father's Deutsche trove. Was there a way to monetize it? Belton told Val that she had an idea of someone who might be willing to pay him. That afternoon, she texted: "It's a go." Val gave her his PayPal and bank account details. Soon $1,000 arrived—and Belton described it as a down payment, "something for starters."* The money was from someone named Glenn Simpson, who Belton wrote was a "really great guy" who was doing opposition research on Trump and Deutsche Bank.

"Wow, that's awesome," Val replied.

Two hours later, a little before eight o'clock on a mild Portuguese evening, Val's phone rang. It was January 26, 2017, the third anniversary of his father's death.

---

* Belton says she "was not party to any financial deal Val may have reached with anyone."

CHAPTER 34

SPYCRAFT

For two decades, Glenn Simpson had been a reporter's reporter, mostly at *The Wall Street Journal*, dredging up explosive stories about political corruption. He was so renowned in Washington journalism circles that a C-Span camera crew once trailed him as he sifted through documents in a federal public-records room. In addition to his reporting chops, Simpson was notorious in the *Journal*'s Washington bureau for belching, scratching his bare belly in view of colleagues, and leaving his desk strewn with half-eaten sandwiches. He was tall and dark-eyed and had a noticeable crick in his neck, a relic of a long-ago car accident. He was often frowning.

In 2009, Simpson and a colleague decided to leave journalism and launch a research company, Fusion GPS, that would cater to hedge funds, corporations, and law firms looking for dirt on their rivals. Drawing on Simpson's reporting skills, Fusion built a large network of clients.[1]

As the 2016 presidential campaign got under way, a conservative website bankrolled by the hedge fund magnate Paul Singer hired Fusion. Its assignment: investigate Trump. Once Trump locked up the Republican nomination, Democrats hired Fusion to search for connections between Trump and Russia. Simpson hooked up with Christopher Steele, a retired British spy who on Fusion's behalf started compiling materials about Trump's dalliances with Russia over the years. He wrote a series of memos outlining what he had gleaned—including that Russia had damaging materials on Trump and that officials in the Trump campaign had been in contact with the Kremlin—and the result was what would become known as the Steele Dossier. On January 10, 2017, the dossier burst into public view when BuzzFeed published the document.

Trump lashed out. Fox News and other conservative outlets joined the chorus. The rest of the media swarmed. Simpson was shoved from the shadows into a white-hot international spotlight.

Two weeks later, he phoned Val.

Like countless others, Val had marveled at the dossier's sensational gossip. Now here Simpson was on the phone, trying to get the star-struck Val to divulge whatever he had on the new president and his relationship with Deutsche. Without going into details, Val said he had gobs of information about all sorts of things at the bank. Simpson agreed to pay $10,000—half up front, half upon delivery—for the materials. The conversation lasted only a few minutes. Anxious that he was being spied on, Simpson didn't want to talk over an unsecured phone line. They switched to an encrypted chat program called Signal; Simpson said they should meet in person. "Let's get you here asap," he messaged.

They decided to meet two days later on Saint Thomas, in the U.S. Virgin Islands. Simpson texted Val an American Express card number to book plane tickets and asked him to start searching for some specific topics. "Any Russia stuff at all," Simpson requested. He added that he was eager for emails or documents related to Renaissance Technologies—the huge hedge fund that Deutsche had worked with to help save it billions in taxes. Simpson was especially curious about any materials on Renaissance's enigmatic leader, Robert Mercer, who along with his daughter Rebekah had become a leading financier of Trump, Steve Bannon, and Breitbart News. "Be safe and I will see you tomorrow," Simpson signed off.

The weather in Saint Thomas was balmy, and Val and Glenn alternated between sifting through Bill's files in a hotel suite and sitting at a picnic table on the beach, drinking beers and smoking cigarettes. Simpson was slightly manic, chattering constantly about Trump and Fusion's financial struggles and the high likelihood that, at that very moment, they were under government surveillance. He told Val that he hoped that any damaging information on Mercer, Trump, or Deutsche would prove valuable to current or prospective Fusion clients. But to both men's dismay, they found no bombshells in Bill's email accounts. There were scant mentions of Trump. The name Mercer hardly came up. There was a lot on Renaissance, but that ground had already been well trodden by Bob Roach's Senate investigation.

Simpson, however, was not ready to quit. He invited Val to return with him to Washington; once there, Val shacked up in a guest room in Simpson's white colonial. One morning, Val was on the front porch, smoking a Marlboro. Simpson joined him and noticed a small rip in the corner of one of his window screens. "Were you messing with my window?" Simpson demanded. "Did you leave the house last night?" Val denied it, but Simpson eyed him suspiciously. "Let's see what the video shows," he said. He escorted Val into his office, flipped on a computer monitor, and pulled up a feed from an infrared camera trained on the front of his house. The grainy footage showed Simpson's son trying to pry the screen off the window. Simpson didn't apologize, but he seemed to relax a little. Val was probably not a spy.

The two men spent the next several days together. They talked about Trump and Christopher Steele and their fathers. Val confided to Simpson about his difficult childhood and his disappearing father and the void that Bill had filled and then vacated. And they plowed through more of Bill's files, which by now Simpson had copied onto his own computer.

Simpson hired a retired auditor from Deutsche to comb through the materials, too. The auditor had left the bank years earlier, angry about many of the same ethical transgressions that had bothered Broeksmit, not least the derivatives that had helped torpedo Monte dei Paschi. He blamed the bank's troubles largely on the reckless management style of Anshu's Army. He had vented about this over the years to journalists, whistleblowers, lawyers, and regulators at the Securities and Exchange Commission and the New York Fed, which was apparently how he had appeared on Simpson's radar. Now he was a Fusion contractor.

The auditor had worked alongside Broeksmit at times in the past, including when he was trying to rein in Troy Dixon, and he found it a little creepy now to be pawing through the dead man's emails. His desire to punish Deutsche helped him overcome his queasiness. He eventually found something interesting. Attached to one of the email chains Broeksmit had received in advance of a DBTCA board meeting was an Excel spreadsheet. To an untrained eye, the spreadsheet looked meaningless, just thousands of rows of numbers under indecipherable headings. But the auditor's eyes were well trained. The document was a snapshot, as of October 8, 2013, of DBTCA's outstanding exposures to hundreds of financial institutions—how much Deutsche owed them and how much they owed Deutsche. It was no secret that the bank

did extensive business with most of the world's biggest banks—
that was part of the reason that the IMF, in 2016, had branded
the company as the world's most systemically dangerous bank—
but what jumped out at the auditor as he scrolled through this
spreadsheet was just how much business, mostly via derivatives,
Deutsche had been doing with Russian banks. There were tens
of millions of dollars outstanding with VTB. Alfa-Bank—another
large, oligarch-controlled Russian lender—was on Deutsche's
list, too. (VTB and Alfa both were under American sanctions.)
And the spreadsheet showed that a network of more obscure
companies—like Russian International Bank and Russian Joint-
Stock Commercial Roads Bank and Russian Mortgage Bank and
Russian Commercial Bank (Cyprus) Limited, to name a few—
also were doing tens of millions of dollars of business with
Deutsche. And that was just on this one particular day that the
spreadsheet captured in the fall of 2013, and only in the one
DBTCA unit of Deutsche. There was no telling how much other
business was happening on other days and in other parts of
Deutsche.

The spreadsheet alone didn't prove anything nefarious—there
wasn't enough information for that. But it was a tantalizing clue
as to just how deeply entangled Deutsche was with Russia and
just how little—despite everything that was already public,
thanks to Deutsche's repeated scrapes with Western law enforcement and regulatory agencies—was really known about what
the bank was up to.

Those answers lay hidden inside Deutsche. Short of theft or a
very lucky break with a very disgruntled employee, the only way
to crowbar open those electronic vaults was for a government
body to issue a subpoena. Simpson and Fusion didn't possess such
authority. But Simpson knew some powerful people—and now
he sent Val to meet them.

———

After nearly twenty years working for the Senate's investigative committee, Bob Roach had switched to the Senate Banking Committee, where he became the chief investigator for the panel's Democrats. In the fall of 2016, as allegations swirled about the Kremlin's efforts to skew the election in Trump's favor and of Trump's supposedly being in Putin's clutches, one thing had jumped into Roach's mind: his old nemesis, Deutsche Bank. There was no doubt that the bank had extensive business dealings with Russia, and those dealings included acting as a conduit for dirty money to get out of the country and into the Western financial system. Deutsche, of course, was the only reliable connection that Trump, his family, and his company had to the mainstream banking world. And Eric Trump had blurted that Russians financed the family's golf projects—even though Deutsche had made the Doral loans.

Perhaps this was more than a coincidence. Maybe Deutsche was what connected Trump to Russia. The rumor that had been ricocheting around Washington, New York, and London was that VTB had in the recent past funneled dirty money to Trump via Deutsche. VTB certainly seemed connected to Trump. Felix Sater, who had once rented the penthouse suite at Trump's 40 Wall Street building, claimed that VTB was facilitating travel and other arrangements for the future president's team in 2016 as they discussed a possible Trump Tower project in Moscow.* And there was no doubt that VTB had deep, long-standing ties to Deutsche. Now the theory was that one of the reasons that Deutsche had been willing to take such risks on loans to Trump was that it wasn't actually taking the risks at all: VTB had agreed

---

* A VTB spokesman denies this.

to secure the loans; if Trump defaulted, Deutsche could collect whatever it was owed from the Russian bank. In effect, that meant that VTB was the one lending to Trump—a direct financial connection between the Russian government and the American president. Deutsche executives insisted this was false, but that didn't stop the rumor from spreading.

Simpson and Roach had known each other for nearly two decades, back to when Simpson, then at *The Wall Street Journal*, was digging into offshore shell companies at the same time that Roach was investigating tax avoidance. Both men were rumpled and indefatigable and accustomed to being underestimated, and now they lived within walking distance of each other and chatted regularly. In February 2017, Simpson suggested that Roach meet Val and peruse his father's files. Roach was happy to oblige; it wasn't every day that someone offered you an unfiltered look at documents from inside a company like Deutsche.

One afternoon, Val—by now staying in a suite Simpson had rented for him at a hotel near the White House—showed up to visit Roach at the Dirksen Senate Office Building on Capitol Hill. Roach still had the rectangular body and sharp jaw of a onetime wrestler; now he had added a flip-top phone and a bunch of cheesy dad jokes to his homespun repertoire. He led Val into his cramped office, amid towering piles of binders, books, and paperwork. Roach had prepared a bundle of printouts for Val: news articles and other materials about Deutsche's years of working with Russian oligarchs and other Putin cronies. They included clippings from a few days earlier, when Deutsche had been penalized by British and New York regulators for the Russian mirror-trading scheme. After agreeing to pay $629 million to settle the cases, the bank pointed at Tim Wiswell, who had been fired in 2015, as "the mastermind of the scheme."[2]

Roach told Val that he was looking for a Trump connection to

Russia via Deutsche. They spent several hours at a small table, huddled over Val's laptop. Val struck Roach as hopelessly scatter-brained, like a burned-out hippie, but the investigator was expe-rienced in dealing with difficult witnesses. Guys like this often didn't realize the value of what they possessed, and the trick was to not get too discouraged or impatient with their idiosyncrasies.

That evening, after a short Senate tour, Val agreed to leave Roach with a digital sampling of some of his father's files. After Roach glanced through the materials, his curiosity was piqued. He knew what the natural next step was: The banking committee should subpoena Deutsche for all of its records related to Trump. But there was no way that any of the Republicans who controlled the banking committee would sign off on a subpoena that had the potential to turn up damaging information about their party's oc-cupant of the White House. (The Democrats, in the minority, didn't have the authority to issue subpoenas on their own.) Nor was there appetite for months- or years-long investigations that might lead to unexpected places. Roach broached the issue of trying to subpoena Deutsche, and his Democratic bosses waved him off.

A week later, Val rented a red Nissan Pathfinder and drove to Phil-adelphia, where he procured a few grams of heroin. His next stop was New York City. Simpson had asked Val to meet with a man there named John Moscow, an attorney at the law firm Baker-Hostetler. Moscow was a minor legend in New York legal circles. He had spent thirty-two years as a prosecutor in the Manhattan district attorney's office, renowned for his victories on big corpo-rate fraud and money-laundering cases. He decamped to private practice in 2005, his Rolodex brimming with contacts in the gov-ernment, at central banks, at top-tier law firms—and with plenty of journalists, including Simpson. (Most recently, Moscow had hired Fusion to help a BakerHostetler client—a Russian company called Prevezon—that was accused of participating in the theft of hundreds of millions of dollars from the hedge fund of an American investor, Bill Browder. Fusion's job was to dig up dirt on Browder. Simpson produced a 600-page dossier. The relationship between Simpson and Moscow was thus cemented.)[3]

Val rode an elevator up to BakerHostetler's headquarters in a Rockefeller Center skyscraper. Moscow occupied a corner office. A wall was crowded with framed photos of him with decades' worth of government bigwigs. Through floor-to-ceiling windows, Val admired the views of midtown Manhattan, its office towers aglow in the evening sky. With his straggly hair and wearing a T-shirt and hoodie, Val was not a conventional visitor to these plush offices. He had snorted some heroin before coming, and he was feeling good—focused, confident, carefree. He unfurled his by-now-well-practiced spiel, explaining who his father was, all the stories Val had leaked to the media, what might still lurk in his father's files, and on and on. Moscow requested a peek, and Val opened his laptop and gave a little multimedia presentation.

Moscow didn't know what to make of his unusual guest. The guy seemed manic—he was talking in rapid-fire bursts—and Moscow wondered if perhaps he was on drugs. Val peppered his monologue with finance buzzwords, but he clearly didn't know much about how Wall Street really worked. And yet . . . he had a cache of documents that appeared to be authentic and could be extremely valuable. Moscow asked if he could have a copy of the files. Val initially balked—he was beginning to worry that he was diluting the value of his possessions by not guarding them more closely—but eventually agreed to share the materials. A BakerHostetler aide came in and copied the files onto a thumb drive.

Back in the Manhattan DA's office, Moscow had gotten to

know a forensic accountant named Sean O'Malley. The two men had stayed in touch over the years. Now O'Malley was leading a team of anti-money-laundering agents at the New York Fed who were investigating. Moscow told O'Malley that he had something interesting to share, and then delivered him a USB stick containing Val's items. The circle was thus complete. Many of the files were related to the scramble inside Deutsche and DBTCA to pacify the very unhappy New York Fed, in the stress tests, in the mirror-trade investigations, and in the bank's accounting and financial reporting—in some cases by masking its problems. Now the materials were in the hands of the very regulator the bank had been so angering.

O'Malley must have been thrilled. The Fed had been struggling to get its hands on internal Deutsche documents; BaFin, the German regulator, was only gradually moving away from its practice of protecting its turf from foreign authorities. While it was possible for American regulators to subpoena documents from Deutsche, it wasn't as easy as it sounded. That made Val's trove especially useful.

A few months later, on a Tuesday afternoon at the end of May, the Fed's years of frustration with Deutsche culminated in an eighteen-page legal agreement with the bank, known as a cease-and-desist order. Like the order the Fed had imposed on DBTCA twelve years earlier in relation to the Latvian money laundering, this one demanded that the bank take immediate action to prevent its customers from using Deutsche to engage in financial crimes. Unlike the 2005 order, this one came with a $41 million penalty attached—a small but symbolic escalation in the severity of the Fed's wrist-slapping. The central bank explained that its latest examination of DBTCA had "identified significant deficiencies" in its risk management and its compliance with anti-money-laundering laws. Because of DBTCA's staffing shortages and stone-age technology—the problems that Broeksmit had repeatedly emailed his colleagues about—billions of dollars of suspicious transactions had washed through DBTCA between 2011 and 2015. The Fed's order was public, but in secret it imposed a more draconian punishment: It downgraded the bank's financial status to "troubled"—a classification that reflected its managerial and financial woes and set it up for years of intense regulatory scrutiny and limits on its operations.[4] After so many years of running wild, DBTCA was finally being put on a tight leash.

Back in Washington, Simpson had lost patience with Val. His irresponsibility, his never-ending nagging about wanting to be part of Fusion's sleuthing, and his spending on Simpson's Amex had all gone too far. "You're acting like a vagabond," Simpson finally exploded.*

For his part, Val was sick of Simpson, who had paid only half of the $10,000 he had promised. "Don't talk to me like you're my father," Val snarled.

"Well," Simpson snapped, choosing words packed with emotional dynamite, "you need someone to act like your father."

---

* Simpson's lawyer says this quote is inaccurate. Val says Simpson authorized in advance all purchases on his credit card.

CHAPTER 35

A NOTE FROM THE PRESIDENT

D onald Trump's newly opened hotel, a couple of blocks down Pennsylvania Avenue from the White House, was booming. The president regularly showed up there for a steak dinner or political fundraiser. A number of top administration officials—including Steven Mnuchin, now the Treasury secretary—took up residence in suites that started at more than $1,000 a night. Interest groups trying to influence federal policy hosted events in the hotel's grand ballroom. Foreign dignitaries and their entourages, hoping to score points with the White House, booked blocks of rooms. The hotel's Benjamin Bar and Lounge—where visitors could sip $10 draft beers in Oval Office–like splendor—became the preferred Washington hangout for the Trump crowd.[1]

Deutsche Bank's money had built the Trump International Hotel. And barely a month into his presidency, Trump was spending a surprising amount of time thinking about his long relationship with his loyal German bank.

Mike Offit was at the Yale Club in Manhattan for a lunch hosted by Business Executives for National Security, an organization of which he was a member. Offit and a few others were chatting with a four-star general about America's arsenal of nuclear weapons. His iPhone buzzed. Offit knew he should ignore it, but he couldn't resist, and he pulled it out of his pocket. He had a new email from something called EOP. Offit opened the email and saw that EOP stood for the White House Executive Office of the President. *How strange*, he thought. The message instructed him to open an attached PDF file. Offit touched the icon and a document appeared on his screen. It was a scanned printout of the email he had sent Trump four months earlier, advising the underdog presidential candidate to blame hedge funds for his companies' bankruptcies. In a black Sharpie, a message was scrawled diagonally across the top of the printout. Offit instantly recognized the tall, squished handwriting: "Mike—Such a cool letter. Best wishes, Donald."

Offit had known Trump for decades, but this was his first time communicating with a president of the United States. He got goose bumps. The most powerful man in the world had sent him a handwritten response to his half-baked email. Offit couldn't help but wonder if the president didn't have more important things to do with his time. What on earth had prompted him now, months after the email was sent, to read it and reply? It reminded Offit of the note he'd received nearly two decades earlier: "Thanks for all of your help—you are a <u>great</u> friend," Trump had penned on the rendering of the planned Trump World Tower. The difference was that the earlier note had a clear purpose: to reward Offit for arranging a loan and to encourage him to do it again.

"Look at this!" Offit exclaimed to the general. "I just got a note from the president!"

"What do you mean, you got a note from the president?"

Offit handed him the phone so he could see for himself. The

general's eyes widened. "Wow," he said. "That's more of a response than we can get out of him." The general asked what Offit's relationship was with the president. "I loaned him half a billion dollars," Offit crowed.

That was on February 21, 2017. One week later, on a warm, rainy evening in Washington, the presidential motorcade pulled up at the Capitol for Trump's first address to a joint session of Congress. In contrast to his hell-raising "American carnage" inaugural oration a month earlier, this speech was calm and conciliatory. Trump had hewed, more or less, to the teleprompter text and had sounded, more or less, like a normal Republican. (Back at the White House that night, relieved aides would give him a standing ovation.[2]) After stepping down from the lectern, Trump shook hands with the dignitaries in the audience. In the front row were the Supreme Court justices. Trump moved down the line until he got to Anthony Kennedy. As Trump pumped the justice's hand, Kennedy congratulated him on a successful speech. "Very nice, thank you," Trump replied. "Say hello to your boy," he added, patting the justice's arm. "Special guy."

The eighty-year-old justice was tickled to hear the president praising his son and remembering the help that Justin Kennedy had provided years earlier to finance Trump projects that no other banks would touch and that even within Deutsche had been deeply controversial. That help had continued even after Kennedy left Deutsche; he had his own finance and real estate firm and had worked with other members of the Trump family, including Kushner. (Kennedy in 2011 helped restructure the overwhelming debt that the Kushner Companies had on their flagship skyscraper at 666 Fifth Avenue in Manhattan.[3] That same year, coincidentally or not, Kennedy landed for the first time on a list of the hundred most powerful people in New York real estate—a ranking published by Kushner's *New York Ob-*

server.) And he regularly socialized with Don Jr. and Ivanka Trump.

"Your kids have been very nice to him," Justice Kennedy said to the president.

"Well, they love him, and they love him in New York," Trump cooed. "He's a great guy." The president turned to the chief justice, John Roberts. "You've got a good guy," he said, gesturing at Kennedy.

Justin Kennedy was at home, watching Trump's speech on TV. This veteran financier, so accustomed to rubbing shoulders with the rich and famous, watched as Trump shook his father's hand and exchanged pleasantries. He couldn't help but feel impressed. Later that night, he called his father. "What did he say?" Justin asked.

"He says hi to you!" the proud father exclaimed.

Trump's flattery was part of a coordinated White House charm offensive designed to persuade the aging justice—for years, the court's pivotal swing vote—that it was safe to retire, even with an unpredictable man in the Oval Office. Milking the family connection via Deutsche Bank—whose offices the elder Kennedy had repeatedly visited over the years—was a central part of the strategy. For a notoriously dysfunctional White House, this was a rare instance of savvy scheming. The campaigning had begun weeks earlier, at an inaugural lunch in the Capitol, when Ivanka was seated beside Justice Kennedy. She had talked his ear off about her great relationship with Justin. She described how they first got to know each other in 2005 when Deutsche made the big loan to finance the Chicago skyscraper that Ivanka was in charge of, and how it had only grown deeper in the ensuing years. Afterward, Justice Kennedy invited her to visit the Supreme Court as a VIP guest. A few weeks later (two days after the White House emailed Offit), Ivanka showed up at the Supreme Court with her five-year-old daughter to hear a case about arbitration agreements.[4] The next month, Justin Kennedy and his brother were guests at the White House's Saint Patrick's Day celebration.[5]

In June 2018, Anthony Kennedy announced his retirement. Trump now had the opportunity to nominate his second Supreme Court justice* and to fundamentally alter the high court's composition. The prospect of tipping the balance in a decisive conservative direction ensured that any Republicans who were losing confidence in their party's unconventional president now reaffirmed their commitment to the success of the Trump administration. On the Saturday in October 2018 when Brett Kavanaugh was sworn in, Kennedy was there to witness the occasion.

Deutsche Bank in previous decades had helped stabilize Trump's floundering business. Now—indirectly, through past relationships and loans—it had helped stabilize his floundering presidency.

After leaving Zurich Insurance in shame, having been blamed for his colleague's suicide, Joe Ackermann had been expected to fade into retirement. But in 2014 he got a call about a job opportunity in Cyprus. The Mediterranean island's banks had been decimated by their reckless lending, as well as by the country's economic crisis. Some prominent financiers now were looking for bargain-basement acquisitions. The country's largest lender, the Bank of Cyprus, soon got new owners: Wilbur Ross, an American investor and Trump's future Commerce secretary, and Viktor Vekselberg, a Russian oligarch with ties to the Kremlin. Ross and Vekselberg drew up a short list of candidates to run the place, and Ackermann was their choice to be chairman. Ackermann—such

---

* The prior year, he had successfully nominated Neil Gorsuch to fill Antonin Scalia's seat.

a Russophile that he had entertained Putin's offer to run the Kremlin's investment fund—was impressed by Vekselberg's credentials and convinced himself that the Russian was a good, honest man. (The United States imposed sanctions on Vekselberg and his company in 2018.[6]) Ackermann took the job.

Even after the collapse of its economy and financial system, Cyprus had remained a portal for Russians to launder money into the European Union and the eurozone. That scared many big banks away from doing business there. Not Deutsche. It continued to help Bank of Cyprus, with Ackermann now at the helm, convert foreign currencies into dollars and euros—a crucial cog in any international money-laundering machine. The Bank of Cyprus relationship lasted into at least 2015—and Deutsche's Cypriot work in general lasted much longer. Well into Trump's presidency, employees in Deutsche's anti-money-laundering offices in Florida would be flagging suspicious transactions their bank was doing on behalf of various Cypriot lenders. Ackermann was long gone from Deutsche, but here was one more sign of his lingering legacy.

Deutsche was beginning to look like a zombie. It had been losing money for years. Tens of billions of dollars of derivatives—likely representing billions of dollars of fresh losses—continued to pollute its balance sheet. The bank's shares were at their lowest level since they debuted on the New York Stock Exchange shortly after 9/11, and they were down 92 percent from their 2007 peak. Investors, regulators, and even some of the bank's senior executives had fundamental doubts about the institution's viability.

A few months earlier, just days before Trump was sworn in as president, the Obama administration's Justice Department pummeled Deutsche Bank with a $7 billion penalty—among the largest fines ever imposed on a bank—for ripping off investors and borrowers through its fraudulent sale of mortgage-backed securities. A parade of federal prosecutors and politicians blasted the bank and its traders and executives for their recklessness and greed. Deutsche's acquisition of MortgageIT, including the destructive manner in which its production was revved up just as the mortgage market was melting down, was a key element of the case. The settlement agreement quoted extensively from internal emails and chat messages in which Deutsche traders, supervisors, and salesmen candidly acknowledged that they were tricking investors and misleading customers. Most of the misconduct was a decade old, and plenty of other banks had engaged in similar behavior, but the enormous financial penalty further drained Deutsche's drying well of capital.

And more problems loomed. In early 2017, shortly after Trump's inauguration, British and German journalists had emailed the bank's public relations department and informed them that they were writing a story about a previously undisclosed Russian money-laundering scheme involving the bank—the sprawling Laundromat operation. This was the first that senior Deutsche executives had heard of this about-to-erupt scandal. Weary bank officials started investigating. They soon realized that Deutsche had been moving money—as much as $80 billion—for thousands of "high-risk entities" in various countries. An internal presentation to the supervisory board concluded that the scheme exposed the bank's senior executives to potentially severe government penalties.[7]

To employees, the eras of Ackermann and Jain had become parables for the perils of growing too fast, pursuing profits above all else, not caring about clients' integrity, not taking the time to integrate businesses. Deutsche still had a tangled nest of more than a hundred different internal technology systems that didn't interact properly—and that was after the bank had managed to cut the number by more than half. There was something like fifty petabytes—each petabyte being a million gigabytes—of incompatible data crammed into various computer servers around the company. "You don't even know where the problems are or where to start," confessed an employee tasked with cleaning up the mess. "Regulators tell us, 'What you've got is the skeleton of a child in the body of an adult.' "

Gallows humor became the order of the day. Some employees noted that the bank's blue-slash logo resembled a falling domino. Conspiracy theories about Bill's suicide blossomed. A popular one held that he had wanted to come clean about high-level malfeasance but was warned he would be thrown under the bus, personally paying the price for the bank's sins. Memories of Edson Mitchell had all but vanished. "He is forgotten," said one mid-level employee, who had heard rumors of his "racy lifestyle" but was pretty sure his name was "Edsall."

Back in Jacksonville, Deutsche's anti-money-laundering watchdogs were reaching the breaking point. They'd been chafing for years under a succession of regional executives whom many staff members perceived as imperious and incompetent. More than a few compliance officers—trained at other financial institutions to view themselves as a crucial shield against financial crime—quit in frustration at what they saw as Deutsche's haphazard setup, in which employees were incentivized to churn through transactions as quickly as possible, with little regard for the potential problems they uncovered. (One employee would recount how she was instructed to stop highlighting transactions involving companies exposed in the massive leak known as the Panama Papers. Another was told to pipe down when protesting a transaction in which money was wired to a prominent sanctioned Russian.) Now, as Deutsche swiveled between trying to cut costs and trying to beef up its compliance programs, longtime staffers watched with dismay as the bank brought in hundreds of outside consultants—many of them young and inexperienced, all of them cheaper than full-time employees—to supplement the anti-money-laundering workforce. With the influx of rookie newcomers, veteran managers couldn't shake the feeling that they were being set up to fail.

There was one elite arm of the anti-money-laundering squad that seemed to be doing all right. It was called the Special Investigations Unit, and it consisted in part of former police and military officials who were considered the best of the best in their field. Their job was to review the most complicated and sensitive transactions. Starting in 2017, that assignment included anything associated with the new president and his dozens of legal entities. When some of those accounts—including the one belonging to the Donald J. Trump Foundation, soon to be shut down after New York prosecutors accused it of operating as a political slush fund—started moving money outside the United States, the investigations group took a look. Employees concluded the transactions were suspicious enough that they should be reported to the government. As had happened with Tammy McFadden the prior year, suspicious activity reports were created, sent up the ladder for approval—and then dismissed.[8] Deutsche officials denied it, but it was hard to avoid the impression that bank higher-ups were going to bat for their most powerful customer.

On December 4, 2017, a German newspaper reported that Robert Mueller, the special counsel investigating Russia's interference in the presidential election, had subpoenaed Deutsche, demanding records related to its relationship with Trump.[9] Within hours, a number of American news organizations had published their own stories, with anonymous sources confirming that Mueller's office had issued the subpoenas. Trump woke up that morning, scanned the headlines on his phone, saw the news about the subpoena, and exploded. "I know my relationships with Deutsche Bank," the president barked at his lawyer, John Dowd, in a seven A.M. phone call. "I'm telling you, this is bullshit!"[10] Dowd organized a phone call with Mueller's team. One of the prosecutors assured Dowd that the news reports had been wrong; Mueller's team hadn't subpoenaed Deutsche for Trump's records. (It turned out that the special counsel had subpoenaed Deutsche for the records of Paul Manafort, Trump's onetime campaign manager.) Word of Trump's fury circulated around Washington. To any government official paying attention, this was a powerful signal: Investigate Deutsche and risk the president's wrath.

For the bank, this was a thick silver lining to the ominous cloud of Trump. And here was another: The Trump administration was rapidly relaxing government regulations designed to hem in Wall Street. The Consumer Financial Protection Bureau was neutered. Joseph Otting, who had previously worked for Steven Mnuchin, was installed atop the Office of the Comptroller of the Currency, a powerful federal regulator, and promptly loosened the reins on the country's biggest banks. Advocates of tough industry oversight exited the Federal Reserve. The administration watered down the Volcker Rule, which restricted banks from engaging in so-called proprietary trading—what had been Deutsche's lifeblood. At the very end of 2017, the Labor Department disclosed in the Federal Register that it was cutting a break to Deutsche and four other banks that had admitted to criminal misconduct in their manipulation of interest rates. Under federal law, companies that are convicted of violating securities laws aren't allowed to manage employees' retirement plans unless they get a waiver from the Labor Department. Now, in a manner that seemed crafted to minimize public attention, the Trump administration granted multiyear waivers.[11]

This was all good news in Frankfurt, but the Justice Department's investigation into Deutsche laundering money for Putin's associates via the mirror trades still loomed. (Deutsche's previous civil settlements with American and British regulators didn't affect the criminal investigation.) In the final months of the Obama administration, all signs had pointed to charges soon being filed against bank employees and probably the bank itself. At the very least, a multibillion-dollar financial penalty looked all but certain.

Something curious, however, had happened as soon as Trump took the oath of office. The investigation had gone silent. Week after week, Deutsche's lawyers and executives wondered when they would get an update. At first they worried that the delay spelled trouble. Perhaps, after campaigning as a populist, after vowing that he was "not going to let Wall Street get away with murder," Trump planned an aggressive crackdown on banking malfeasance. Perhaps, after having his election victory tarnished by Russian interference, Trump would try to dispel those suspicions with a high-profile assault on Russian money laundering.

But as months passed, and nothing happened, executives' fears faded. One source of relief was the realization that two of the Justice Department's most powerful prosecutors, Geoffrey Berman and Robert Khuzami, both had previously represented Deutsche. Berman, whom Trump had appointed as the U.S. Attorney for the Southern District of New York, had defended the bank and its employees in tax-evasion cases. Khuzami had been one of Dick Walker's first hires at Deutsche back in 2002 and later had become its top internal lawyer and later still represented the bank when he worked at an outside law firm—and now he was Berman's second-in-command. It was the old revolving door that had allowed Deutsche (and plenty of its peers) to co-opt its pursuers by hiring them, except that now it was happening in reverse. These two men were among those deciding Deutsche's fate.*

Bank executives soon concluded that Russia was off-limits, too hot to handle, for the Trump administration. So, it seemed, was Deutsche.

Paul Achleitner, the bank's chairman, was on a two-week vacation in the Peruvian Andes when the news broke that he had been secretly trying to replace John Cryan as CEO. Cryan had known Achleitner was getting antsy—the pace of improvement on his watch was sluggish at best, and the bank's recent warnings that its finances remained weak had further shellacked its stock price—but he hadn't realized his job was in imminent peril. Achleitner had canvassed top executives at banks like Goldman Sachs to gauge their interest in the job, a tactic virtually guaranteed to leak to the media. Within hours of the publication of articles about Achleitner searching for a new CEO, the bank was engulfed in a leadership crisis.

Achleitner cut short his vacation—Machu Picchu would have to wait—and accelerated his hunt for a new CEO. This was his second time in three years replacing the bank's leaders. One candidate after another rebuffed him; the top job at Deutsche seemed like a poisoned chalice. Meanwhile, the bank's board of directors very much preferred someone who could steer their German bank back to the simple things that it had been good at before a parade of CEOs had chased Wall Street riches.

There were a few senior executives currently at the bank who

---

* Khuzami stepped down from the U.S. attorney's office in March 2019.

fit that mold, and a leading contender soon emerged. He was
German, a Deutsche lifer, someone who'd been at the bank basically since high school. He had worked in different parts of the
company, including retail banking and the legal department, as
well as on three continents. He was forty-eight years old, with a
boyish face and spiky hair.

On April 8, Achleitner unveiled the bank's new CEO. It was
Christian Sewing—the same man who had warned decades earlier about Deutsche forgetting its heritage, the same man who
had nixed the final Trump loan, the same man who had presented what looked like a whitewash about the investigation into
Bill Broeksmit's suicide. Now he would be running the entire
company.

Sewing was surprised by what the new gig entailed. This was a
company with more than 90,000 employees—even as the bank's
finances crumbled, Deutsche had managed to expand its workforce by some 12,000 employees over the past decade—yet investors and journalists tended to view the bank through a
CEO-centric prism. Everything that happened at Deutsche would
henceforth be framed as a success or failure of Sewing. Everything he did or said was scrutinized and could be dredged up
months later to undermine a decision he made or an action the
bank took. The smallest slip of his tongue had the potential to
anger one constituency or another: investors or colleagues or
union members or a particular journalist or German regulators
or American regulators or the president of the United States. It
was unnerving.

A year into the job, Sewing remained healthy and fit—nearing
fifty, he still had the taut body of a high-caliber tennis player. But
deep creases lined his forehead. His once-spiky hair drooped,

thinned, and grayed. His face looked weathered, the boyish sheen scraped away. The job was hard. There were no attractive answers about how to clean up the bank's many messes or how the company might make money in the future. The bank's largest shareholders for the past few years—predating Sewing—included Qatar's royal family,* a shadowy Chinese conglomerate, and the American private equity firm Cerberus. These investors were not patient.

Nor, it turned out, was the German government. Senior officials in Berlin doubted the bank's viability. It didn't have a clear identity or direction. The threat of having to bail out this monstrously large institution was omnipresent. Leading politicians pushed Sewing and Achleitner to consider radical changes—including, on the eve of the bank's 150th anniversary, merging with another troubled German lender, Commerzbank. Sewing didn't want to be the one responsible for bringing the curtain down on what once had been a proud national icon, but he didn't see much of a choice. The combined companies would still be called Deutsche Bank, but it would be a fundamentally different institution—as if the clocks had been turned back to a time before the bank's plunge into Wall Street. Negotiations between Deutsche, Commerzbank, and the German government dragged on for months, only to unravel when all parties concluded that merging two bad banks wasn't as likely to create one healthy bank as it was to result in a single very sick one. Deutsche Bank would have to go it alone.

As weeks passed, it became clear how treacherous that solitar

---

* When Qatar made its investment, its financial adviser was Michele F
sola. A lawyer who had previously represented Faissola later ended u
Deutsche's supervisory board at the behest of the Qataris.

path would be. The bank's shares sank to their lowest levels ever—down 95 percent from their 2007 apex. Employees bailed. So did customers, including loyal ones like the hedge fund Renaissance Technologies, which had remained one of Deutsche's biggest clients even after the companies' tax-avoiding scheme was brought to light. Now Renaissance started pulling money out of its accounts—a sign of just how nervous everyone was about Deutsche's solvency.[12] Sewing and Achleitner scrambled to devise a plan that would prove to investors, customers, employees, and regulators that this crippled bank had the capacity to recover, albeit in a much smaller form.

After endless media and market speculation, the plan was unveiled on a pleasant Sunday afternoon in July 2019. It called for Deutsche to exit most of its remaining sales-and-trading businesses—the heart and soul of the Wall Street juggernaut that Edson Mitchell and Anshu Jain and Bill Broeksmit had constructed. Tens of billions of dollars of unwanted assets—many of them the derivatives that for years had been unnerving investors and regulators—would be disposed of. Some 18,000 jobs would disappear, representing about 20 percent of Deutsche's workforce. A number of top executives—including the head of the investment-banking business and the head of regulatory affairs—were shown the door. The goal was to weed out anything that wasn't related to helping German individuals and European companies do business at home and abroad. The hope was that this would turn out to be at least modestly profitable.

It was Sewing's third and presumably final stab at crafting a recovery plan for the bank he had joined as a teenager thirty years earlier. Back in 2004, in the midst of Deutsche's anarchic stampede for short-term profits, he had complained to Hugo Bänziger that the bank was forgetting its heritage—and then resigned when his concerns fell on deaf ears. Now Sewing framed his vision for the company's future in nostalgic terms.

"We lost our compass in the last two decades," he confessed. "It is my personal purpose to connect this bank with what it used to be."[13] Given Deutsche's ugly past, that didn't inspire much confidence in the bank's future.

EPILOGUE

Val had rented a room in a ranch house on top of a hill in Culver City, California, not far from Sony Pictures' studios. He had three roommates, no car, no job. He subsisted on the $2,800 that Alla's banker wired him once a month; for all the trauma that had transpired, she couldn't bring herself to pull the financial plug on her first-born child. Val stalked social media for clues about what his mother and sisters were up to. In the spring of 2018, he noticed that Alla had paid someone named Marie using the money-transfer app Venmo. The name sounded familiar, and Val realized he'd been following her on Instagram. She was an artist based in L.A. He started liking dozens of her old posts. Val thought that her art was beautiful and that she was, too. Maybe this was a way to infiltrate his mom's life.

Marie had grown up in France and Australia. She'd met Alla in an art class in New York a couple of years earlier, back when Alla was in mourning. They had become friends, and Alla confided in Marie about Bill, the circumstances of his death, her attempts to bounce back, and her falling-out with her son. So when Marie noticed Val tracking her on Instagram, she was intrigued. Alla, however, demanded that Marie block him from seeing her account, and when Marie hesitated, Alla took her phone and did it for her. Marie's curiosity was piqued by the intense reaction, and she unblocked Val later that day.

When Marie first heard from Val, she was in Australia to display a series of her surrealistic oil paintings. "Hi, is this Marie, who is also a friend of my mother?" Val asked her in an Instagram message. He had hatched a bizarre plan: He would befriend her, win her confidence, sleep with her, and lure her into spilling some of his mother's secrets. Somewhere in the back of her mind, Marie had flirted with the idea of contacting Val. Now she replied swiftly. "Your mum is very against this," she texted.

"She's against everything," Val replied.

"You seem like an interesting character," Marie answered. Dozens of messages zipped between them. Then Val called her. He found her French accent sexy. She found his voice captivating. She also wondered if he might be a lunatic. She didn't need that in her life right now; she was separated from her husband and was the primary caretaker of their six-year-old boy. When her plane landed in Los Angeles a few days later, Val called her at the airport. "I need to see you right now," he insisted.

"No, I have to see my son," she said, laughing. A week later, though, she got a babysitter and met Val at a trendy, pharmacy-themed bar called Apotheke. Marie sat in the club's patio, smoking cigarettes, waiting for her date to arrive. When he walked in, one thought flashed through her mind: trouble. Val was tall and skinny and had a scraggly beard and a halfhearted ponytail. Marie thought he looked cool and handsome. He exuded charisma. Their conversation bounced along, Marie's nervousness fading. Val made her feel at ease. So did the vodka and then the cocaine. They went home together.

Marie could tell that Val was trying to extract information from her about his mother. He wasn't hiding it. He was furious with Alla and wanted to hurt her. "Fucking her good friend seemed like a pretty good strategy," Marie smirked when I spoke to her later. Their relationship blossomed. In September 2018, Val took Marie up to San Francisco and introduced her to Pegi Young. The three of them spent hours at her ranch that afternoon. Marie could see how much Val and Pegi cared for each other; around her, Val seemed vulnerable—and happy. Back in L.A., Val moved into Marie's apartment, in an artists' commune near Chinatown, which she occupied with her son. Marie didn't tell Alla that she was living with Val; instead, she engaged in long text message exchanges with Alla, trying to tease out information about Bill and Deutsche and Michele Faissola and her relationship with her lost son.

On November 6, 2018, riding a wave of anti-Trump anger, Democrats seized a majority in the House of Representatives. Republicans still controlled the White House and the Senate, but Trump for the first time faced an opposition party with tangible power. Nancy Pelosi became the House Speaker, and two of Trump's most vocal congressional critics, Maxine Waters and Adam Schiff, took over powerful committees. Waters became chairman of the House Financial Services Committee, which was responsible for overseeing the banking industry, and Schiff took charge of the House Intelligence Committee. Running those panels, the two California Democrats now had the ability not only to advance their favored legislation but also to issue subpoenas. One of the first things they did was to announce that their committees would jointly investigate Trump's relationship with Deutsche.

The investigation by Schiff's panel—which wanted to know whether Trump was in hock to the Kremlin and if Deutsche had somehow served as a financial intermediary between Russia and Trump—would be led by a pair of former federal prosecutors in

New York, Daniel Goldman and Dan Noble. The focus of Waters's committee was Trump's personal finances, including whether he or the bank had received special treatment at the hands of the other. The panel already had a large staff of finance experts, but it didn't have anyone with a specialty in Deutsche. As it happened, Bob Roach was tired of languishing in the minority party. In early 2019, after decades in the Senate, he agreed to move to the other side of Capitol Hill, where he joined the Financial Services Committee. Twenty years earlier, he had started his pursuit of Deutsche by investigating the ties between a private banker and Mexico's Raúl Salinas. Now he would rejoin the hunt for his white whale, investigating the ties between a private banker and Donald Trump.

Rosemary Vrablic figured it was only a matter of time until she was summoned to testify before a congressional committee about how she had stage-managed the bank's Trump relationship. In private conversations with journalists and government officials, Deutsche executives had been downplaying senior executives' involvement in, and even knowledge of, all the loans to Trump, insisting that it was Vrablic and her old boss Tom Bowers who had unilaterally masterminded the whole arrangement. Vrablic was still employed by Deutsche (Bowers was long gone), but she worried that she was about to be publicly hung out to dry. She took solace in the fact that she had extensive email chains and internal documents that showed how the loans to Trump and his family had been blessed up and down the chain of command. Just to be safe, she printed out some of the materials and stashed them in her Park Avenue penthouse.

On January 1, 2019, Pegi Young died of cancer. Val hadn't realized she was sick, and he felt like he had, one more time, lost a family member without any warning. "The world is darker & colder without pegi," he tweeted, posting a photo of them hugging. "I'm devastated & shocked & don't know what to say." He began sleeping all day and getting so stoned that he was "like a zombie," Marie told me.

Besides searching for the truth about Deutsche Bank, Val had been trying to drum up Hollywood interest in his life story—a project that had ground to a halt when Pegi died. One evening, though, a film producer invited Val to a small dinner party at a house she was renting up in the Hollywood Hills. Among the guests was Moby, the electronic music legend. "The dinner had an accidentally survivalist theme, as we had to make dinner with whatever food the previous tenant had left behind," Moby recalls. "So we had vegan spaghetti, slightly stale bread, and a surprisingly wonderful salad." It turned out that Moby and Adam Schiff were pals; Schiff, a fellow vegan, was a regular guest at Moby's plant-based L.A. restaurant, Little Pine. When Moby heard Val's haunting story, and the fact that he was in possession of a trove of internal Deutsche materials, he made some introductions. In early 2019, Val and Daniel Goldman, the ex-prosecutor working for Schiff, had a preliminary phone call. Val outlined what he had and offered to help. Goldman, just starting to work on the investigation, hadn't realized that one of DBTCA's board members had committed suicide and that the banker's son had retrieved his electronic files.

Goldman wanted those files—so much so that he sent Val to meet with Schiff in his district office in L.A. Val showed up wearing orange-laced sneakers and a Grateful Dead shirt. The congressman, in a suit and tie, ushered Val out after barely fifteen minutes. It was hard to believe that this guy was for real. But the intelligence committee needed information, and Val undoubtedly had some. The committee soon wrote Val a formal letter, signed by Schiff, requesting that he load his father's materials onto "an encrypted thumb drive" and mail it to Washington.

Val, however, wanted something in return, preferably money. He pushed Goldman to fly him to D.C. and to hire him as a paid consultant as the committee combed through the Broeksmit files. Goldman resisted—there was zero chance that he was about to let Val hang around the committee's heavily secured chambers. Instead, he appealed to Val's sense of patriotism. "Imagine a scenario where some of the material that you have can actually provide the seed that we can then use to blow open everything that [Trump] has been hiding," Goldman urged. "In some respects, you and your father vicariously through you will go down in American history as a hero and as the person who really broke open an incredibly corrupt president and administration." But Val wouldn't budge, insisting that he needed to supervise the committee's work. Goldman finally snapped. "I can guarantee you that I have spent exponentially more time talking to you about getting these documents than I have to Deutsche Bank itself," he hissed. "You are proving to be very, very difficult to deal with."

Val wasn't the only source of frustration. The two committees in April issued subpoenas to Deutsche for its records related to the Trump and Kushner accounts—everything from personal financial information to any records related to suspicious activity reports tied to the accounts. In the hands of congressional Democrats, the materials could become a Rosetta Stone to unlock Trump's innermost financial secrets. For that reason, when the president learned of the subpoenas, his lawyers sued to block Deutsche from complying. The dispute spent months winding through the federal court system. In the midst of that process, the intelligence committee in June issued a new subpoena—this one to Val. It demanded that he promptly hand over everything in his possession related to Deutsche. Val grudgingly complied.

"My apologies," the FBI special agent wrote, "but I have just been handed your information which you had sent some time ago via email to the U.S. Department of Justice." More than two years had passed since Val submitted the form on the department's website inviting someone to call him to discuss what he'd found in his father's Deutsche files. Now a call was organized, and the FBI agent, based in Manhattan, told Val that he was interested, very interested, in taking a look at whatever he had retrieved from Bill's accounts. The agent told Val that he and a partner would fly to L.A. in the near future to talk in person. He didn't say what he was investigating, and Val couldn't help but wonder if he was walking into a trap. Was he about to get busted for assisting North Korean hackers or stealing his mother's money or moving drugs across international borders?

In February 2019, the two agents—both with backgrounds in counterintelligence and currently on a squad focused on banking malfeasance—flew to California. Their meeting took place the same day that Michael Cohen, Trump's former lawyer, testified on Capitol Hill that the president had routinely exaggerated his wealth in order to win loans from Deutsche Bank. Val, wearing a partly unbuttoned paisley shirt, arrived at the bureau's field office in a federal building downtown. The agents met him in the tenth-floor lobby, where portraits of President Trump watched over visitors, and escorted him upstairs.

The meeting lasted three hours. Val munched on Kit Kats and raspberry-flavored fig bars and drank coffee and Coke and smoked his e-cigarette and unspooled his story a final time. The agents told him they had started out investigating Deutsche's money laundering in Russia—the notorious mirror trades—but they had widened their scope to focus on an array of potential criminality at the bank. They were interested in DBTCA. They were interested in Monte dei Paschi. They were interested in the Fed's stress tests. (Soon the same agents would be in touch with a number of Deutsche whistleblowers. One of the employees who had complained to the SEC about how the bank was hiding billions of dollars in losses on derivatives got a call. So did Tammy McFadden, the former compliance officer who had raised concerns about Kushner's company moving money to Russians. These former employees were more than happy to help bring the bank to justice.)

If Deutsche executives had been listening in on Val's interview, they would have been deeply unsettled. The bank's confidence that the federal investigations into its crimes in Russia and elsewhere were wrapped up, neutered, had been misplaced. These two special agents, along with a team of their colleagues and federal prosecutors, were still on Deutsche's trail—though it remained far from clear where this criminal investigation would go or whom it would touch. The agents didn't think the crimes that occurred throughout the bank were the work of lone low-level employees—they suspected that this was the product of a culture of criminality that pervaded Deutsche. Tim Wiswell— Wiz, the supposed mastermind of the mirror trades—appeared to be a "fall guy," a "scapegoat," they explained. And now someone with a potentially valuable cache of documents was sitting in a large conference room in an FBI field office, being plied with sugary snacks—and the possibility of power.

"You're holding documents that only people within the inner circle of Deutsche would ever see," the first agent told Val.

"What we've been up against is stonewalling," the other agent chimed in. "Clearly things went on in Deutsche Bank which weren't kosher. What we're up against is all those bad acts are being pushed down on the little people on the bottom."

"The low-hanging fruit," the first agent added.

"And the larger bank in its entirety is claiming ignorance and that it's one bad player. But we know what we've seen, it's a culture of just—"

"Fraud and dirt," Val interjected, thrilled to be part of this. He called me from a Lyft afterward. His adrenaline was still pumping. "I am more emotionally invested in this than anyone in the world," he said. "I would love to be their special informer."

A couple of months later, a padded manila envelope arrived at Marie's apartment, addressed to Val. The return address was the FBI's Manhattan headquarters. Inside was a thumb drive. Val had concluded that the materials he'd guarded for the past five years belonged in the FBI's hands—a decision made easier when the agents agreed to help Marie and her son secure visas so they could legally remain in the United States. The agents had told Val that once he had loaded his goods onto the miniature drive, someone would come by to pick it up. Val texted me a photo of the envelope. It had three postage stamps, each depicting a household pet: a mouse, a guinea pig, and a parrot.

"Guess I'm the mouse," he wrote. I asked him why, and he responded within seconds, invoking a fable. "Because I can take down an elephant."

In death, Bill Broeksmit became a symbol: of what ails Deutsche Bank, of the destructive power of institutional greed, of how Wall Street lures even well-intentioned people away from their moral and ethical principles, of the relentless pressure that bears down on those who stand up for what they believe is right.

Broeksmit was no saint, but he was a moral man—no easy feat in an amoral industry, one in which instant profits trumped all else. Survival, to say nothing of success, required constant compromises. Broeksmit had ethics, one of his former colleagues told me, but they were "trader ethics." He didn't want to pull the wool over anyone's eyes, but he did want to make money—for himself, for his employer, for customers, for shareholders—and that sometimes required being aggressive. Broeksmit wouldn't kill an unethical transaction; he would tweak it. A little sleight of hand—with MortgageIT, for example—was acceptable if it was within the letter of the law.

That is part of what made his ethical code palatable to his peers. Being part of their system gave him the credibility to critique that system, to argue that sometimes everyone should take a step back from the system's norms and revert to a more conservative baseline. The fact that Broeksmit ultimately failed—Deutsche's mile-long rap sheet is testament to that—reflects less on him than on the institution and, in fact, the entire banking system.

Broeksmit may have found solace and discipline in his effort to walk the line at work, a way to sequester his inner demons and mental anguish. But that firewall seems to have ruptured as his fears grew that he, too, had been complicit in something shameful and that it would be exposed via government investigations. He absorbed his professional failures, took them personally, as if they belonged to him rather than to the out-of-control bank that would have been on an even more treacherous crash course had it not been for his periodic pumping of the brakes. With the benefit of hindsight, it is hard to imagine a worse place for someone like Broeksmit to have worked than Deutsche, with its endless cutting of corners and hostility to the rule of law. Then again, Deutsche might have been the industry's worst offender, but it was hardly the only criminal entity. Just about every scandal that engulfed the bank during the past two decades also swept over at least one or two other rivals. Maybe Broeksmit was doomed the moment he entered the industry, long before he met Edson Mitchell and then followed him to Deutsche.

Ultimately, although his longtime employer played a role in his decision to die, Deutsche Bank did not kill Bill Broeksmit. Instead, the bank—through the years of recklessness, greed, immorality, hubris, and criminality that emanated from its dark towers—killed itself.

ACKNOWLEDGMENTS

This book would not exist were it not for the extensive cooperation of my sources. Quite a few took professional or personal risks to speak to me, while others dug up painful memories. I am grateful for their help and patience.

None more so than Val Broeksmit. Over the past five-plus years, we have spent what must be hundreds of hours talking on the phone, meeting in person, and exchanging text messages. This hasn't always been easy for either of us. Val, so eager for his and his father's stories to be told, dealt with repeated delays and fended off numerous other journalists following this project's inception in early 2018. This has been the most intense source relationship I've ever had, and I have learned much about Val—and also about myself. Thank you, Val, for your patience and trust.

I am immensely grateful to *The New York Times*. A few months after arriving from *The Wall Street Journal* in September 2017, I told my bosses, Rebecca Blumenstein, Ellen Pollock, and Adrienne Carter, that I planned to write this book in my spare time. They were less than thrilled, predicting (accurately, it turned out) that it would distract me from my day job. I am thankful for their patience and good humor (even you, Adrienne!).

Ellen, Adrienne, Randy Pennell, and Nick Summers helped turn my Deutsche factoids and musings into *Times* articles. All three of them—as well as Mohammed Hadi and Ashwin Seshagiri— repeatedly picked up my slack. Dean Baquet and Matt Purdy provided more-or-less constant inspiration. Thank you, too, to Joe Kahn and David McCraw.

Quite a few of my *Times* colleagues generously contributed reporting or research or introduced me to sources. Among them: Sue Craig, Emily Flitter, Ben Protess, Jessica Silver-Greenberg, Jesse Drucker, William Rashbaum, Kitty Bennett, Jo Becker, Matina Steuis-Gridneff, and Susan Beachy. Natalie Kitroeff and Emily Flitter read drafts of the manuscript, and their advice made it better. (Thanks as well to William Cohan.)

I also am in debt to some of my former *Wall Street Journal* colleagues. Jenny Strasburg was the one who initially pushed to dig into the circumstances of Bill Broeksmit's death, and she has consistently inspired (and irritated) me with her deep sourcing and sheer doggedness. Bruce Orwall, the bureau chief when I was in London, encouraged our Deutsche Bank passions and is perhaps the greatest editor and mentor in journalism today. Kirsten Grind and Keach Hagey were early supporters of this book, giving me well-timed confidence boosts.

My agent, Dan Mandel, immediately embraced this project and has been a steady advocate throughout. At Custom House and HarperCollins, Geoff Shandler offered wisdom, pushed me for more, and improved every page of this book with his meticulous line-by-line editing. His assistant, Molly Gendell, kept things on track. Maureen Cole, in charge of publicity, wisely urged me to avoid early overexposure on radio and TV. Kyran Cassidy provided much-needed legal counsel. Thanks as well to Nancy Inglis, Ryan Shepherd, Liate Stehlik, Ben Steinberg,

Rachel Weinick, Andrea Molitor, Fritz Metsch, Ploy Siripant, and Ed Faulkner.

Finally, my family.

My parents, Peggy and Peter, provided motivation and fuel—and emotional support during sleepless nights when I worried, among other things, that I would never get this done. From the other side of the world, Liza and Jay were the source of infectious enthusiasm. Nick and Jords asked tough questions that forced me to think harder about the way I was telling elements of this story.

Henry and Jasper didn't help on the book, but they bring me pure joy (most of the time!), and this project took me away from them on so many nights and weekends. Thank you to Kristina Monteleone for serving as something of a surrogate parent.

This brings me to Kirsten. This could not have happened without her. The night that I told her my idea for this book, she was on board—even though she must have known it would put an enormous strain on our family. While I obsessed at all hours about Deutsche Bank, while I immersed myself with sources, while I agonized over draft after draft, while I shirked my parenting responsibilities, she kept our lives running. She handled my many ups and downs. She dispensed sage advice. Oh, and she read four versions of this manuscript!

Thank you, Kirsten. I love you.

ENDNOTES

This book is based mainly on my interviews with a wide variety of sources, most of whom agreed to speak on the condition that they not be identified. In this section, I have identified information that comes from public sources, such as news articles, books, or court filings. In addition, for each chapter, I have included in italics a brief description of the types of other sources that I relied on. Most of the information that is not specifically attributed in this section is derived from these other sources.

PROLOGUE

Interviews with Broeksmit family members and friends. Interviews with Deutsche executives.

1 Trump's requested Turnberry loan: David Enrich, Jesse Drucker, and Ben Protess, "Trump Sought a Loan During the 2016 Campaign. Deutsche Bank Said No," *New York Times*, February 2, 2019.

1. A CRIMINAL ENTERPRISE

1 Villard's train ride and family history: Alexandra Villard de Borchgrave and John Cullen, *Villard: The Life and Times of an American Titan*, 2001, 64–67.
2 Deutsche's initial losses on Villard: Lothar Gall, "The Deutsche Bank from Its Founding to the Great War," in Lothar Gall et al., *The Deutsche Bank: 1870–1995*, 1995, 62.

3 Early history of the bank: Gall, "The Deutsche Bank," 2, 12, 107.

4 Descriptions of Georg von Siemens: Christopher Kobrak, *Banking on Global Markets: Deutsche Bank and the United States, 1870 to the Present*, 2008, 4–24.

5 "my colleague was hailed": Gall, "The Deutsche Bank," 48–49.

6 "Armed to the teeth": Villard de Borchgrave and Cullen, *Villard*, 350.

7 "It is a little hard to understand": Kobrak, *Banking on Global Markets*, 38.

8 Good money after bad: Villard de Borchgrave and Cullen, *Villard*, 349–53.

9 Villard's downfall: Kobrak, *Banking on Global Markets*, 65, 94.

10 "wool pulled over its eyes": Gall, "The Deutsche Bank," 62.

11 Deutsche's rapid growth: Kobrak, *Banking on Global Markets*, 23.

12 Statues: Ibid., 229.

13 "at worst an opportunist": Ibid., 261.

14 Overruled by colleagues: Harold James, "The Deutsche Bank and the Dictatorship, 1933–1945," in *The Deutsche Bank: 1870–1995*, 294–96.

15 Aryanizations and the SS: Ibid., 294–321.

16 Swastikas in annual reports: Historical Association of Deutsche Bank, http://www.bankgeschichte.de/en/docs/Chronik_D_Bank.pdf.

17 Nazi gold: Alan Cowell, "Biggest German Bank Admits and Regrets Dealing in Nazi Gold," *New York Times*, August 1, 1998.

18 Auschwitz: John Schmid, "Deutsche Bank Linked to Auschwitz Funding," *New York Times*, February 5, 1999; and Ian Traynor, "Deutsche Bank Auschwitz Link," *The Guardian*, February 4, 1999.

19 No record of Abs objecting: James, "The Deutsche Bank and the Dictatorship," 351.

20 British support for reunifying Deutsche: Carl-Ludwig Holtfrerich, "The Deutsche Bank 1945–1957: War, Military Rule and Reconstruction," in *The Deutsche Bank: 1870–1995*, 371.

21 Deutsche's revival: Ibid., 371–485.

22 Abs at Eisenhower's Inaugural: Kobrak, *Banking on Global Markets*, 263, 303.

23 Reciting German poetry: Stefan Baron, *Late Remorse: Joe Ackermann, Deutsche Bank, and the Financial Crisis*, 2014, 25.

24 Herrhausen's early years: Associated Press, "Herrhausen a Giant Among Bankers," November 30, 1989, and Steven Greenhouse, "Deutsche Bank's Bigger Reach," *New York Times*, July 30, 1989.

25 "As the world becomes our marketplace": Reuters, "Deutsche Bank Plans to Follow Acquisition Path," March 12, 1989.

26 Herrhausen's rising star: Greenhouse, "Deutsche Bank's Bigger Reach," *New York Times*.

27 "The banker is all-powerful": Dan Morgan, "Slain Banker Personified Germany's Hopes," *Washington Post*, February 19, 1990.

28 "a real European bank": Richard Rustin and E. S. Browning, "Deutsche Bank Seeks Grenfell for $1.41 Billion," *Wall Street Journal*, November 28, 1989.

29 Herrhausen assassination: *Wall Street Journal*, "Terrorist Murder Stuns a Germany Euphoric Over Rapprochement," December 1, 1989; and Ferdinand Protzman, "Head of Top West German Bank Is Killed in Bombing by Terrorists," *New York Times*, December 1, 1989.

30 Red Army Faction communique: *Dialog International*, "Alfred Herrhausen Assassinated 20 Years Ago," November 29, 2009.

2. EDSON AND BILL

Interviews with family members, friends, and former colleagues of Edson Mitchell and Bill Broeksmit.

1 "Maine's most infamous businessman": Colin Woodard, "Notorious Egg Seller 'Jack' DeCoster Gets Jail Time for Salmonella Outbreak," *Portland Press Herald*, April 13, 2015.

2 Edson's upbringing: Jen Fish, "Edson Mitchell Jr., Deeply Religious Man and Avid Maine Outdoorsman," *Portland Press Herald*, March 9, 2004.

3 "I began to realize": Arthur Andersen Hall of Fame Roundtable, DerivativesStrategy.com, March 1998.

4 Reverend Jack's history: *Chicago Tribune*, "Death Notice: Rev. John S. Broeksmit Jr.," August 25, 2011.

5 "a certain amount of education pedigree": Austin Kilgore, "New MBA CEO Robert Broeksmit Is Ready to Be the Lender's Advocate," *National Mortgage News*, October 14, 2018.

6 Cocaine in the bathrooms: Janet M. Tavakoli, *Decisions: Life and Death on Wall Street*, 2015.

7 "the whitewater": Pat Widder, "Trillions at Stake in the Swaps Market," *Chicago Tribune*, June 22, 1992.

8 Extra Girl Scout cookies: Tavakoli, *Decisions.*

9 "Derivatives such as these": Lawrence Malkin, "Procter & Gamble's Tale of Derivatives Woe," *New York Times*, April 14, 1994.

10 Robert Citron: Davan Maharaj and Shelby Grad, "Seducing Citron: How Merrill Influenced Fund and Won Profits," *Los Angeles Times*, July 26, 1998.

11 Orange County's wager: Laura Jerseki, "Merrill Lynch Officials Fought Over Curbing Orange County Fund," *Wall Street Journal*, April 5, 1995, A1.

12 $2.8 billion portfolio: Leslie Wayne, "The Master of Orange County," *New York Times*, July 22, 1998.

13 "The potential adverse consequences": Michael G. Wagner, "Merrill Executives Saw O.C.'s Disaster Coming," *Los Angeles Times*, May 19, 1995, A1.

14 Missives didn't work: Jerseki, "Merrill Lynch Officials Fought Over Curbing Orange County Fund."

15 "uncanny accuracy": Wagner, "Merrill Executives Saw O.C.'s Disaster Coming."

3. WALL STREET'S GREAT MIGRATION

Interviews with Deutsche and Merrill executives and friends, family members, and associates of Mitchell and Broeksmit.

1 Shares were up 30 percent: Dan Morgan, "Slain Banker Personified Germany's Hopes," *Washington Post*, February 19, 1990.

2 "chaste souls": Ullrich Fichtner, Hauke Goos, and Martin Hesse, "The Deutsche Bank Downfall," *Der Spiegel*, October 28, 2016.

3 Soviet Union outposts: Historical Association of Deutsche Bank, "Deutsche Bank, 1870–2010," www.bankgeschichte.de/en/docs/Chronik_D_Bank.pdf, 142.

4 "Deutsche Lynch": Christopher Kobrak, *Banking on Global Markets: Deutsche Bank and the United States, 1870 to the Present*, 2008, 323–28.

5 Deutsche hadn't reviewed his financial statements: John Eisenhammer, "All Fall Down," *The Independent*, June 17, 1995.

6 Goldman's role on Deutsche Telekom: Patrick Jenkins and Laura Noonan, "How Deutsche Bank's High-Stakes Gamble Went Wrong," *Financial Times*, November 9, 2017.

7 Kopper in Madrid: Fichtner, Goos, and Hesse, "The Deutsche Bank Downfall."

8 An erudite Brit: Anne Schwimmer and Ron Cooper, "The Raid on Merrill Lynch," *Investment Dealers' Digest*, June 19, 1995.

9 Mitchell saw derivatives as key: Arthur Andersen Hall of Fame Roundtable, DerivativesStrategy.com, March 1998.

10 "NFL-type salaries": Schwimmer and Cooper, "The Raid on Merrill Lynch."

11 "a genuine opportunity": Ibid.

12 2,000 employees: Deutsche Bank's 1995 annual report.

13 "more time with his family": Michael Siconolfi and Laura Jereski, "Merrill Lynch's Stock-Derivatives Chief to Take Leave," *Wall Street Journal*, January 12, 1996.

14 "love to have him back": Anne Schwimmer, "Merrill's Broeksmit Will Go on Paid Leave of Absence in March," *Investment Dealers' Digest*, January 15, 1996.

4. FORCES OF DARKNESS

Interviews with Deutsche executives and their friends and family members.

1 "Douche Bank": Ed Caesar, "Deutsche Bank's $10-Billion Scandal," *The New Yorker*, August 29, 2016.

2 "nothing we were proud of": Clive Horwood and John Orchard, "The Bankers That Define the Decades: Hilmar Kopper, Deutsche Bank," *Euromoney*, June 14, 2019.

3 "I'm God": Ullrich Fichtner, Hauke Goos, and Martin Hesse, "The Deutsche Bank Downfall," *Der Spiegel*, October 28, 2016.

4 Losing him would be a disaster: Daniel Schäfer and Michael Brächer, "Deutsche Bank Chief Economist Lashes Out at Former CEO Ackermann," *Handelsblatt*, May 23, 2018.

5 Bottles of Beck's: Matthew Connolly, *Teethmarks on My Chopsticks: A Knucklehead Goes to Wall Street*, 2018, 153–54.

6 Anshu had recently graduated: Tom Buerkle, "The Outsiders," *Institutional Investor*, May 4, 2006.

7 Chasing tigers in India: Christoph Pauly and Padma Rao, "Anshu Jain Mixes Success and Controversy," *Der Spiegel*, September 14, 2011.

8 Edson told Anshu to do the trade: Marcus Walker, "Making Its Mark: Deutsche Bank Finds That It Has to Cut German Roots to Grow," *Wall Street Journal*, February 14, 2002.

5. PROJECT OSPREY

Interviews with Deutsche executives and government officials.

1 Project Osprey: Christopher Kobrak, *Banking on Global Markets: Deutsche Bank and the United States, 1870 to the Present*, 2008, 334–35.

2 "We were brain dead": Carol Loomis, "A Whole New Way to Run a Bank," *Fortune*, September 7, 1992.

3 "trolling the fringes": Laurie P. Cohen and Matt Murray, "Exit Interview at Bankers Trust Triggered Federal Investigation," *Wall Street Journal*, March 15, 1999.

4 audiotapes of phone calls: Loomis, "A Whole New Way to Run a Bank."

5 Bankers Trust's size: Deutsche Bank's 1999 annual report.

6 Breuer flew to Washington: Paul Thacker, "Inside the SEC's Abandoned Deutsche Bank Investigation," *Forbes*, September 20, 2011.

7 "no takeover talks": Ibid.

8 *Übernahmegespräche*: Matt Taibbi, "Is the SEC Covering Up Wall Street Crimes?" *Rolling Stone*, August 17, 2011.

9 29 percent of profits: Deutsche Bank's 1999 annual report.

10 85 percent of profits: Deutsche Bank's 2000 annual report.

6. TRUMP'S BANKERS

Interviews with Mike Offit, his colleagues, and other Deutsche and Wall Street executives, and photos and other documents provided by Offit and other sources.

1 A Baltimore bookie: Sidney Offit, *Memoir of the Bookie's Son*, 1995.

2 "an elemental world": Mike Offit, *Nothing Personal: A Novel of Wall Street*, 2014, 7.

3 Blizzard: Robert D. McFadden, "New York Shut by Worst Storm in 48 Years," *New York Times*, January 9, 1996.

4 Ingram's blank check: Landon Thomas Jr., "Ex-Goldman Trader Stung in Arms Plot, Shocks Colleagues," *New York Observer*, July 2, 2001.

5 Trump's organized-crime ties: Michael Rothfeld and Alexandra Berzon, "Donald Trump and the Mob," *Wall Street Journal*, September 1, 2016.

6 "Donald risk": Susanne Craig, "Trump Boasts of Rapport with Wall St., but It's Not Mutual," *New York Times*, May 24, 2016.

7 Cohan interview: Transcripts of unpublished interviews provided by Cohan.

8 Fred Trump's loans: David Barstow, Susanne Craig, and Russ Buettner, "Trump Engaged in Suspect Tax Schemes as He Reaped Riches from His Father," *New York Times*, October 2, 2018.

9 State of upheaval: *Commercial Mortgage Alert*, "Trump Taps Deutsche to Refinance 40 Wall," September 11, 2000.

10 Offit relationship with Trump: David Enrich, "A Mar-a-Lago Weekend and an Act of God: Trump's History with Deutsche Bank," *New York Times*, March 18, 2019.

11 Felix Sater's penthouse: Andrew Rice, "The Original Russia Connection," *New York*, August 2017.

7. RIPTIDE

Interviews with government officials, Deutsche executives, and their friends and family, and photos and other documents provided by sources.

1 "kindergarten-like attitude": Christopher Rhoads and Erik Portanger, "How an American Helped Torpedo the Dresdner Deal," *Wall Street Journal*, April 18, 2000.
2 "Please don't underestimate": Ibid.
3 Wave of cheering: Janet Guyon, "The Emperor and the Investment Bankers: How Deutsche Lost Dresdner," *Fortune*, May 1, 2000.
4 The ratio had flipped: Marcus Walker, "Making Its Mark: Deutsche Bank Finds That It Has to Cut German Roots to Grow," *Wall Street Journal*, February 14, 2002.
5 A professional secretary: Ibid.

8. THE LAST DAY

Interviews with government officials, Deutsche executives, and their friends and family, and photos and other documents provided by sources.

1 Blue ribbons: Michael R. Sesit and Anita Raghavan, "Deutsche Bank Hit Many Costly Snags in Its American Foray," *Wall Street Journal*, May 4, 1998.
2 All-time best parties: The list was compiled by efinancialcareers.com.
3 Sex-discrimination lawsuit: BBC News, "Bank in Sex Case Payout," January 18, 2000.
4 Timing, location, and altitude of Mitchell flight: National Transportation Safety Board, "NTSB Identification: NYC01FA058," January 9, 2001.
5 Warden's plane: Associated Press, "Wreckage of Plane Found in Rangeley Area," December 23, 2000.
6 SEC investigation and Walker's recusal: Matt Taibbi, "Is the SEC Covering Up Wall Street Crimes?" *Rolling Stone*, August 17, 2011.
7 "Dick Walker probably knows more": Associated Press, "Deutsche Bank Hires Former S.E.C. Official," October 2, 2001.
8 Hantavirus and large men with earpieces: Matthew Connolly, *Teethmarks on My Chopsticks: A Knucklehead Goes to Wall Street*, 2018, 237–38.
9 Ackermann thought it showed commitment: Tom Buerkle, "The Outsiders," *Institutional Investor*, May 4, 2006.

10 Waistcoat and bow tie: Marcus Walker, "Making Its Mark: Deutsche Bank Finds That It Has to Cut German Roots to Grow," *Wall Street Journal*, February 14, 2002.

11 An enormous tombstone: Nicholas Varchaver, "The Tombstone at Ground Zero," *Fortune*, March 31, 2008.

9. ACKERMANN

Interviews with Deutsche executives and government officials.

1 Mels: Tom Buerkle, "The Outsiders," *Institutional Investor*, May 4, 2006.

2 Javelin thrower: Stefan Baron, *Late Remorse: Joe Ackermann, Deutsche Bank, and the Financial Crisis*, 2014, 81.

3 Broken-legged skiers: Peter Koenig, "It's War—Deutsche Bank vs Germany," *The Sunday Times* (London), November 7, 2004.

4 Memorizing ratios: Marcus Walker, "Making Its Mark: Deutsche Bank Finds That It Has to Cut German Roots to Grow," *Wall Street Journal*, February 14, 2002.

5 Tinkering with smoke detectors: Baron, *Late Remorse*, 23.

6 Boasting about relationships: Ullrich Fichtner, Hauke Goos, and Martin Hesse, "The Deutsche Bank Downfall," *Der Spiegel*, October 28, 2016.

7 4 percent returns: Deutsche Bank's 2003 annual report.

8 "youthful smile": Baron, *Late Remorse*, 32.

9 $30 million bonuses: Daniel Schäfer and Michael Brächer, "Deutsche Bank Chief Economist Lashes Out at Former CEO Ackermann," *Handelsblatt*, May 23, 2018.

10 Loan volumes shriveled: Baron, *Late Remorse*, 60.

11 Quotes from internal Deutsche correspondence about sanctions: Federal and state regulatory settlements with the bank.

12 Accounts of soldiers killed in Iraq: *Neiberger et al v. Deutsche Bank*, 1:18-cv-00254-MW-GRJ, filed December 28, 2018.

13 Deutsche higher-ups knew: New York Department of Financial Services, announcement of penalties against Deutsche Bank, November 4, 2015.

14 Commanding a tank battalion: Bänziger's LinkedIn profile: www.linkedin.com/in/hugo-banziger-3086538/.

15 Colonel in the Swiss reserves: Baron, *Late Remorse*, 25.

16 United Financial acquisition and Charlie Ryan: Liam Vaughan, Jake Rudnitsky, and Ambereen Choudhury, "A Russian Tragedy: How

Deutsche Bank's 'Wiz' Kid Fell to Earth," *Bloomberg News*, October 3, 2016.

17 "Russia is hot": Buerkle, "The Outsiders."

18 VTB's links to FSB and Kremlin: Luke Harding, "Is Donald Trump's Dark Russian Secret Hiding in Deutsche Bank's Vaults?" *Newsweek*, December 21, 2017.

19 Deutsche's loan to VTB: Jenny Strasburg and Rebecca Ballhaus, "Deutsche Bank in Late 2016 Raced to Shed Loan It Made to Russian Bank VTB," *Wall Street Journal*, February 2, 2019.

20 "our good relationship": Nailya Asker-Zade, " 'The Global Economy Is in an Unstable Situation,' " *Vedomosti*, June 30, 2011. As republished at: www.db.com/russia/en/content/1597.htm.

10. THE MAR-A-LAGO PRIZE

Interviews with Deutsche executives and others with direct knowledge of the events described.

1 Friederich Trump's barbershop: Gwenda Blair, *The Trumps: Three Generations That Built an Empire*, 2000, 110.

2 Move to 60 Wall Street: Historical Association of Deutsche Bank, http://www.bankgeschichte.de/en/docs/Chronik_D_Bank.pdf, 221.

3 GM Building mortgage: *Commercial Mortgage Alert*, "Deutsche to Fund Trump Buyout of GM Building," May 28, 2001.

4 Atlantic City casino refinancing: *Casino City Times*, "Trump Approved for $70 Million Bank Loan," June 21, 2002.

5 Taunting investors: Riva D. Atlas, "After His Gloom Went Over Like a Lead Balloon, Trump Tries to Sell Happiness, in Junk Bonds," *New York Times*, May 7, 2002.

6 story after preposterous story about his hijinks: David Enrich, "A Mar-a-Lago Weekend and an Act of God: Trump's History with Deutsche Bank," *New York Times*, March 18, 2019.

7 Trump's default on the junk bonds: Associated Press, "Trump Casinos File for Bankruptcy," November 22, 2004; Emily Stewart, "The Backstory on Donald Trump's Four Bankruptcies," *TheStreet.com*, September 15, 2015.

8 Trump Chicago tower plans: *Donald J. Trump et al. v. Deutsche Bank et al.*, filed November 3, 2008.

9 Flights on the 727: Anupreeta Das, "When Donald Trump Needs a Loan, He Chooses Deutsche Bank," *Wall Street Journal*, March 20, 2016.

10 Trump's $788 million net worth: Deposition of Donald Trump in lawsuit against Timothy O'Brien, 37.

11 Deutsche's fee and additional exposure: *Trump v. Deutsche Bank.*

12 Client parties at Mar-a-Lago: *BondWeek,* "Seen 'N Heard," October 15, 2004.

13 Trump's golf-course interview with Deutsche: Enrich, "A Mar-a-Lago Weekend and an Act of God: Trump's History with Deutsche Bank."

14 "Exceptionally well-equipped": Deutsche Bank's 2005 annual report.

15 Consultants were hired: Karina Robinson, "Steering Deutsche," *The Banker,* May 1, 2004.

16 Merger talks with Citigroup: Mark Landler, "A Chip in the Global Game of Bank Reshuffling," *New York Times,* March 23, 2004.

17 Citigroup and Deutsche's sizes: Each bank's 2004 annual report.

18 German poll: Armin Mahler, "The World According to Josef Ackermann," *Der Spiegel,* October 29, 2008.

19 Board member resigns in protest: Peter Koenig, "It's War—Deutsche Bank vs Germany," *The Sunday Times* (London), November 7, 2004.

20 "bit of a politician": Mark Landler, "Big at Home, But Not Much Heft Globally," *New York Times,* August 26, 2005.

21 Merkel's dinner for Ackermann: Mahler, "The World According to Josef Ackermann."

11. DER INDER

Interviews with Deutsche executives and documents provided by sources.

1 "Indian 'bond junkie' ": *The Economist,* "A Giant Hedge Fund," August 26, 2004.

2 Misra's industry awards: Nicholas Dunbar, *The Devil's Derivatives: The Untold Story of the Slick Traders and Hapless Regulators Who Almost Blew Up Wall Street . . . and Are Ready to Do It Again,* 2011, 100.

3 Removing smoke detectors: Tom Braithwaite, "SoftBank's $100bn Vision Fund Needs Wall St Trader to Come Good," *Financial Times,* August 25, 2017.

4 "Mr. Basis Point": Suzi Ring, Gavin Finch, and Franz Wild, "From a $126 Million Bonus to Jail," *Bloomberg News,* March 19, 2018.

5 Leverage ratios: Adam Tooze, *Crashed: How a Decade of Financial Crises Changed the World,* 2018, 88.

6 Project Maiden: Internal Deutsche Bank presentation about transactions and its risks.

7 The world's biggest bank: Patrick Jenkins and Laura Noonan, "How Deutsche Bank's High-Stakes Gamble Went Wrong," *Financial Times,* November 9, 2017.

12. FIREMAN

Interviews with Deutsche executives and others with direct knowledge of events and documents provided by sources.

1 $4 million: Jennifer O'Brien, "Skip Soggy Gigs," *The Sun*, July 11, 2008.

2 "how to avoid an oncoming train": Daniel Schäfer and Michael Brächer, "Deutsche Bank Chief Economist Lashes Out at Former CEO Ackermann," *Handelsblatt*, May 23, 2018.

3 "best credit trader in the world": Scott Patterson and Serena Ng, "Deutsche Bank Fallen Trader Left Behind $1.8 Billion Hole," *Wall Street Journal*, February 6, 2009.

4 Mechanics of Lippmann's trades: Nicholas Dunbar, *The Devil's Derivatives: The Untold Story of the Slick Traders and Hapless Regulators Who Almost Blew Up Wall Street . . . and Are Ready to Do It Again*, 2011, 149–64; and Lippmann testimony to Financial Crisis Inquiry Commission.

5 "I'm short your house": Gretchen Morgenson and Louise Story, "Banks Bundled Bad Debt, Bet Against It and Won," *New York Times*, December 23, 2009.

6 Deutsche's profits, Lippmann's bonus: Dunbar, *The Devil's Derivatives*, 216.

7 "After some initial criticism": Historical Association of Deutsche Bank, http://www.bankgeschichte.de/en/docs/Chronik_D_Bank.pdf, 237.

8 Fed loans to Deutsche: A. Blundell-Wignall, G. Wehinger, and P. Slovik, "The Elephant in the Room: The Need to Deal with What Banks Do," *OECD Journal: Financial Market Trends*, vol. 2009/2.

9 $18 million payday: Armin Mahler, "The World According to Josef Ackermann," *Der Spiegel*, October 29, 2008.

10 "most powerful banker in Europe": Jack Ewing and Liz Alderman, "Deutsche Bank's Chief Casts Long Shadow in Europe," *New York Times*, June 11, 2011.

11 "relatively strong today": Mahler, "The World According to Josef Ackermann."

12 Derivatives relative to overall balance sheet: Blundell-Wignall, Wehinger, and Slovik, "The Elephant in the Room."

13. "THIS GUY IS A DANGER"

Interviews with Deutsche executives and lawyers, lawyers for Trump, and journalists who interviewed the participants.

1 "a great monument to the city": Transcript of Trump interview with William Cohan.
2 Nobody was buying his luxury apartments: Anupreeta Das, "When Donald Trump Needs a Loan, He Chooses Deutsche Bank," *Wall Street Journal*, March 20, 2016.
3 Deutsche's countersuit: *Deutsche Bank Trust Company Americas v. Donald J. Trump*, filed November 26, 2008.

14. THE PENDULUM SWINGS

Interviews with Deutsche executives, Rod Stone, and U.S. and European government officials.

1 Fifty-to-one leverage ratio: A. Blundell-Wignall, G. Wehinger, and P. Slovik, "The Elephant in the Room: The Need to Deal with What Banks Do," *OECD Journal: Financial Market Trends*, vol. 2009/2.
2 Deutsche's sales-tax refunds: Richard T. Ainsworth, "VAT Fraud Mutation, Part 3," *Tax Notes International*, March 28, 2016.
3 Surnamed Lawless: Ruling in UK court case EWHC 135 (Ch), High Court of Justice, Chancery Division, by Mr. Justice Newey, January 30, 2017.
4 "Because we're that greedy": Laura de la Motte and Volker Votsmeier, "Deutsche Bank's Emissions Fraud," *Handelsblatt*, February 15, 2016.
5 Executives pulled the plug: Ainsworth, "VAT Fraud Mutation, Part 3."
6 Nearly $250 million: de la Motte and Votsmeier, "Deutsche Bank's Emissions Fraud."
7 "risk-affirming climate": Yasmin Osman, "Deutsche Bankers Sentenced in CO2 Scam," *Handelsblatt*, June 14, 2016.
8 Bonus of more than $100 million: U.S. Justice Department, "Statement of Facts in Deferred Prosecution Agreement with Deutsche Bank AG," April 23, 2015.
9 "mountains of money": Frauke Menke, BaFin Letter to Deutsche Bank Management Board, May 11, 2015, accessible at graphics.wsj.com/docu ments/doc-cloud-embedder/?sidebar=0#2167237-deutsche.
10 Business Integrity Review Group: Menke, BaFin Letter.
11 $570 million of fees: U.S. Senate Permanent Subcommittee on Investi-

gations, "Abuse of Structured Financial Products: Misusing Basket Options to Avoid Taxes and Leverage Limits," July 22, 2014, 6.

12 Monte dei Paschi foundation's budget: David Enrich and Deborah Ball, "European Drama Engulfs the World's Oldest Bank," *Wall Street Journal*, October 26, 2011.

13 Faissola's role with Monte dei Paschi: Vernon Silver and Elisa Martinuzzi, "How Deutsche Bank Made a $462 Million Loss Disappear," *Bloomberg BusinessWeek*, January 19, 2017.

14 Deutsche's profits and bonuses from Paschi: Ibid.

15. CLUELESS OLD MAN

Interviews with Deutsche executives, traders, and Eric Ben-Artzi, and documents provided by sources.

1 Dixon's $14 billion trade: Matt Scully, "A $541 Million Loss Haunts Deutsche Bank and Former Trader Dixon," *Bloomberg News*, June 22, 2016.

2 $541 million in losses: Ibid.

3 Israel's refusenik: Chris McGreal, "I Realized the Stupidity of It," *The Guardian*, March 10, 2003.

4 Inside the envelope: Nicholas Kulish, "Letter Bomb Sent to German Bank Chief," *New York Times*, December 8, 2011.

5 "bloodsuckers": *Der Spiegel*, "Deutsche Bank Package Carried 'Functional Bomb,' " December 8, 2011.

6 Ackermann's globe-trotting: Stefan Baron, *Late Remorse: Joe Ackermann, Deutsche Bank, and the Financial Crisis*, 2014, 25–26.

7 Merkel seeks advice: Christoph Pauly and Padma Rao, "Anshu Jain Mixes Success and Controversy," *Der Spiegel*, September 14, 2011.

8 Suicide and other consequences: Marcus Walker, "Greek Crisis Exacts the Cruelest Toll," *Wall Street Journal*, September 20, 2011.

9 Attacks on Ackermann: "Deutsche Bank CEO Ackermann Slammed," *Der Spiegel*, April 14, 2011.

10 A locus for activists: Justin Elliott, "Occupy HQ: A Bailed-Out Bank," *Salon.com*, November 3, 2011.

16. ROSEMARY VRABLIC

Interviews with Deutsche executives and Vrablic's friends and family members.

1 Ursuline School: Twitter post by the Ursuline School, April 26, 2017, twitter.com/ursulinenr/status/857331407038935040.
2 "Be a lady": Transcript of Vrablic interview with *Mortgage Observer,* December 14, 2012.
3 Combat money laundering: Bank of Israel, "Sanctions Committee Decisions on Infringements by Bank Leumi of the Prohibition on Money Laundering Law," June 28, 2015.
4 "Little Rosemary": Vrablic interview with *Mortgage Observer.*
5 More than $50 million to invest: Evelyn Juan, "Deutsche Gets Bank of America Private-Bank Duo," Dow Jones Newswires, September 14, 2006.
6 "a few assets and many homes": Jacqueline S. Gold, "Duo Make Private Bank Jewel in B of A's Crown," *American Banker,* March 24, 1999.
7 Scholarship: The Ursuline School, "Bernice & Joseph Vrablic Memorial Scholarship," www.ursulinenewrochelle.org/page.cfm?p=907.
8 *New York Times* ad: *New York Times,* October 11, 2006, C2.
9 Vrablic at Kushner's *Observer* party: Patrick McMullan Company, "Jared Kushner and Peter Kaplan Present the Relaunch of the New York Observer Website," April 18, 2007, www.patrickmcmullan.com/ev ents/5b3ef4fb9f92906676448199/.
10 Trump's exaggerated asset valuations: David Enrich, Matthew Goldstein, and Jesse Drucker, "Trump Exaggerated His Wealth in Bid for Loan, Michael Cohen Tells Congress," *New York Times,* February 27, 2019.
11 Trump's Chicago and Doral loans, and the fight within Deutsche: David Enrich, "A Mar-a-Lago Weekend and an Act of God: Trump's History with Deutsche Bank," *New York Times,* March 18, 2019.
12 "a great relationship": William D. Cohan, "What's the Deal with Donald Trump?" *The Atlantic,* March 20, 2013.

17. ANSHU ASCENDANT

Interviews with Deutsche executives, their friends and family members, and government officials, and documents provided by sources.

1 A sweltering day: Stefan Baron, *Late Remorse: Joe Ackermann, Deutsche Bank, and the Financial Crisis,* 2014, 248.

2 More than 7,000 shareholders: Jack Ewing, "Ackermann Hands Over Reins of Deutsche Bank," *New York Times*, May 31, 2012.

3 Buffet tables: Baron, *Late Remorse*, 248.

4 Protests outside: Edward Taylor, "Deutsche's Ackermann Bows Out with Euro Warning," Reuters, May 31, 2012.

5 "I have done my duty": Ewing, "Ackermann Hands Over Reins of Deutsche Bank."

6 Ackermann blamed Jain: Baron, *Late Remorse*, 201.

7 Pulled out an iPad: Taylor, "Deutsche's Ackermann Bows Out with Euro Warning."

8 The golden nameplate: Jack Ewing, "Regulators Said to Have Pressed for Exit of Deutsche Chiefs," *New York Times*, June 9, 2015.

9 Normal protocol for seeking BaFin approval: Mark Schieritz and Arne Storn, "Frau Menke Stoppt Mr. Jain," *Zeit Online*, March 22, 2012.

18. DUMPING GROUND

Interviews with Deutsche executives and their friends and family members, and documents provided by sources.

19. 5,777 REQUESTS FOR INFORMATION

Interviews with Deutsche executives and their friends and family members, and documents provided by sources.

1 More than two dozen Deutsche officials investigated: Laura de la Motte and Volker Votsmeier, "Deutsche Bank's Emissions Fraud," *Handelsblatt*, February 15, 2016.

2 Confidential internal report: Deutsche Bank, "US Regulatory Management Report," August 2013.

3 Employees told regulators to talk to Broeksmit: "Bundesbank Questions Ex-Deutsche Bank Employees in U.S." Reuters, June 27, 2013.

4 Bittar firing and conviction: Suzi Ring, Gavin Finch, and Franz Wild, "From a $126 Million Bonus to Jail," *Bloomberg News*, March 19, 2018.

5 $200 million in revenue: New York State Department of Financial Services, consent order against Deutsche Bank, January 2017.

6 won work with the father's company: Securities and Exchange Commission cease-and-desist order against Deutsche Bank, August 22, 2019.

7 "quite galling": Luke Harding, "Is Donald Trump's Dark Russian Secret Hiding in Deutsche Bank's Vaults?" *Newsweek*, December 21, 2017.

8   Deutsche profits via Laundromat: Luke Harding, "Deutsche Bank Faces Action over $20bn Russian Money-Laundering Scheme," *The Guardian*, April 17, 2019.

9   Young, handsome Tim Wiswell: Liam Vaughan, Jake Rudnitsky, and Ambereen Choudhury, "A Russian Tragedy: How Deutsche Bank's 'Wiz' Kid Fell to Earth," *Bloomberg News*, October 3, 2016.

10   Wiswell's promotions: Ed Caesar, "Deutsche Bank's $10-Billion Scandal," *The New Yorker*, August 29, 2016.

11   His squad devised a plan: NYDFS, 2017.

12   Mirror-trade mechanics: Caesar, "Deutsche Bank's $10-Billion Scandal"; NYDFS, 2017; and Vaughan, Rudnitsky, and Choudhury, "A Russian Tragedy."

13   More than $10 billion: Financial Conduct Authority, Final Notice vs. Deutsche Bank, January 30, 2017.

14   Relatives and friends of Putin: Irina Reznik, Keri Geiger, Jake Rudnitsky, and Gregory White, "Putin Allies Said to Be Behind Scrutinized Deutsche Bank Trades," *Bloomberg News*, October 16, 2015.

15   "We lived like rock stars": Vaughan, Rudnitsky, and Choudhury, "A Russian Tragedy."

16   chief anti-money-laundering officer: NYDFS, 2017.

17   money they were seeking to use: Caesar, "Deutsche Bank's $10-Billion Scandal."

18   greater internal vetting: Financial Conduct Authority, "Final Notice," January 30, 2017, https://www.fca.org.uk/publication/final-notices/deutsche-bank-2017.pdf.

19   Not-always-squeaky-clean: Andrew E. Kramer, "Russian Fund Under Scrutiny for Loan to Company Linked to Kremlin," *New York Times*, January 22, 2016.

20   Nobody asked follow-up questions: FCA Final Notice, 2017.

20. STRESS

Interviews with Deutsche and Zurich Financial executives, government officials, and Broeksmit family members, friends, and lawyers.

1   Wauthier's suicide: David Enrich and Andrew Morse, "Friction at Zurich Built in Months Before Suicide," *The Wall Street Journal*, September 4, 2013.

2   Financial-crime chief quit after six months: Jenny Strasburg, "Deutsche Bank's Anti-Financial-Crime Chief to Quit Post," *The Wall Street Journal*, January 4, 2017.

3 BaFin inquiry scheduled for 2014: Vernon Silver and Elisa Martinuzzi, "How Deutsche Bank Made a $462 Million Loss Disappear," *Bloomberg BusinessWeek*, January 19, 2017.

4 Jain urged Carney to back off: Harry Wilson, "Carney Switches Bank of England Focus to Conduct Risks," *Daily Telegraph*, January 26, 2014.

21. VALENTIN

Interviews with Val and his friends, family members, therapist, and foster brother, and family photos.

1 Alla Broeksmit's refugee experience: Alla Broeksmit, "Compasses" (master's thesis).

2 "a mass exodus": "Russian Families Start Life All Over in U.S.," *Daily Dispatch* (Moline, Illinois), December 8, 1978.

3 Homeless shelter, Val is neglected: Circuit Court of Cook County, Illinois, Juvenile Division, "Petition for Adjudication of Wardship in the Case of Cherednichenko, Valentin," Case 82-8001, May 6, 1982.

4 Alla couldn't be found: Cook County sheriff's notice, filed with Circuit Court of Cook County, Case 82-8001, September 21, 1982.

5 Rocky Mountain Academy as a cult-like experience: Kevin Keating, "Suit Says School for Troubled Teens Set Stage for Abuse," *The Spokesman-Review*, April 1, 1998.

6 John Avila suicide: Kevin Keating, "Boy Hangs Himself in Dormitory," *The Spokesman-Review*, July 19, 1994.

22. LIFE EXTINCT

Interviews with Broeksmit family members and friends. Family photos. Police and ambulance reports.

23. EVERYTHING IS UPSIDE DOWN

Interviews with Broeksmit family members and friends and Deutsche officials. Family photos. Written descriptions of the memorial. Broeksmit suicide notes. Emails and text messages provided by Val.

1 "a friendly note": Jenny Strasburg, Giles Turner, Eyk Henning, and David Enrich, "Executive Who Committed Suicide Anxious Amid Deutsche Bank Probes," *Wall Street Journal*, March 25, 2014.

24. NO REASON FOR CONCERN

Interviews with Deutsche executives.

1 Cypriot bank got suspicious: Liam Vaughan, Jake Rudnitsky, and Ambereen Choudhury, "A Russian Tragedy: How Deutsche Bank's 'Wiz' Kid Fell to Earth," *Bloomberg News*, October 3, 2016.
2 Description of scheme and Deutsche's ignoring of Cypriot inquiries: FCA Final Notice, 2017.
3 "no reason for concern here": New York State Department of Financial Services, consent order against Deutsche Bank, January 2017.
4 "had to prioritize": Ibid.
5 After prodding from the Kremlin: James Shotter, Kathrin Hille, and Caroline Binham, "Deutsche Bank Probes Possible Money Laundering by Russian Clients," *Financial Times*, June 5, 2015.
6 Deutsche discovers scheme: FCA Final Notice, 2017.
7 Wiswell's wife: NYDFS, 2017; Vaughan, Rudnitsky, and Choudhury, "A Russian Tragedy."
8 Bags of cash: Ed Caesar, "Deutsche Bank's $10-Billion Scandal," *The New Yorker*, August 29, 2016.
9 Sanctions penalty: New York Department of Financial Services, announcement of penalties against Deutsche Bank, November 4, 2015.
10 The bank's defense in Renaissance hearing: Barry Bausano and Satish Ramakrishna, written testimony before Senate Permanent Subcommittee on Investigations, July 22, 2014.
11 "He knew as well as I did": Transcript of Senate Permanent Subcommittee on Investigations hearing, July 22, 2014.

25. THE FIRST LEAK

Interviews with Val and other Broeksmit family members, friends, and acquaintances. Photos, emails, and documents provided by Val. Interviews with Deutsche executives and board members and others with direct knowledge of the events.

1 Dutch bank murder-suicide: Maarten van Tartwijk, "Former ABN Amro Executive Committed Suicide After Killing Wife, Daughters, Police Say," *Wall Street Journal*, April 8, 2014.

26. THE NORTH KOREANS

Interviews with Val and other Broeksmit family members and friends. Val's emails. Interviews with people with direct knowledge of the events.

1 Gambino's suicide and role at Deutsche: David Enrich, Jenny Strasburg, and Pervaiz Shallwani, "Deutsche Bank Lawyer Found Dead in New York Suicide," *Wall Street Journal*, October 24, 2014.
2 Val's Fox interview: Fox Business, "Sony Threatens to Sue Musician over Hacking Tweets," December 23, 2014, video available at https://video.foxbusiness.com/v/3958928360001/.
3 Stress-test article: Charles Levinson, "Former Risk Chief Warned Deutsche Bank on Stress Test, Emails Show," *Reuters*, March 12, 2015.

27. NO CONFIDENCE

Interviews with Deutsche executives and board members.

1 Sewing's father: Dirk Laabs, *Bad Bank: Aufstieg und Fall der Deutschen Bank*, 2018, 498.
2 7,000 outstanding legal actions: James Shotter, Laura Noonan, and Martin Arnold, "Deutsche Bank: Problems of Scale," *Financial Times*, July 28, 2016.
3 Jain at World Economic Forum: Martin Arnold and Tom Braithwaite, "Anshu Jain in Davos Regulation Clash with Jack Lew and Mark Carney," *Financial Times*, January 23, 2015.
4 "repeatedly misleading us": Eyk Henning and David Enrich, "Deutsche Bank to Pay $2.5 Billion to Settle Libor Investigation," *Wall Street Journal*, April 23, 2015.

5 Board members were appalled: Daniel Schäfer and Michael Maisch, "Riding with the King," *Handelsblatt*, May 13, 2016.

6 Menke descriptions: Heinz-Roger Dohms, "Allein gegen das Kapital," *Cicero*, June 26, 2014.

7 Emoting without strategizing: Eyk Henning, David Enrich, and Jenny Strasburg, "Deutsche Bank Co-CEOs Jain and Fitschen Resign," *Wall Street Journal*, June 7, 2015.

8 "I don't want to stand in the way": Thomas Atkins, "Jain Puts Deutsche Bank on World Stage, but Leaves It in Limbo," *Reuters*, June 7, 2015.

9 Customers consider moving money: Henning, Enrich, and Strasburg, "Deutsche Bank Co-CEOs Jain and Fitschen Resign."

10 Achleitner had already scouted out replacements: Ibid.

11 "the anti-Anshu": Schäfer and Maisch, "Riding with the King."

12 On their way out within months: Arno Schuetze, "Deutsche Bank Restructures Business, Removes Top Executives," *Reuters*, October 18, 2015.

28. TRUMP ENDEAVOR 12 LLC

Interviews with Deutsche executives and others with direct knowledge of the events.

1 Old Post Office dimensions: U.S. General Services Administration, "Old Post Office, Washington, DC," https://www.gsa.gov/historic-buildings/old-post-office-washington-dc.

2 Trump's winning bid for Old Post Office: U.S. General Services Administration, "GSA Selects the Trump Organization as Preferred Developer for DC's Old Post Office," February 7, 2012.

3 Skepticism about Trump's bid: Jonathan O'Connell, "You May Not Take Donald Trump's Candidacy Seriously, but Take Another Look at His Real Estate Business," *Washington Post*, June 21, 2015.

4 "Every bank wants to do the deal": Ibid.

5 Deutsche claim to Trump assets: House Committee on Transportation and Infrastructure, Democratic staff, "Breach of a Lease: The Tale of the Old Post Office in the Swamp," July 12, 2017.

6 "I'm borrowing money": Cohan's transcript of unpublished interview with Trump.

7 Titan Atlas: Shawn Boburg and Robert O'Harrow Jr., "Donald Trump Jr. Stumbled While Trying to Make a Mark in the Business World," *Washington Post*, February 4, 2017.

8 The gauzy profile: Carl Gaines, "Deutsche Bank's Rosemary Vrablic

and Private Banking's Link to CRE Finance," *Commercial Observer*, February 6, 2013.

9 Kushner's personal loan: Jared Kushner financial documents, reviewed by *New York Times*.

10 Trump signed Doral loan during campaign: Brian Bandell, "Trump Boosts Loan on Doral Golf Resort," *South Florida Business Journal*, August 13, 2015.

29. THE DAMAGE I HAVE DONE

Interviews with Val and his friends, therapist, and fellow rehab and sober-living residents, as well as interviews with Broeksmit family members and friends. Emails, photos, and documents provided by Val.

30. PERSON OF INTEREST

Interviews with Val and his friends and with Broeksmit family members and friends. Emails and documents provided by Val.

1 "He explained he was being investigated": Mitchell and Moore letters to coroner.

2 Mentioned in a confidential EU report: Dirk Laabs, *Bad Bank: Aufstieg und Fall der Deutschen Bank*, 2018, 490.

3 Results of Broeksmit review: Justice Department Statement of Facts (draft), April 15, 2015, disclosed in *USA v. Connolly*, Exhibit 399-12.

4 Phone call about ignoring Justice Department: Justice Department Statement of Facts (draft).

5 FBI agents summoning Deutsche executives: Matthew Connolly, *Teethmarks on My Chopsticks: A Knucklehead Goes to Wall Street*, 2018, 331–34.

6 Risk group approved Paschi deal: Vernon Silver and Elisa Martinuzzi, "How Deutsche Bank Made a $462 Million Loss Disappear," *Bloomberg BusinessWeek*, January 19, 2017.

31. SIENA

Interviews with Val, his girlfriend and other friends, his therapist, Luca Goracci, Deutsche executives and board members.

1 "mounting concerns": Evelyn Cheng, "Deutsche Bank Crisis: How We Got Here, and Where We Are," CNBC.com, September 28, 2016.

2 "the most important net contributor": International Monetary Fund, "Germany Financial Sector Assessment Program," June 2016.

3 Surveillance footage: Michael Gray, "Why Are So Many Bankers Committing Suicide?" *New York Post*, June 12, 2016.

4 returned to their car: Ibid.

5 Foundation's yearly distribution had shriveled: Rachel Sanderson, "Siena Faces Life after 500 Years of Monte dei Paschi Largesse," *Financial Times*, August 2, 2016.

32. ROSEMARY IS THE BOSS

Interviews with Mike Offit, Tammy McFadden, other Deutsche employees and executives, and journalists who interviewed several characters (and related emails and transcripts).

1 Bannon's radicalization: Michael C. Bender, "Steve Bannon and the Making of an Economic Nationalist," *Wall Street Journal*, March 14, 2017.

2 Kushner's biggest lending facility: Kushner financial documents, reviewed by *New York Times*.

3 Kushner's loan for old *New York Times* building: Will Parker, "Jared Kushner Looks to Be Still Tied Up in 229 West 43rd Street Retail Condo," *The Real Deal*, March 6, 2017.

4 Clinton attacks: Glenn Kessler and Michelle Ye Hee Lee, "Fact-Checking Clinton's Speech on Trump's Business Practices," *Washington Post*, June 22, 2016.

5 Trump describing Vrablic as CEO: Susanne Craig, "Trump Boasts of Rapport with Wall St., but It's Not Mutual," *New York Times*, May 24, 2016; transcript of Susanne Craig interview with Donald Trump.

6 "These are guys that shift paper around": James B. Stewart, "A Tax Loophole for the Rich That Just Won't Die," *New York Times*, November 9, 2017.

7 Epstein at Deutsche: David Enrich and Jo Becker, "Jeffrey Epstein Moved Money Overseas in Transactions His Bank Flagged to U.S.," *New York Times*, July 23, 2019.

8 Tammy McFadden: David Enrich, "Deutsche Bank Staff Saw Suspicious Activity in Trump and Kushner Accounts," *New York Times*, May 19, 2019.

33. DO NOT UTTER THE WORD "TRUMP"

Interviews with Deutsche executives, board members, and consultants. Interviews with Val and his acquaintances, and photos and video footage.

1 "we don't rely on American banks": Bill Littlefield, "A Day (and a Cheeseburger) With President Trump," WBUR, May 5, 2017.
2 Deutsche's sale of VTB loan: Jenny Strasburg and Rebecca Ballhaus, "Deutsche Bank in Late 2016 Raced to Shed Loan It Made to Russian Bank VTB," *Wall Street Journal*, February 2, 2019.
3 "It looks terrible": Keri Geiger, Greg Farrell, and Sarah Mulholland, "Trump May Have a $300 Million Conflict of Interest with Deutsche Bank," *Bloomberg News*, December 22, 2016.
4 Vrablic's attendance at Trump's Inaugural: David Enrich, "A Mar-a-Lago Weekend and an Act of God: Trump's History with Deutsche Bank," *New York Times*, March 18, 2019.

34. SPYCRAFT

Interviews with Val and people with whom he interacted. Val's text messages, emails, photos, and receipts. Interviews with Deutsche executives.

1 Background on Simpson: Matt Flegenheimer, "Fusion GPS Founder Hauled from the Shadows for the Russia Election Investigation," *New York Times*, January 8, 2018.
2 "the mastermind of the scheme": Ed Caesar, "Deutsche Bank's $10-Billion Scandal," *The New Yorker*, August 29, 2016.
3 The Moscow-Simpson-Browder nexus: Marie Brenner, "The Mogul Who Came in from the Cold," *Vanity Fair*, Holiday 2018/19.
4 Fed deemed Deutsche "troubled": Jenny Strasburg and Ryan Tracy, "Deutsche Bank's U.S. Operations Deemed Troubled by Fed," *Wall Street Journal*, June 1, 2018.

35. A NOTE FROM THE PRESIDENT

Interviews with and photos from Mike Offit. Interviews with Deutsche executives and employees.

1 Trump hotel details: Katie Rogers, "Trump Hotel at Night: Lobbyists, Cabinet Members, $60 Steaks," *New York Times*, August 25, 2017.

2 Trump's standing ovation: Glenn Thrush, Twitter post, October 29, 2018, https://twitter.com/GlennThrush/status/1056983892928970752.

3 Kennedy's work on restructuring Kushner debt: Eliot Brown, "Rescue for a Developer," *Wall Street Journal*, July 7, 2011.

4 Ivanka Trump at Supreme Court: Betsy Klein and Ariane de Vogue, "Ivanka Trump and Daughter Go to the Supreme Court," CNN, February 23, 2017.

5 Kennedy at St. Patrick's Day celebration: Shane Goldmacher, "Trump's Hidden Backchannel to Justice Kennedy: Their Kids," *Politico*, April 6, 2017.

6 Vekselberg: Andrew Higgins, Oleg Matsnev, and Ivan Nechepurenko, "Meet the 7 Russian Oligarchs Hit by the New U.S. Sanctions," *New York Times*, April 6, 2018.

7 Internal presentation shows management exposure: Luke Harding, "Deutsche Bank Faces Action over $20bn Russian Money-Laundering Scheme," *The Guardian*, April 17, 2019.

8 Trump suspicious activity reports: David Enrich, "Deutsche Bank Staff Saw Suspicious Activity in Trump and Kushner Accounts," *New York Times*, May 19, 2019.

9 German newspaper story on Mueller subpoena: Christopher Cermak, "Mueller's Trump-Russia Investigation Engulfs Deutsche," *Handelsblatt*, December 5, 2017.

10 Trump's explosion: Bob Woodward, *Fear: Trump in the White House*, 2018, 326–27.

11 Labor Department waiver: David Sirota and Josh Keefe, "Trump Administration Waives Punishment for Convicted Banks, Including Deutsche—Which Trump Owes Millions," *International Business Times*, January 9, 2018.

12 Renaissance bailing: Sonali Basak, Donal Griffin, and Katherine Burton, "RenTech Has Been Pulling Money from Deutsche Bank for Months," *Bloomberg News*, July 5, 2019.

13 "We lost our compass": Jack Ewing, "Deutsche Bank Layoffs Begin as Workers Feel Turnaround Plan's Impact First," *New York Times*, July 8, 2019.

EPILOGUE

Interviews with Val, Marie, Moby, Deutsche executives, and government officials. Photos, text messages, and documents provided by Val and Marie.

INDEX

=====